'Our capacity for play...can become drowned in a life full of prescriptions, responsibilities and fears. In *Playful Awakening* Gammage brings back to life the magical, mysterious, liberating significance of play as a source of health and transformation, not just for children but for us all. She shows us that when we see the play of our reality, we discover how much lighter, kinder and more joyful our world can then be.'

— *Rob Preece, author of* The Psychology of Buddhist Tantra,
The Wisdom of Imperfection *and* Feeling Wisdom

'We learned: "hard work" is the key to success, play is kids' stuff. This fascinating, deep dive into play rejoins the two. That marriage produces more creative and innovative work, more authentic lives and healthier relationships.'

— *Bowen F. White, MD, author of* Why Normal Isn't Healthy *and*
Founding Board Member, The National Institute for Play

'In [Di Gammage's] comprehensive look at play...the reader can begin to appreciate its richness and life-affirming reality.'

— *Stuart Brown, MD, Founder, President, The National Institute for Play*

T0301234

of related interest

Practical Zen

Julian Daizan Skinner
Foreword by Miyamae Shinzan Gyokuryuji
ISBN 978 1 84819 363 5
eISBN 978 0 85701 321 7

Cultivating Qi
The Root of Energy, Vitality, and Spirit

David W. Clippinger
Foreword by Grandmaster Nick Gracenin
ISBN 978 1 84819 291 1
eISBN 978 0 85701 254 8

The Buddha's Children
Buddhism and Childhood Spirituality

Alexander von Gontard
ISBN 978 1 78592 038 7
eISBN 978 1 78450 289 8

Playful Awakening

Releasing the Gift of Play in Your Life

Di Gammage

Foreword by Stuart Brown, MD

Jessica Kingsley *Publishers*
London and Philadelphia

Please see pages 10–11 for a list of permissions granted. Every effort has been made to trace the copyright holders for the purpose of permission. The publisher apologizes for any omissions and errors incurred and would welcome notification of any corrections or omissions that need to be included in future editions of this work.

First published in 2017
by Jessica Kingsley Publishers
73 Collier Street
London N1 9BE, UK
and
400 Market Street, Suite 400
Philadelphia, PA 19106, USA

www.jkp.com

Library of Congress Cataloging in Publication Data
A CIP catalog record for this book is available from the Library of Congress

British Library Cataloguing in Publication Data
A CIP catalogue record for this book is available from the British Library

ISBN 978 1 84905 150 7
eISBN 978 0 85700 350 8

Printed and bound by CPI Group (UK) Ltd, Croydon, CR0 4YY

Contents

Foreword

PLAY... 'Who are we without it?'

'The reason we play is simply because it is fun and pleasurable to engage in. It makes us feel connected to LIFE, otherwise we would not do it.'

What does it mean to live completely within our human capacities? And how can we most effectively embrace and achieve fulfilment as we identify and activate those capacities?

Read this book carefully, and in the process gain access to paths toward fulfilment through play that often otherwise are elusive.

So Di Gammage, in her comprehensive look at PLAY in these pages, shown through her lifetime lenses of clinical exposure, is able to place play in its broadest contexts. And in this process, the reader can begin to appreciate its richness and life-affirming reality. Through direct observation and prodigious scholarship, the mosaic of play that unites the spiritual, psychological and biological is presented.

Play is a deeply embedded survival drive that needs to be understood, appreciated and enacted throughout our lives. What is often missed about play and is addressed clearly here are its healing qualities and its place in the remediation of children dispossessed by the horrors of trauma and abuse. Like an overturned iceberg, that which is usually hidden in the depths (about play) becomes lucidly visible.

The traditions of Buddhism and the ancient wisdom of Hinduism are interwoven into the body of this book, as are the reverberations of Jung's contributions and other relevant scholars such as Joseph Campbell, as their works amplify the place of play in the overall scheme of things.

I left its pages feeling affirmed in my embrace of play, more compassionate for kids who suffer from early trauma, and deepened by her embrace of the wisdom traditions of the East.

I have written elsewhere that play is largely accountable for our existence as sentient intelligent beings. Di Gammage weaves an intricate tapestry that provides a colourful foundation for these contentions.

Stuart Brown, MD
Founder, President, The National Institute for Play

Acknowledgements

To my editor, Jessica Kingsley.

All the children and adults who have taught me about the gift of play in healing. My supervisees and my dramatherapy, play therapy and child psychotherapy students.

The Abbey Community in Sutton Courtenay, Yolande Anastasi, Blandine Anderson, Renee Barange, Lorna Bird, Susie Boyd, Rob Burbea, Hannah Burgon and the Sirona team, Jo Christensen, Jo Clarke, Maya Cockburn, David Cowell, Helen Cross, Rob Dighton, Gillian Eckley, Sara Fairfax, the Gammages of Maidenhead, Jo Hardy, Alison Hepburn, Caz Hoar, Chris Hoggett, Ned Hoste @ nedof2h. net, Richard and Vicki Hougham, Robyn Michele Jones, Jackie Juno, the Karuna Institute, Moira Lake, Fiona Lothian, Mary Maxfield, Bozena Merrick, Andrew Motion, Nagamudra, Kay Parkinson, Lia Ponton, Rob Preece, Ian Reece, Carol Richards and the Dartington Trust, Denise Robson, She-Wolf, Franklyn Sills, Maura Sills, Daniel Stolti, Ian Strang, Amy Urry, Vajrasara, Jessica Williams Ciemnyjewski, Angela Willow, Jan Wilson, and Vicky Zerva and the Athyrma team.

Special thanks to Mary Booker and Sarah Scoble, my literary midwives, and to Anna Trevone for showing me the way.

Matthew, Tabitha and Dexter.

My parents – Shirley and Derrick Grimshaw.

Permissions

Finding a Way Through

For those who feel the weight of a damp hessian
sack filled with the rubble of grief,
I can tell you 'It will pass.'

For those who drop to the bottom of a well that has been
dried out by a depression deemed unquenchable,
I can tell you 'There is a way through.'

For those who waver on the edge of the labyrinth
for fear of what feeling life might mean,
I can tell you 'Enter, it is worth it.'

For those lost in the myriad of chambers of the
mind's endless wondering and wrangles,
I can tell you 'Drop into your heart.'

For those who catch a run-away train that abandons
the present for 'what-ifs' and worry,
I can tell you 'Be here now.'

For this moment holds fierce beauty,
The bitter and the sweet,
And the taste of one ignites the other,
Both exist in perfect balance,
Shadow and light.
When dark times beckon
Keep it simple.
Walk out on the land,
Breathe,
Through cloud,
On wet stone,
Across water,
The light is there.

Anna Trevone

Prologue

While training to be a drama teacher, I was given the task of directing a short piece of theatre. In the college library I stumbled upon a play entitled *The Cloak* by a playwright I had never heard of before. Clifford Bax's surreal and intriguing play is set in 'a world of spirits' and depicts an encounter between an Angel, an Unborn Spirit and 'One Newly Dead'. We first meet the Angel conversing with the fervent Unborn Spirit, eager for her birth on Earth, but before the Angel can show her the way to go, the Angel has a harder and more pressing task: that of persuading the Dead One, whose arrival is imminent, to remove her richly decorated, highly elaborate cloak. The Angel explains:

> *I am waiting here to guide*
> *The footsteps of a woman who has just died, –*
> *For when they slip their bodies and, as men say,*
> *Are dead, all human spirits pass by this way.*
> *From heaven they go forth simply-clad, like you,*
> *But, as years pass, they let the whirring brain*
> *Weave no thoughts but of self-glory and self-gain.*
> *These, though not visibly to their mortal view,*
> *Become a cloak, a richly-patterned cloak,*
> *That hides their true selves as a flame in smoke;*
> *And having worn it (there*
> *On earth) so long, they will not cast it by,*
> *But think they are the garment which they wear.*
> *It is my task to teach her that before*
> *She enters heaven her separate self must die,*
> *And she become simple as you once more.*[1]

Inevitably, the Dead One resists, having worked on the cloak her 'whole life through, making it from a thousand threads and scraps'.[2] This intricate design makes her who she is. It is unique. There is no other cloak like hers. She clings to her garment and pleads with the Angel, who, despite her compassion, remains intractable. To lose her personality, her identity, her protection – what would this mean?

In deciding to explore the subject of play, its role in the creation of identity (the cloak) and its wider manifestations including theatre, art and dance, I realized I had been involved in this enquiry for many years. More recently, I was reminded of *The Cloak* when I came across a Zen story retold by Mark Epstein. In this story, an elderly Chinese monk sets out on a long and arduous journey to seek enlightenment which he believes he will find in an isolated cave. He meets another old man travelling down the mountain towards him who is carrying a huge bundle of sticks on his back. This man, unbeknown to the monk, is the bodhisattva, Manjushri.[3] Manjushri stops and asks the monk where he is going. The monk tells him of his mission, declaring that he will stay in the cave until he realizes awakening or he will die trying. The elderly monk senses this old man is not all he may appear to be and enquires, 'Tell me, do you know anything of this enlightenment?' Upon being asked this question, Manjushri drops his bundle on to the ground and in that moment the old monk is enlightened… Epstein comments, 'In an instant he, too, had put down his whole defensive organisation, the entire burden.'[4] The newly enlightened monk, disorientated and confused, asks, 'What now?' But the bodhisattva does not reply; he simply smiles, picks up his bundle and continues on his way. We are not told what happens next to the monk. We do not know whether he gradually falls back to sleep (the enlightening experience being a one-off phenomenon that is not integrated into the rest of his life) or whether he is able to maintain his enlightened position, staying awake to what is within and around him in this world. Many people may claim to have such enlightening experiences, where there is sudden, astonishing clarity as if a bright, white light momentarily illuminates the darkness; sustaining and cultivating such awareness is another issue altogether.

The old monk's experience might be described as a 'spiritual awakening' where a sudden realization strikes the individual with such force that he or she feels to be broken down or broken open. Every sinew of mind and body is affected, every comfortable self-belief (comfortable owing to its familiarity) is swept away in an instant and, whatever happens thereafter, the person knows they and the life they have led can never be quite the same again. This disorientation and revelation is resonant to a client in therapy who, through their creative enquiry, makes a sudden and powerful discovery about themselves which can be a deeply shocking and disturbing experience. This is akin to Bax's idea of the cloak, constructed so painstakingly over the years to provide safety and solace – our 'defence against the world' – being torn away to expose the nakedness beneath, perhaps to reveal the nothingness that Bax's deceased character most dreaded. Such an experience is literally 'mind-blowing'. It could be described as traumatic, where trauma is understood to be an experience which threatens to overwhelm the system, rendering the individual powerless and disconnected from him or herself and from the world of relationships beyond (leaving aside the question of whether the experience has a pleasant or unpleasant source). It is utterly tumultuous. There is nothing gentle about this. It is no wonder that the recently deceased individual in Clifford Bax's play resisted the Angel's instruction with such fearful opposition. In such a moment, our whole identity, who we understand ourselves to be, is shot through like a lightning bolt, threatening to destroy everything in its path. At such times, what we believed to be impenetrable, solid and reliable proves to be nothing of the sort.

This book is an exploration of the part play has in the construction of our identity – in other words, the cloak. That creation that we weave around ourselves that both protects and imprisons us. I am also curious how play can facilitate the re-examining and reworking of the cloak. What is it that the cloak protects? Who are we without it? Are we really nothing, as feared by Bax's character, and, if so, how would that be? The monk's awakening has an extreme quality that is total and all-consuming. Perhaps there are other forms of awakening that are less visibly dramatic but nevertheless life-altering for the recipient? As a play therapist and dramatherapist, and as a client of therapy myself, I have witnessed and experienced numerous 'moments of awakening', 'ah-ha' flashes, some lasting a millisecond – blink and it is missed – some seeming to inhabit suspended time, and others accompanied by great cathartic release. Every one of them is unique, precious and awesome in its own right; every one of them is a privilege to behold. I have seen children, in their everyday play as well as in the context of play therapy, experience moments of surprise when some new awareness emerges. These moments of awakening in psychotherapy could be described both as a 'gradual unfolding' and a (re)connection, a tapping into something bigger. John Welwood[5] describes unfolding as a process throughout life that leads to new discoveries and revelations. Welwood recognizes two kinds of unfolding: horizontally, where new discoveries and developments build in a progressive way, and vertically, which is more like the monk's experience on the mountainside, 'a sudden and surprising… emergence, in which a larger, deeper kind of awareness unexpectedly breaks through into consciousness, allowing us to see things in a radically new light'.[6] This psychological unfolding and connection and the spiritual awakening experienced by the monk are not, I would suggest, necessarily the same. There may be a psychological unfolding without an accompanying spiritual awakening. During the course of this book, in several different contexts, I will introduce the idea of a spectrum or continuum. And here is the first one. Here I am proposing that our psychological and spiritual selves are intrinsically united, as are our physical, social, emotional, sexual and intellectual selves. We are multifaceted beings. All aspects of ourselves are interrelated.

The perspective taken in this enquiry is a transpersonal one – or psychospiritual as it is known in the domain of Core Process psychotherapy[7] – for I am interested in bringing together spiritual and psychological aspects. Humanistic and transpersonal psychologist Abraham Maslow held the belief that spirituality is an innate part of human nature and that spiritual realization is the ultimate in human development, describing a 'Fourth psychology'.[8] In contrast to the Third Force which is concerned with humanness, personal identity and self-actualization, the Fourth Force relates what is beyond the personal to the transpersonal, beyond our Earthbound existence to include the whole cosmos. Eastern philosophies, predominantly Buddhism, have much to offer the Western psychological world. I will also draw upon other spiritual and religious traditions to shed light upon this multifaceted and diverse enquiry. I work from the premise that no one spiritual tradition holds The Truth. The founding father of the transpersonal approach is Carl Jung, and in his exploration of depth psychology he drew upon mystical Christianity, Shamanism and Eastern philosophies. The Buddha advised not to have blind faith, rather to explore for oneself what others are proposing in an attempt to discover one's own truth.

Furthermore, I also believe all aspects of us are in relationship to all other beings. I am not saying anything new here. The tradition and practice of Buddhism is rooted in the understanding of interconnectedness and non-separateness.

The model of psychotherapy training I studied, Core Process, at the Karuna Institute in Devon, UK, is a contemporary manifestation of Buddhist psychology and philosophy, contemplative practice and Western psychology. During my practice as a Buddhist psychotherapist I have been privileged to witness many discoveries and reconnections. As a drama and play therapist, I have witnessed to my great delight and surprise (my own 'ah-ha' moments) that the medium of play has a great deal to contribute to the process of discovery and reconnection both to self and to Source. Source describes our sacred or spiritual ground; some may recognize it as God, Goddess, the Universal, the Infinite, Emptiness, the Truth, the Numinous, and the Dynamic Ground,[9] for example.

This book is an enquiry into the complex nature of play: its part in the creation of the cloak that enables survival in this imperfect relational world *and* the role of play in the process of awakening that encompasses the psychological, intellectual, physical, social and spiritual sphere, reminding us that life is more than just surviving: it is about thriving. It is about being connected to something bigger than the individual self.

In the writing of this book, I have been reminded many times of Indra's Net.[10] Indra is a Hindu god who created a vast net covering the universe. The net portrays the nature of reality where all things are connected over space and time. At each join in the net sits a shining jewel. The surface of each jewel is multidimensional so that it reflects everything else. Each jewel reflects every other jewel and is reflected by every other jewel, thus portraying the nature of absolute reality in its vastness, infinity and holography. And so it is with play. There is no way I can re-present play completely and entirely to you, the reader, for it is both simple and exquisitely profound. It has infinite possibilities. I can only offer you my very humble contribution and my wish that, like a jewel in Indra's Net, it may be recognized for its part in this rich tapestry we call life.

At the heart of this book are my clients' personal accounts of their healing through Buddhist psychotherapy and the arts therapies – in particular, play and dramatherapy. As therapy is a joint practice through which the therapist, as well as the client, is transformed, it is also an account of my own healing. It has often been said to me – and in turn I find myself repeating this to my own students and supervisees – that 'we meet the clients we need to facilitate our own healing'. Through the acceptance of non-separateness, this statement is obvious. Joint enquiry, when understood within the context of spaciousness, far from encroaching on the client's therapeutic space, expands the space to include the other person, the therapist, and thus the relationship. We are social beings. We are relational beings. All our wounding happens in relationship, and all our healing happens in relationship.[11]

The healing has the capacity to enrich and deepen the experience of living, releasing stuck patterns and conditioning and allowing us to be present to ourselves and each other in ways we perhaps never imagined. It is the transformation from being asleep to wakening up. It is an honour for me to be given this opportunity to share my clients' bravery and a privilege to experience their trust to have me alongside them as they travel their own paths of unfolding and reconnection. I hope I meet the challenges before me with clarity, courage and the skill required.

Clifford Bax's play takes place in the land of spirit, where the earthly being is seen struggling with the challenge of removing their cloak in order to enter whatever lies beyond. This book is not an enquiry into what might lie beyond our earthly existence. This is the realm of conjecture or faith. Here is an enquiry into how we live our lives *now*, in the present and from moment to moment. How life can be lived as fully and as authentically as possible according to one's true nature in Buddhism, termed as our Buddha or Being nature. A life that at the point of death, when all is dissolving, when all identity is disintegrating and we encounter our own 'angels', we may be afforded the opportunity to reflect upon a life well lived and say, yes, I am ready. At the risk of seeming morbid, it is helpful to hold our own mortality in the picture during this enquiry. Death, I was once told, provides the backing on the glass that creates a mirror. It allows life to be reflected back to us. Elisabeth Kübler-Ross spent much of her professional life exploring our relationship to death and dying.[12] She noticed that many people show the most extraordinary creativity when consciously involved in their own dying process. Kübler-Ross was of the view that we all possess such gifts but they are often obscured by our trivial, often negative, frequently materialistic preoccupations which waste much precious time and energy. She believed that when we are able to engage in the reality of our own mortality, we become much freer, creative souls. Do we have to wait until we *know* we are dying (in real rather than abstract terms) before we can afford ourselves the opportunity to live life more freely and more creatively?

In my work as a psychotherapist, I hear my clients frequently ask this question. Many clients express a wish to feel free to create relationships that are not constrained by mistrust, craving or fear. Buddhist nun Pema Chödrön asks, 'Do the days of our lives add up to further suffering or to increased capacity for joy?'[13] This is, she adds, an important question.

Can psychotherapy support people in bringing awareness to the layers of defences that make up the cloak – to enquiry into the fabric, the weft and weave of this protective garment, so that it may be re-evaluated? Consciously reworked, reshaped, rewoven, to better suit the individual and to permit a more creative engagement with life? My client Natalie arrived at our first meeting with a quote – 'Tell me, what is it you plan to do with your one wild and precious life?' – from the Mary Oliver poem 'The Summer Day':

Who made the world?
Who made the swan, and the black bear?
Who made the grasshopper?
This grasshopper, I mean –
the one who has flung herself out of the grass,
the one who is eating sugar out of my hand,
who is moving her jaws back and forth instead of up and down –
who is gazing round with her enormous and complicated eyes.
Now she lifts her pale forearms and thoroughly washes her face.
Now she snaps her wings open, and floats away.
I don't know exactly what a prayer is.
I do know how to pay attention, how to fall down
into the grass, how to kneel down in the grass,
how to be idle and blessed, how to stroll through the fields,
Which is what I have been doing all day.
Tell me, what else should I have done?
Doesn't everything die at last, and too soon?
Tell me, what is it you plan to do
with your one wild and precious life?[14]

Playful Awakening: Releasing the Gift of Play in Your Life is not only about therapy. Its message is about rediscovering what each of us, without exception, already has, and how we might free that potential of play to serve and enrich life. Not only our own individual life, however, for the very nature of play is its expansiveness and infectiousness. Through our own play we touch the lives of others. Through play we make manifest our interconnectedness.

The book is divided into three sections: Act 1, Act 2 and Act 3.

Act 1, Scene 1 introduces the Universality of Play and, in Scene 2, works towards a definition of this subject that encompasses the cave paintings of homo sapiens, a toddler's earliest forays, Shakespeare's plays and Mozart's symphonies, together with poetry, classical art and dance. Although not the focus for this book, we also touch upon the importance of play in the field of scientific endeavours. Human beings are meaning makers. Our brains, minds and bodies have developed over millennia because we have been curious about the world and what it means – how it all works and why. We are innately curious about ourselves and each other. We are playful in our nature. What happens if…why did that happen…why is this so? Human beings, for better or for worse, will push everything and anything to its limits. Chögyam Trungpa Rinpoche urges us to live our lives as an experiment,[15] and what better way to do that than through play? Staying with the metaphor of the cloak as a defined self, we will explore how our unique identity forms from early life in Scene 3, and in Scene 4 we explore the role of play in weaving the cloak.

Act 2, Scene 1 focuses on the experience of Falling Asleep – how we cut off from our deeper nature – and raises the question: Is falling asleep avoidable or inevitable? We return to play in Scenes 2, 3 and 4 where we will explore *The Day of the Square Yellow Sun* – Obstacles to Play, having internalized the judgments of significant others in our lives – parents, teachers, the societies and cultures that shape us – who may have told us we couldn't draw, act, sing or dance so that we learn to close down those precious parts of ourselves in order to avoid further suffering. We learn from our societies that as adults we no longer *should* play because life is far too serious for such trivia, isn't it? Here, too, we will explore the concepts of 'deadly' play.[16] In the final scene of this act, we raise the question: Is there a shadow side to play relating to the risks and dangers of playing?

Act 3 opens with *The Call from the Great Below* – Aspiration to Awaken. The Call is a phrase taken from the 7000-year-old Sumerian myth of Inanna. We explore the question: If awakening is such a life-enriching, joyful endeavour, then why do we human beings not welcome it enthusiastically and without reservation into our lives? This scene introduces what Buddhist tradition considers the essential conditions for awakening, known as the Four Great Catalysts of Awakening or the Brahma Viharas. These conditions are recognized as essential in cultivating the courage, tenacity and trust needed for awakening.

The following scene, Manifestations of Play, is a celebration of some of the great gifts to humanity from the arts that we can enjoy and share today. Here I draw upon well-known and lesser-known contributors, admittedly reflecting my own aesthetic viewpoint.

Scene 3 is concerned with play's relationship to well-being across the spectrum from play for surviving to thriving. This scene introduces the arts therapies and provides case studies which illustrate the intentional application of play for the purpose of healing. Play for survival is a testament to those who have lived through and been trapped in the most abhorrent life-threatening circumstances and have revealed the human spirit's capacity to use play not only for physical survival in such extremes of terror but to protect the life force from lasting harm. We will draw upon personal accounts from those who have suffered violation to show just how astonishing we humans are and the extraordinary power of play.

The final scene examines the possibility of Staying Awake, raising the question: How, in this beautiful yet imperfect world that exists and we have co-created, can we develop a lasting resilience that allows us to live our wild and precious lives as fully as we are able? Calling for a shift from 'tabloid to myth',[17] as Hougham describes it, and to paraphrase his words so that the uniqueness of each individual can expect more than operation and domesticity…it can be *realized*.

ACT 1

THE UNIVERSALITY OF PLAY

All the world's a stage
And men and women merely players;
They have their exits and their entrances,
And one man in his time plays many parts…[1]

The adverb 'merely' has a modern-day meaning of 'only as specified and nothing more'; however, there is another now-obsolete meaning – 'simply, purely, altogether, entirely' – which offers quite a different sense to the meaning of being 'players'.

We begin our enquiry with play: what play is and where it might be found.

When we speak of play, many may immediately associate it with children and perhaps only with children. Indeed, play is what children do naturally, given the opportunity. They meet and make sense of their world through the medium of play – in particular, those experiences that carry an emotional meaning. Play is often referred to as *the* language of children. Play in the development of a self in the creation of a cloak, an identity, is explored later, but straightaway let us challenge the myth that play is *only for children*. It could be argued that play is probably most common during the times when we are growing in our understanding of ourselves, our environments and our social relations; hence, play is associated with children and childhood. Yet it is illogical and shortsighted to believe that *only* children have a capacity to grow in these areas and that when we are adults we stop developing.

Play is something many adults struggle to engage in because, as we grow up and take on responsibilities in the world, other things take over or get in the way. In the West, we are familiar with phrases such as 'stop messing/playing around and get on with your work', so the word 'play' becomes synonymous with messing around: play is something someone does when they are not doing something worthwhile and important. We are told that the opposite of play is work, and work is what adults do, isn't it? Such phrases go hand in hand with others such as 'stop being childish', which is usually intended as an insult. So we learn that play and playing belong to children, not to the serious world of being adults, and our capacity to play becomes obscured by layers of responsibility – to our own, our children's and the world's detriment. It has not always been so. Dr Stuart Brown[2] said, 'Play is more than just fun.'[3] He draws our attention to a 16th-century painting by Netherlandish Renaissance artist Pieter Bruegel, showing a joyous and complex scene of sheer playful delights. Against a European courtyard backdrop, adults and children of all ages are depicted engaging in, according to Brown, over a hundred variations of play including rough-and-tumble, imaginative, storytelling and object play. Life and vitality are positively bursting from the canvas. Brown contrasts this to a cover story published by the *New York Times Magazine*[4] extolling the values of play, and yet only children are depicted in the image. Brown concludes, 'I think we may have lost something in our culture.' Medic Bowen White[5] has pioneered an approach as a medical clown, undertaking significant humanitarian work with his clown colleagues including the renowned physician Patch Adams, made famous by Robin Williams in the film which took his name. White believes that in society today 'we are all being acculturated to devalue play and fun or to relegate it to some later, after work time frame'.[6] He goes on to note that we have a way of separating play off from the rest of our lives – if we are working, play is excluded; if we are playing, work is excluded. White fundamentally challenges this 'bivalent', dualistic viewpoint. He shows how being a playful doctor can succeed in engaging desperate and traumatized patients where conventional approaches fail.

Furthermore, in so many so-called civilized societies today, children's play as defined in this book is in serious jeopardy as consumerism becomes god and many parents are worried for their children's futures in this highly pressurized world. For these parents, play is an extravagance the contemporary child cannot afford. Perhaps it is the parents, driven by their fear of what might become of their offspring, who cannot afford this space for play? Folklorist and play theorist Brian Sutton-Smith describes the opposite of play not as work but as depression.[7] This is a sobering thought.

Thankfully, many disciplines still do understand the importance of play for both children and adults and regard it as a necessity throughout life for the growth and evolution of the individual and society. Play is the root of creativity and thinking. Einstein, arguably one of the greatest thinkers of all time, is reputed to have said that play is more important than knowledge. Play is innate in every human being, whether they choose to cultivate it or not. Stuart Brown holds the view that fundamentally play is largely accountable for our existence as sentient, intelligent beings. Paul Harris[8] argues how a child's capacity to imagine alternative possibilities – in other words, to play – makes a significant and continuing contribution to intellectual and emotional development and *lasts a lifetime.*

If we are able to play, we can bring a lightness and softening that allows for a loosening around how we perceive ourselves, others and our own thinking. Play allows us to open up and question concepts, beliefs and assumptions that we perhaps were not even aware we held, offering us opportunities to deepen our understanding of ourselves, others and the world we share together. Play is universal, however much it is ignored, obscured or derided. Scratch the surface and there we will find it – a little rusty perhaps, but nevertheless present.

Negative or dismissive attitudes towards play often arise from our failure to grasp the overall purpose of free play because its values are often not linear, goal-orientated and immediate (discounting the obvious gains of fun, joy, laughter). It is not always easy to link a particular form of play to a desired outcome, and maybe we need to question the validity of trying to do so. The relationship of play to our evolutionary trajectory is abstract and, more often than not, oblique. The 'evidence' is there if we wish to discover it. Harris makes a convincing argument for the link between the emergence of modern humans – homo sapiens – some 40,000 years ago and the engagement in cave painting, refinement of tools, the creation of jewellery and burial rituals which could be considered as forms of play.

Game designer Jane McGonigal[9] speaks of the population in the Kingdom of Lydia in Asia Minor over two and a half thousand years ago. On the brink of starvation and in grave danger of wiping themselves out completely through warring, the Lydian ruler in desperation invented a dice game using sheep knuckles. The ruler decreed that his people would alternate their days – one day eating, the next playing, the next eating and so on. They survived for 18 years in this way. When it was eventually safe to venture out, the Lydians were able to find the resources they needed. In the 21st century, Stuart Brown cites an experiment carried out on rats wherein two groups of young rats are observed managing an intrusive threat in their environment. One group of rats have had a normal upbringing in which they were able to play freely together; the rats in the other group were deprived of play in their early life. Both groups have the same reaction to the danger, withdrawing to a safe hiding place; however, after a while curiosity gets the better of the playful group and they begin, tentatively at first until their confidence grows, investigating and exploring the alien presence among them. Upon discovering the intruder to be benign, the rats in this group resume their normal business. Those in the play-deprived group, however, remain hidden, too afraid and lacking in basic curiosity and self-trust. Consequently, this group fails to eat and starves. The playful group is able to take a risk whereas the non-playful group is not and suffers immensely as a result.[10]

We might expect to see play at work in familiar creative fields of endeavour such as theatre, art, music and dance, subjects we will enquire into more deeply throughout this book. However, the arts do not have the monopoly on play. Scientist and evolutionist Charles Darwin[11] described the creation of new variations in species as 'sports' that, if found to be advantageous to the species, would be passed on to future generations through the DNA. These were (and are) happy and fortuitous events in nature. Diversities in species would be eradicated if found to be useless for the species' survival – hence, only the fittest and the most adaptable survive. Paul Schoemaker[12] suggests that in the field of scientific endeavours more than half of the discoveries in healthcare have an accidental origin. He claims that such fortuitous breakthroughs as the discovery of penicillin by Alexander Fleming come about by creating opportunities for serendipity, being open-minded enough to recognize even the smallest observations and curious to explore further – all aspects of play.

Play is evident, for instance, in such diverse spheres as cooking, such as the playful curiosity of celebrity chef Heston Blumenthal, and biomedical engineering, in which Chris Toumazou[13] works alongside biomedics, atomic physicists, biologists and engineers and talks of a 'playground of innovation', encouraging his colleagues to be disruptive in the pursuit of discovery. Toumazou is known to ask the questions that most others would not think to ask, and his intuitive approach has led to groundbreaking inventions. Educationalists have long been fascinated by the role which play has in children's learning and have sought to increase international awareness of its importance. Anthropologists have studied play directly, exploring the role of play in adults' ability to make sense of and challenge societal norms and create new ones. Primatologist Isabel Behncke Izquierdo understands play to be evolution's gift from the bonobo apes she studies to human beings. She describes play as 'the chemistry of yes!' that epitomizes the essence of openness and discovery, adding that 'it is the only space where uncertainty is really fun, otherwise uncertainty is awful, it's scary'.[14]

In her prize-winning memoir *H is for Hawk*, Helen Macdonald records the exact moment she realized that hawks play. Macdonald had read all there was to read about goshawks and had never known this about them, yet her willingness to observe that upturned head and narrowed eyes – which she understood as play signs – led to her scrunching up balls of paper and watching her goshawk grabbing and gnawing at them. Next she rolled up a magazine, telescope-like, and peered through it. Her goshawk rewarded her efforts by ducking her head to reciprocate the gesture. Passing sounds through the tube of magazine resulted in her hawk 'shaking her tail rapidly from side to side and shivering with happiness'.[15]

Researcher and writer Brené Brown, in developing a concept she describes as 'Wholeheartedness'[16] that embodies authenticity and a sense of worthiness, recognized play's central position in this way of living life. Brown noticed people who were having fun and celebrating the simple fact of being alive. She was puzzled by these folk until she realized they were simply playing, not so much organized play as in sports, hobbies and crafts, but spontaneously seizing the moment. Brown describes them as 'fooling around' – Jonathan Kay, acclaimed storyteller and exponent of the Archetypal Fool, has much to add on this point. We will meet Jonathan Kay later.

Play, although culturally and socially influenced, can cross boundaries quite effortlessly. Where play adheres to particular rules, such as in football or other sports, the newcomer will need to learn the basics but will quickly understand the general idea and will certainly appreciate the emotional aspects – the excitement, tension, frustrations and joy – that a good game of football can evoke. Teasing, another form of play, is understood to be extremely culturally specific. Judy DeLoache and Alma Gottlieb collated anthropological information about teasing in different parts of the world in relation to child-rearing practices.[17] Their findings were diverse. In one of these societies, the Beng tribe of the Ivory Coast, children are taught by their parents to insult their grandparents to enable the youngsters to feel freer and more relaxed with elderly relatives. Play theorist Brian Sutton-Smith comments that the study demonstrates how such complex play practices initiate the young into their society. Teasing, as with other forms of play, is a way of helping to socialize. How would such behaviour be seen in Western cultures? There is, of course, a fine line between teasing and tormenting, and what may be teasing to one may be experienced as bullying to another.

Play manifests through humans and lives through the human endeavour. But it is not only humans who play; animals play too – including dogs, cats, horses, gerbils and seals, as well as the bonobos studied by Isabel Behncke Izquierdo. Play crosses species' boundaries – humans play with dogs and cats, horses with dogs. There is much documentary evidence to show that animals, as with all sentient beings, share our inherent capacity for play. In his TED lectures, Stuart Brown shows his audience the most astonishing series of photographs captured by German photographer Norbert Rosing showing the play between a starving polar bear and a husky dog. It is extraordinary because the dog could so easily have been supper to the great beast. Instead, they became playmates – not once, but repeatedly over a number of days until the ice freezes and the bear can go hunting for seal. A question arises: Can it only be play when the participants have an awareness of it not being 'real'? Recently, I saw one of my cats chasing a leaf across the lawn. Was he playing? Did he know it was only a leaf and not a mouse to catch and eat?

There are as many ways to play as there are beings who play, for play is less about the actual activity and more about the mental state of the player. This said, there are commonly recognizable play signs such as soft eyes (in contrast to the predator's stare), and for animals such as dogs, the classic play bow, tail wagging, play-bite invitation, jaw-wrestling play, head-jockeying play (as seen in black bears[18]) and flat hair as opposed to raised hackles; all these signs clearly evident in the polar bear and husky dog. Essentially, play signs convey to the other that we are non-threatening. Bowen White makes the observation that humans and animals have a 'play face' that is instantly recognizable to fellow players regardless of culture.

Some years ago, I had the opportunity to facilitate a week-long play therapy residential for trainee child psychotherapists in South Wales. In beautiful surroundings, we were a short walk from the sea. On our first glorious morning in late autumn, the group asked if we might venture down to the beach. It was agreed on the condition that we went there as our child-selves, not as adults, so as to avoid discussions of assignments and the like. So that this group of 'children' did not have an adult accompanying them, which would have changed the dynamics, it was also necessary that I too engaged as my child-self. Many revelations were made that morning (Plato is reputed to have said we can learn more about each other in an hour of playing than in years of talking), but what really struck me was the experience in the children's playground on the way to the beach. There we encountered a three-year-old boy with his mother. He instantly recognized our play faces and seemed completely unaware of our size and shape as adults. To the child, we were fellow playmates. He was open and engaging, and, of course, we responded similarly. What was equally interesting was his mother's reaction to us, which was one of trepidation tinged with fear. I noticed her hastily looking around for our carers/minders and her confusion when none could be seen, as if, in this playful state, we needed the holding of adults in the environment. Unlike her son, the mother was not able to recognize our play signs as non-threatening. As the group leader, I was instantly faced with a dilemma: should I take the time to explain our behaviour to her, instantly taking me out of my child-self and into 'responsible adult'? I chose not to do this and instead urged the group to head on down to the beach, leaving the playground sooner than we might have otherwise. We departed to the exuberant waves of a little boy and the great relief of his mum. This is the play face that White speaks of inviting another to play. It is important to note here that the invitation to play is just that: an invitation – one that the child, but sadly not his mother, was able to accept at that time.

Play exists both within and outside the realms of conventional time and space. It occupies both a timeless zone and a multidimensional domain. A Greek tragedy may have been written 2000 years ago by

Socrates and yet, when we see it live at the theatre, it is happening in the here-and-now for us, just as when a child plays out the argument she witnessed between her parents that morning, it is happening in the here-and-now for her. Sally Jenkinson makes the remark about only a handful of adults walking on the moon, yet millions of children having done so in their play. In *The Genius of Play*,[19] Jenkinson offers us the Oxford Dictionary translation of the term 'genius' as being 'attendant, tutelary spirit'. This sense of play as spirit resonates through many others' understanding of this phenomenon we are calling play.

In works of music, art, sculpture or literature, for instance, we have tangible evidence of other people's playful endeavours and can be moved to tears by a piece of music written hundreds of years ago, and who knows how future generations will respond to music composed today? Cave drawings in remote locations in Wales have recently been discovered dating back at least 10,000 years. Sculptor Emily Young uses rocks that are over 3.5 billion years old. She mused, 'I often wonder who might be looking at them should they last another 3.5 billion.'[20] Could we imagine who? In a world where monetary investment is so risky ('cash is trash, art is smart'), investment in a Young sculpture may be a canny speculation (further to 'cash is trash, art is smart' comes 'art is no longer about the soul, it's a unique alternative asset as it is not tied to one currency – unlike a Mayfair apartment…'[21]).

Although creations may last for centuries or even millennia, play essentially lives in the present moment – in the immediate. It exists in that moment of hearing, seeing, touching and being emotionally stirred by the piece of music, a sculpture or the rhythm that moves our bodies. We experience play through our bodily senses, and although we may be able to call upon a memory of a song or a fragrance, our senses only operate in the present moment. Play brings the 'then' into 'now' and the 'there' into 'here'. These qualities of play are especially significant when we explore the role of play in the healing process in the creative arts therapies – drama, art, music, dance movement, bibliotherapy and play therapy itself.

It is perhaps the field of psychological healing and specifically psychoanalysis that has led us to understand that the lack of play in our lives does not only mean a shortage of creative ideas, although this would be bad enough. A lack of play cuts to the very heart of what it is to be human and could be a factor in life and death. Stuart Brown[22] has carried out more than 6000 'play histories' of individuals from very diverse backgrounds including psychiatric patients, artists, scientists and serial murderers. Brown has identified, through his extensive research, that the ability to play is fundamental not only for happiness but in the creation and maintenance of social relationships. Brown challenges the view that play is simply a means of rehearsal for later life, such as lion cubs rough-and-tumbling, chasing and catching one another as preparation for future hunting. Instead, he offers the observation that when there is a notable deficit in play behaviour in the early years, animals still become competent hunters, but what they struggle to do is make the distinction between friend and enemy. In other words, they fail to read social behaviours and subsequently act inappropriately aggressively, or they withdraw from social situations, just as the unfortunate rats did. Animals that have not had enough play in childhood do not recognize the 'play faces' of others. Human beings are social, relational beings and we cannot survive without each other. Play facilitates our understanding of each other's emotional states and behaviours and offers opportunities for responding sensitively and fittingly.

Psychoanalyst and paediatrician Donald Winnicott says, 'It is in playing and only in playing that the individual child or adult is able to be creative and to use the whole personality, and it is only in being creative that the individual discovers the self.'[23] Stuart Brown corroborates, saying that 'true play that comes from our own inner needs and desires is the only path to finding lasting joy and satisfaction in our work'.[24] Work can be as diverse as any conventional paid work or being in a personal relationship or parenting children. Winnicott further stressed the vitality of play in the therapeutic relationship:

> Psychotherapy takes place in the overlap of two areas of playing, that of the patient and that of the therapist. Psychotherapy has to do with two people playing together.[25]

Bowen White expands on Winnicott's statement by adding that play, as well as creating psychological space for relationships, also releases energy that can be used for problem solving and other creative endeavours.

Play, in many fields of study, is recognized as 'a self-motivating activity that serves a reflective and reflexive function…of the individual and culture [enabling] growth and understanding'.[26]

Petrūska Clarkson introduces the concept of *physis*,[27] which seems to correspond to Göncü and Perone's understanding of play. *Physis* is, according to Guerrière,[28] the life force that allows for healing, growth and creativity. It appears to be an energy that is available to but not necessarily originating from the individual; an energy that can be tapped into and used for the greater good. Clarkson suggests that medical practitioners have long known about this healing force, and those attuned and humble enough regard themselves as servants to *physis*. She quotes 16th-century physician Paracelsus:

> There is nothing in me except the will to discover the best that medicine can do, the best there is in nature, the best that the Nature of the earth truly intends for the sick. Thus I say, nothing comes from me; everything comes from nature of which I too am a part.[29]

Paracelsus was, among other professions, an alchemist. Alchemy is, in the literal sense, the ancient science that predates chemistry. It was concerned with the transmutation of base substances into gold. Metaphorically, it is a complex system for personal transformation proposed by psychoanalyst Carl Jung, and Paracelsus was a major inspiration to Jung more than three centuries after his death.

Richard Hougham, in his exploration of the nature of creativity, draws on the concept of *duende*. The concept of *duende* was 'dis-covered' by Spanish dramatist, poet and theatre director Frederico Lorca in response to the growing support for fascism in 1930s Spain. This creative force is described by Hougham as 'a force of initiation which resists the censorship of the operational and which may enable the individual…to rekindle a sense of mystery, meaning and location'.[30] Lorca saw *duende* as a 'wind of the spirit…a wind with the colour of a child's saliva, crushed grass, and Medusa's veil, announcing endless baptism of freshly created things'.[31] Hougham tells us that the literal translation of *duende* is a goblin, elf or fairy, deriving from the term *duen de casa*, meaning lord of the house, and refers to a trickster spirit which offers protection yet resists domesticity. *Duende* is, according to Hougham, 'a disruption to the norm, a crack of the whip at the façade of persona, a laugh in the face of dogma and fundamentalism'.[32] *Duende* is both personal and universal, present within all, yet, as Lorca extols, 'one must awaken duende from the remotest mansions of the blood'.[33]

Rob Preece recognized the deep connections between these two disciplines in the 1980s while on retreat in India. For Preece, Jung's understanding of alchemical nature revealed the psychological meaning in Tantric practice, and, conversely, viewing Tantra from a more psychological place served to widen and enhance understanding of Western archetypal psychology. In essence, Tantra centres attention on the vitality and underlying energy of life; delicately interweaving mythical and historical truths to express 'the inner meaning and symbolic nature of our experiences'[34] that connect us with subtle forces which shape and influence life force. The literal meaning of Tantra is *continuity*, referring to 'the continuity and co-emergence of absolute and reality truth, heaven and earth, spirit and matter, emptiness and form, awakening and *samsara*'.[35] Tantra is often popularized as relating solely to sex in the West. Unfortunately, the wider context of our sexuality and its implicit relationship to our life force is usually missed in this reductionist perspective. This vitality includes sexuality indeed, as perhaps the most profound form of creativity; however, our life force cannot be conveyed *only* through our sexuality. From an alchemical view, Jung recognized this vitality as spirit in its relation to libido, but not only libido. For Jung, 'The hallmarks of spirit are first, the principle of spontaneous movement and activity; second, the spontaneous capacity to produce images independently of sense perception; and third, the autonomous and sovereign manipulation of these images.'[36] As Preece comments, 'Jung's view of spirit suggests a phenomenon present in the psyche of each individual, giving rise to the power of imagination.'[37]

Shakespeare understood that we live in a playful universe because, according to his character Jacques, we are all players on this stage of the world. Play lives in and through us. In Buddhism but more commonly found in Hinduism, the Sanskrit word *līlā* has been translated as 'self-willed joy, the play of a child and the work of the god(s)'[38] – it is the divine play of the gods. It is the sport or game played by the bodhisattva.[39] *Līlā* is the creation, destruction and re-creation of everything, not for the outcome, but for the pure joy of the process. It is that quality of spontaneity, mischievousness and mystery found in a young child's play. Although joyful, *līlā* can and does embody terror, sorrow and grief, deception, eroticism and, like Lorca's *duende*, trickery. Hawley argues that one of its main functions is to 'undermine everyday assumptions about life'[40] – in other words, *līlā* reminds us not to take life for granted and not to have preconceived ideas that cause rigidity. According to Robert Goodwin, *līlā* is 'the universe in a work of art, a play, for it is nothing but a transcendental consciousness taking form for its own delight'.[41] Stephen Nachmanovitch[42] describes *līlā* as 'the most difficult and hard-won achievement imaginable, and its coming to fruition is a kind of homecoming to our true selves'.

In the ancient Greek language, the word *athyrma* was used to describe the *action of play*. In the arts and philosophy, it describes not just the psychic energy that inspires the artist or the poet to create but also the feelings that are triggered in the psyche of the audience or the reader on encountering that piece of artwork. It is a word that has been reclaimed by the Hellenic Institute of Play Therapy and Dramatherapy Training Programme in Athens. I spoke with two of its directors, Vicky Zerva and Peter Vagiakakos, to ask them the significance of this word in their training programme. For them, the word encapsulates their intention for the training and most accurately defines how they experience the universal power of play. Interestingly, the term is still in current popular usage, but over the years it has taken a negative connotation. It has come to describe a human being who is a 'puppet in the hands of a god' – a person with no self-determination. In many Greek dramas and especially in the tragedies, human beings were indeed portrayed as being toys to the gods. Take, for instance, Sophocles' Oedipus and the tragedy that befell not only him but his parents, wherein he slayed his own father and mistakenly married his own mother. The truth caused him to gouge out his own eyes and to wander in the wilderness thereafter. As if this was not enough punishment, the curse continued into the next generation. The myth of Dionysus, however, portrays a different relationship between god and human. Dionysus, also called 'the liberator', was the god of music, wine, ecstatic dance and ritual. He set free his followers from their inhibitions and fear, both possessing and empowering them to embody their exuberance that was both exhilarating and, at times, terrifying.

Zerva and Vagiakakos reflected on the way the meaning of powerful early Greek words is often hijacked, perhaps to lessen their potency in the everyday language, such as the Greek word '*daemon*' (δαίμων) or '*daimon*'. In archaic Greek, the word originates from the verb '*dao*' (δάω) meaning 'I have deep knowledge, I have learned'. Thus, a *daimon* is an archetypal being that holds knowledge and truth. James Hillman defines *daimons* as 'figures of the middle realm, neither quite transcendent Gods nor quite physical humans… [T]here were many sorts of them, beneficial, terrifying, message-bringers, mediators, voices of guidance and caution.'[43] In English, the word has been translated to 'demon' –

an enemy to be scared of. We pondered this tendency of the self, the ego, or, as we are defining it in this book, the cloak, to split into good and bad/evil, and our mutual desire to reach deeper within to a place beyond this egotistical duality, to a place where play is recognized as universal, where play is understood as *physis*, *duende* or *līlā*. In this place it is possible to imagine play at work, not to render the human being as a mere puppet but rather as a willing and conscious partner for the expression of something greater than the individual.

Our very universe has been and continues to be a playground – whether you believe in an absolute, divine originator or not, it is a constantly changing and dynamic essence. We are part of this playful universe. Play is the innate gift we are born with, through which we not only make discoveries but can also challenge our findings. Play allows us to dissolve what we think we know to make space for something new and thus far unknown. In this way, play, just like in nature, gives us the means for continual growth. Play serves to remind us to stay open-minded, for:

> In the beginner's mind there are many possibilities; in the expert's there are few.[44]

David Cowell, a Devon-based tradigital artist, has his own understanding of an expert. He says that an 'ex' is a has-been and a 'spert' is a drip under pressure.

Rob Burbea, a teacher at Gaia House, a centre for contemplation in Devon, UK, has taught for several years on the subjects of Image, Mythos and the Dharma – Dharma being the teachings of the Buddha. He states that 'where there is meaningfulness and soulfulness in our lives there is already mythos and fantasy'.[45] Rob's way of teaching is to gently challenge his audience's preconceptions of themselves, the world and the Buddha's teachings. His manner is playful, and the content of his teaching is play in the form of image, fantasy and myth. He suggests that fantasy is prevalent in all our lives; that we inhabit a world comprised of images that are nuanced, complex, only partially graspable like dreams and difficult to articulate. We experience ourselves as images or fantasies, and he stresses this is natural and not a problem as long as we are aware of this. One example he offers is how, in order to engage fully in the sexual act, we not only need to hold an image of our partner as sexually desirable but also of ourselves.

We can imbue another person, a place or a time with our own fantasy as we project our own thoughts, wishes and desires so that the other comes to hold a mythic value for us. Some may say these fantasies are not real, but Burbea questions: So, what is *real*? He suggests that the whole notion of what is real is oversimplified and proposes that there are two realities – objective reality that, by and large, most of us can agree on, and a second, a subjective experiential/imaginal reality which is individual to each person. And he proposes the idea: What if the imaginal world is the primary reality and the objective, the secondary one? Most adults move between both worlds quite seamlessly with an awareness of the difference between the two. In my experience, this distinction is something that children learn and they recognize the difference before the age of ten. As we will explore in subsequent scenes, it appears to be the imaginal reality that first engages the infant and orientates her to the world. It is then in relationship with other that she is introduced to objective reality. Burbea does not privilege one reality above the other and proposes that both have essential value. He acknowledges that some adults may, however, feel anxious and fearful in recognizing the imaginal reality – perhaps fearing this is the way to madness? Drawing upon the work of psychologist Mary Watkins with schizophrenic patients,[46] Burbea highlights the lack of nuance and complexity a patient with such a diagnosis may exhibit with the image. So, for instance, an alien or the CIA is simply an alien or the CIA. In contrast to this, he is proposing a richer, evolving and unfolding enquiry with the image and to refrain from understanding it in a literal way. Engaging this fluidity of meaning is a strong feature of Burbea's practice, as he encourages his students to explore the image through many different qualities and to hold a lightness around its meaning. He likens the work to Keats' 'soul-making', inviting us to enter into a special and dynamic relationship with the image, allowing it to change, allowing ourselves to be changed by it. Once we label an image as this or that, in essence we kill it. As Burbea cautions, 'an image or fantasy cannot be interpreted singularly; it cannot be explained'. It needs to keep a freshness as it is inherently ambiguous and infinite.

This approach wholly resonates with *physis, duende, līlā* and *athyrma*. Paradoxically, these images arise from us but have a feeling of coming from somewhere else, as if they do not belong to us, as if they are moving through us. Burbea suggests they are universal –

'something bigger than what ego wants yet still personal and unique'.[47] He disputes the assumption that the image comes in the service of the self and invites us to ponder the possibility of our being in the service of something greater than ourselves. This is interesting in connection to the two seemingly opposing views of *athyrma* – being a puppet or being a conscious ally to/of the gods (however we choose to understand that term).

In the Buddhist Mahayana tradition, the liminal space that exists in between emptiness which is full of potential (absolute reality) and the material world (relative reality) is recognized in the term *sambhogakaya*. The word *kaya* is translated to mean 'body' in relation to a Buddha, and *sambhogakaya* is often translated as the body of bliss that enjoys the fruits of Buddhist practice. So, a Buddha, an awakened one, is believed to exist in three realms – the *dharmakaya* (the aspect of absolute reality) and *nirmanakaya* (the body that, as in human form, is subjected to the effects of time and space; 'having our entrances and exits', according to Shakespeare's Jacques), with *sambhogakaya* lying between the two where emptiness and form meet.

The three *kayas* are not easy concepts to grasp and so Buddhist teachers will often draw upon a metaphor to help explain them. One such metaphor is that we imagine the *dharmakaya* as space such as a pure blue sky, the *sambhogakaya* as the clouds surrounded by rainbows and the *nirmanakaya* as the rain. The *sambhogakaya* relates to the archetypal, the imaginal Buddha form, and so lies beyond the constraints of space and time. Inhabiting the liminal space of play in between conventional relative reality and absolute reality, *sambhogakaya* acts as an intermediary and is described by Rob Preece as 'the constant vibration of inspiration made manifest'.[48] This intermediary needs to be embodied to be realized; as Preece says, 'like lightning coming to earth, a conductor is required, and humans as part of the natural world, are that conductor'. For as *līlā*, the whole universe is a manifestation of this vitality.

The *sambhogakaya* has a great many archetypal forces that exist in the intermediate between 'ordinary earthbound human consciousness and the level of ultimate, absolute reality'.[49] Sangharakshita reminds us that we do sometimes come into contact with the archetypal world of the *sambhogakaya* in deep meditation, dreaming or aesthetic experience. Perhaps, as Rob Burbea says, that contact is much more available once we open to it.

TOWARDS A DEFINITION OF PLAY

Play transcends all disciplines, if not all discipline.[1]

When we play we are engaged in the purest expression of our humanity, the truest expression of our individuality.[2]

I believe that play, with love, may just be central to living fully, living well.[3]

The world of play does not adhere to everyday reality and the laws that bind conventional time and space. Even though we may not physically move, we can enter the world of play, when conditions permit, where literally *anything* is possible. I could invite you to enter the world of play in this moment by imagining that I am requesting the pleasure of your company in a beautiful, tranquil garden, with softly coloured blossoms of lilac, pink and cream; a gentle, warm breeze; high wispy, white clouds in an otherwise rich blue sky; and a delicate perfume filling the air. The bodily sensations of relaxation, joy and contentment I hope you will be experiencing now are real for you, which you may not have been feeling when you began reading this scene. Yet the picture you have formed in your mind, the play you have engaged in, only exists in your imagination. And now as the image dissolves, perhaps the sensations linger?

Play is transitory in its nature. It comes and goes, and its presence changes us. For an activity to be play, it must be entered into voluntarily and the player can cease playing whenever they wish. Entry into the world of play is thus by invitation, as in the example above. If someone is forced to play or continue playing against their wishes, the activity ceases to be play. If you had not wished to engage in the garden visualization, then cajoling, pressurizing or even threatening you would have been completely fruitless.

Play is paradoxical. It has an absurdity about it. We know it is not of this tangible reality and yet it does have a truth. A truth that is difficult to define because we are trying to do so, for the large part, through the tangible reality of language.

Play inhabits the hinterland that Winnicott calls the 'potential space'.[4] This term, adopted by the paediatrician after observing babies with their parents/carers, is both physical and conceptual in nature. The potential space can literally be observed as the space between the two where play unfolds. It is also a conceptual space as play exists in the psychic domain. Winnicott explains: 'The precariousness of play belongs to the fact that it is always on the theoretical line between the subjective (i.e. inner experience) and that which is objectivity perceived.'[5] For this reason, the image of the garden I had in my mind when describing it is likely to differ from the one that emerged in your mind. Play's unique positioning – on that hypothetical line between the subjective and objective – contributes to its paradoxical nature, existing as it does in a reality outside of the everyday while simultaneously being both real and not real; thus, inhabiting linear and non-linear realms.[6] This capacity to be in linear time and space while occupying non-linear realms, together with its transitory nature, makes play one of the most potent gifts for growth and discovery.

As play is such a potent conveyance, it should come as no surprise, then, that it can be used as a means of exploitation and harm. Entering into the world of play makes us especially vulnerable as our defences (our cloaks) are softened and loosened. Harm inflicted through play is particularly damaging. This is the shadow side of play which we will explore later in the book. That people have had such negative experiences of something that has such potential saddens me greatly. Play has no hidden agenda other than the joy of living and all that entails. When used as a means of revenge or retaliation, it is no longer play. For many, this is their understanding of play and they freeze in terror at the very mention of the word. For far too many, play is about exposure, humiliation and persecution. Once the activity has the energy of vengeance, it ceases to be play. It cannot be. Even though one's personal experiences are subjective and may not be experienced in the same way as someone else's, nevertheless, if 'play' has been injurious, that must be respected. If forced to play, then that person will re-experience the earlier trauma, however much we want to help them. If abusive experiences involving 'play' are left unhealed, it is likely that any future experiences of play, whether intentionally harmful or not, will be felt from this same place of wounding. Play essentially springs from love, not fear; from collaboration, not competition.

As play inhabits the space in between, one way to approach the task of defining play is obliquely, using a visual image. An artist offered this instruction: when drawing a chair, for instance, rather than focusing on the physical lines, draw the spaces in between them. Play inhabits the spaces in between what we generally understand to be concrete, tangible reality. Without the spaces in between the parts of the chair, it would not be a chair, and without the spaces in between concrete, tangible reality, there would be no reality as we understand it. Yet play is clearly not *nothing*. It may be understood as emptiness that is full of potential. It is not only the spaces in between the apparently solid. Play exists in the space between us and the chair, between our conventional understanding of the object (as something to be sat upon) and our imagination. Play can soften the conventional meaning and invite in something else. As Nachmanovitch says, play is a configuring, a breaking apart and a reconfiguring so that we free ourselves from the chair's conventional meaning and apply another 'out of the box' meaning. So in play the chair can become a horse, or a spaceship or a letterbox. In this way, 'we toss together elements that were formerly separate (a chair and a horse) and our actions take on novel sequences (we can ride to the fair, go to Mars, post that letter to an imaginary friend)'.[7]

The unique place that play inhabits gives rise to a quality of elusiveness: it can stretch, evade and sidestep the truth (whatever the truth means). Play is mysterious and magical, mercurial and trickster-like. It is exploratory, taking us out of what we believe we know and into unfamiliar territory. In free play, we simply do not know where we will go and what will be revealed. It opens us up, catches us out, exposes us; play literally plays with us and who we believe ourselves to be. It shows us in ways we do not always wish to be seen. This is why Plato is reputed to have said you can discover more about someone in an hour of play than in a year of conversation.

Play only happens in the present. It brings the past or the future into the present moment, and this aspect is particularly important for therapeutic purposes and is invaluable in the therapeutic context because healing can *only happen in the present*.[8]

This quality of play is clearly very significant in relation to children's growth and learning. What we as adults are likely to overlook is the importance of play in supporting our own self-learning, our own unfolding, believing perhaps that we know who we are and that what is known is constant, unchanging and unchangeable. It is not possible for *anything* to remain unchanged, least of all living, interactive human beings.

Play has the quality of spontaneity about it. Even if we plan beforehand, play's trickster energy will often throw up something new and unexpected. It takes us directly into the mind of the beginner. When wholeheartedly engaged in, playful exploration gives us the freedom to experiment – physically, emotionally, cognitively, socially and spiritually. Play is life-enhancing and life-validating because it is directly connected to the life force. It is the wellspring of *physis*, connecting us to the universal. It gives us the possibility to form and re-form ourselves, and because of play's paradoxical quality – being simultaneously real and not real – it offers us a degree of psychic safety. Echoing Isabel Behncke Izquierdo's words from the previous scene – that play is the only space where uncertainty is welcomed – children's author Michael Rosen describes play as 'trial and error, without fear of failure'.[9]

Play is an unequivocal reminder of the transitory nature of life. Realization of this can create fear. Generally speaking, human beings like to have certainty and control because these make us feel safer. Perhaps play is essentially a frightening experience for many because truly free play takes us into the unknown and brings us face to face with the illusion of stability.

What we know is that play's potential for realization is ever-present and can be summoned in an instant as if it is waiting in the wings only to be invited on to the stage – by the wink of an eye, or intonation of a word, a slight gesture or nod, a joke, tease or a pun, or, as Bowen White describes, our 'play face'. There is usually an invitation to play, a subtle threshold marking beginnings and an ending to the play. This threshold can be crossed and re-crossed repeatedly during play, a feature which can be observed when children play together. Often children will step into play and out of it to clarify, explain, narrate what is happening. This process of witnessing, which involves detaching from and reflecting on, supports the later development of emotional resilience.

Mark Epstein observes that although play cannot be imposed, providing the conditions are favourable, it seems to naturally arise. As he says, '[play's] spirit emerges'.[10] When conditions are unfavourable, such as time constraints, a sense of duty or obligation, guilt or fear, it is challenging to be able to play, though not impossible. The Bible instructs us that we cannot live by bread alone,[11] and so for the population of the Kingdom of Lydia who were starving to death it would seem conditions were far from favourable and yet they *still* managed to play their dice games.

According to anthropologist and linguist Gregory Bateson,[12] another important quality of play is that all players/participants understand that actions and objects are to be interpreted as representational rather than literal (this fits with Rob Burbea's understanding of the image explored in the previous scene). In the previous scene, I noted an observation of my cat chasing a leaf across the lawn and questioned whether the cat was playing. It is my sense that the cat did know, in some way, that it was a leaf rather than a mouse as he made no attempt to eat it. On some level, the cat was playing. Without this basic ability to configure, break apart and reconfigure – that is, apply an out-of-the-box meaning – I would suggest play is thwarted, the problem being that the threshold into the world of play has not been crossed. To even engage in, let alone sustain, play with another if they were unable or unwilling to suspend their disbelief is deeply problematic. Take, for example, a long swath of bright turquoise fabric. If you had imagined the material as a tumultuous river needing to be navigated while your co-player only saw a piece of blue cloth, your play would not advance very far. On the other hand, if you were to play together, then you would still need to have a consensus of what the fabric was representing. If you imagined it to be a river and your co-player envisaged something else, then your collaboration might be challenged. In my experience as a play therapist, I have encountered some children who have been unable to engage in this representational or symbolic level of communication, conditions for play, often safety, not having been available for these children. All these children had suffered extreme early childhood neglect and other forms of abuse or were in deep grief. We will explore obstacles to play in a later scene.

Scott Eberle tells us that the word 'play' is a transitive verb, an intransitive verb, a noun and an adjective![13] Unsurprisingly, play does not 'lie flat on the page'.[14] Nachmanovitch advises us that play is not bound by linear progression, it does not follow numerical stages and it cannot be learned from a manual. He continues, 'Play cannot be defined, because in play all definitions slither, dance, combine, break apart, and recombine.'[15] This has certainly been my experience of play. A metaphor that often springs to mind is when you are desperately trying to squeeze holiday clothes into an undersized suitcase, pushing, catching one errant sleeve and tucking it in here only for another to fly out elsewhere, pushing, pushing, pushing, and then finally the clips acquiesce with your full weight cajoling them. You look up relieved and exhausted only to see the thing you really have to take still lounging mischievously on the chair. This is how it is with play. Play refuses to be boxed and labelled! Stuart Brown cautions that trying to define play is much like trying to explain a joke: 'analysing it takes the joy out of it'.[16]

The reason for our difficulty in trying to define play is convincingly explained by Brian Sutton-Smith.[17] We are trying to describe what is essentially a 'right'-brain phenomenon (as are play's close relations, intuition, creativity and imagination) with the rational and language-orientated 'left' brain. Brown adds that it is so challenging to define play because '[play] is a very primal activity. It is preconscious and preverbal – it arises out of ancient biological structures that existed before our consciousness or our ability to speak.'[18] Play is an experiment in the truest sense of the word and belongs to the territory of 'the spontaneous creative moment' defined by Hougham, which is 'difficult to understand rationally, impossible to predict and dangerous to prescribe'.[19] Brown adds that play in its most fundamental form is a precursor to advanced cognitive structures; indeed, play is arguably *the* vehicle for the development of those intellectual frameworks. Play is most definitely productive; however, the outcome may not be so apparent. If play is the vehicle for intellectual, emotional and social development, who could doubt its productivity? Paul Harris, whom we met in the previous scene, and Stuart Brown would argue that the practice of play has largely contributed to the evolution of human beings on this planet. Play is the wellspring of all creativity. It is the root of daydreaming, comedy, teasing, irony and flirting. There are literally hundreds of ways to play that include skipping, jumping, rolling, cartwheels, rough-and-tumble, solo or group play, board games such as snakes and ladders, chess and draughts, object play, social play, role play and imaginative play and clowning, to name but a few. Many of these apparent categories of play overlap. Play is the root of art, drama, poetry, prose, film, theatre, sculpture, dance, music, ritual, myth, architecture, fashion and innovation.

Play is fundamentally a joyful, playful, fun experience, or it offers, at least, a welcome respite or escape from another situation, especially a distressing one. Whether it is frivolous play or solemn play, it has a pleasurable quality; it energizes us and takes us out of our everyday lives so that for a time we might forget our obligations. Play makes us feel alive and can offer us the opportunity to better equip ourselves to be able to meet our responsibilities, feeling more creative and thus empowered. In realizing potential, play can reignite a sense of reconnection and optimism. It promotes empathy and compassion, and provides the 'oil in the cogs' that make possible secure attachments and elaborate social systems. Drama specialist Amanda Kipling noticed how, when playing games, pupils with particularly complex needs were liberated to form relationships with others.[20] Softening our defences, our cloaks, in order to engage in play makes us especially vulnerable; this is perhaps why children living in unsafe homes might struggle to play and why young animals are most at risk in the wild during their play when their attention is diverted and their guard is down.

Play is a 'mode of being' that has a different feel, texture and quality to everyday reality. It is a state of mind, an attitude, a spirit, so that two people can undertake the same activity but, depending on each person's state of mind, one could be described as playing while the other is not playing. The playful person may be engrossed in the activity, whether it is gardening, singing or baking a cake, for example, in an exploratory, joyful, process-orientated way as opposed to a dutiful, goal-focused, perhaps more self-critical way than the other person. There is something about play for the sheer pleasure of the undertaking, whatever that is; the outcome is a happy coincidence. There might still be a tangible outcome – vegetables, a song or a delicious cake – born out of play, but this is not the primary focus. As a child, whenever my client Susie asked her mother if she could help her in the kitchen – making bread or a cake, for instance – she was always put on washing-up duty. Not surprisingly, she soon tired of washing up (which certainly was not playful for her). As an adult, Susie realized her mother must have felt she had no time to simply play at baking as the pressure of time (a full-time working mother with four children) was always upon her. Throughout her life, Susie developed a very functional relationship with food, lacking adventure and excitement, until she became a grandmother. Susie recently shared a discovery of the joy of baking with her four-year-old granddaughter, Clara. Children are usually more than happy to teach adults how to play if they have forgotten along the way, providing the adults are willing students.

Play can help us resource, escape or avoid. It is the view of educationalist David Elkind that play has such significance in childhood because it is the child's only protection against a world that presents both real and imagined dangers. He believes play always facilitates a manipulation of reality in the service of the self.[21] Although perhaps a child's only defence against the world, play also affords the same protection for the adult. Play mediates the hard truths of life. It enables us to be with the inevitable truth about life – death; as Nietzsche said, 'We have art so that we may not perish by the truth.'[22] Play allows us to stay open and present to possibly overwhelming situations and circumstances, giving us the opportunity to find meaning in the darkest of times. Medical clown and medic Bowen White, whom we met in the previous scene, has made it his business to be with people who are suffering, from life-threatening illnesses and diseases to the horrific experiences of war. He says there is a way of being with suffering that is light, buoyant and spontaneous.[23] In this way, people's hearts connect and both are reminded of their innate vulnerability. He cites as an inspiration an adolescent boy with cancer who underwent prolonged and extreme chemo- and radiotherapy. One day, the boy came for his treatment and before White met him the boy put on the pink plastic pig nose he had brought in a bag. He turned his back as White approached and said something along the lines of 'Doctor White, I think that new medication you gave me is having some strange side-effects!' Was the boy in denial or was he using play to mediate the hard truth of his serious condition? Who can judge?

Play's lack of focus on a particular outcome – that is, it is the process rather than the product that is important – may be another reason why some are so afraid of it. As mentioned earlier, in conventional thinking the opposite of play is usually seen as work. So how do work and play differ from one another? Work can be seen as being focused on outcome and routine, regarded as compulsory, aligned with productivity and being necessary for survival. Could none of these descriptions relate to free play? If we are describing work as drudgery, deadening, boring or enslaving, then surely these descriptions could not be used to define play? The difficulty arises when we employ a generalized bivalent approach to our understanding – play is this, play is not that. It is far more spacious to imagine play and work along the same spectrum. From this perspective, Sutton-Smith's suggestion of the opposite of play as being depression seems all the more self-evident.

Free play			Depression
Improvisation	Organized play, e.g. games and sports, the arts	Outcome-focused and compulsory work	Drudgery, enslavement, deadening 'work'

VanderVen[24] advises against viewing play from a bivalent or dualist position of either/or – such as fantasy/reality, work/play, process/product, freedom/constraint – believing these to be too simplistic to encompass the complexity of play. It is far more helpful to view each of them as existing on a continuum, as with the earlier example of play and work.

Nachmanovitch, with his view on free play, makes a distinction between play and game, where game is recognized as a set form with its own rules, such as a football game, a sonnet or a symphony. Eberle does not hold the same viewpoint as Nachmanovitch, perhaps because of their differing starting places. Nachmanovitch is an artist, not a medical practitioner. As an improvisational violinist, he has cultivated a capacity to respond to his own impulses and the energy from his audience, and to channel that into his violin, creating a spontaneous and original range of notes and melodies. His violin is in conversation with its listeners. Eberle, in contrast, recognizes the importance of rules; they are 'not just for organizing games and making them fair, they keep games interesting and keep games going'.[25] Eberle's understanding encompasses both official, complex, universally acknowledged rules of national sports to instantly arising rules 'noisily negotiated in a neighbourhood pick-up game'. Artists such as Jackson Pollock, Pablo Picasso and George Braque were well known for breaking the so-called rules of art; indeed, in some playful endeavours, breaking or 'vaulting the obstacles' becomes part of the fun and is the root of innovation. The same could not be said in a sport, surely? In the 2015 Wimbledon tennis tournament, Australian player Nick Kyrgios caused controversy when he broke the rules of the game by half-heartedly returning the ball to his opponent, taking time over changing his socks and hugging a ball boy. Although Pollock, Picasso and Braque all caused contention at the time, it is unlikely Kyrgios' actions will be celebrated in the way these artists' have been. Generally, in sport there is a winner and a loser, points or goals are scored, and so the rules have to be consistent for both.

It is, of course, still possible to experience a tennis match or game of football with the energy of *līlā*, with the pure joy of the experience, if, rather than focusing only on the rules, the player permits him or herself to enjoy the physical exhilaration of moving limbs, a sense of togetherness that can accompany a team sport and the sheer thrill of the exertion. If the game is played simply to win (for self-esteem, financial reward, social status or fear of losing), it is unlikely to include the energy of free play that we are describing here (the same could be true for an artist under pressure to produce the next creation demanded by agents and collectors). However, even in a high-powered, high-stakes top-division football match, *līlā* can still infect the player at any time. Such is the energy of free play. Perhaps connected to the fear of loss, Nachmanovitch also cites revenge as an obstacle to free play. It is hard to imagine a game of football being played as an act of malevolence, but transfer that understanding to the Roman 'sport' of setting Christians against lions and the connection is more than apparent.

Using metaphor and imagery can be of value in working towards a definition of play, as in the garden or suitcase examples offered above. The risk here is that you, the reader, may not relate to or resonate with the example. I am using play to define play.

The definition of play we are moving towards here, then, is evidently not the goal-orientated play structured and planned by others in order to achieve a specific outcome. The play described here does not necessarily lead to specific, preordained skills (although it can do), nor is it the play that is 'acceptable only if it leads to utilitarian goals'.[26] Play is an activity primarily for its own sake rather than an outcome, and the outcome of free play cannot be predicted.

It is, as Nachmanovitch says, 'without the why'.[27] The reason we play is simply because it is fun and pleasurable. It makes us feel more connected to life. If it was not so, we would not do it.

So much of our ease around play is contingent on our capacity to be with the unknown – what John Keats described as 'negative capability'.[28] I once knew a woman who could not commit herself to beginning a novel without knowing how it ended. It was, at times, difficult being around this woman, as her anxiety and need for certainty did not only apply to reading novels. Another way of defining uncertainty is a state of suspension, as in Coleridge's phrase 'a willing suspension of disbelief',[29] often used in the theatre to describe the audience's readiness to put aside their rational perception that they are sitting in a theatre watching actors performing a play and instead to enter into the co-creation of an illusion. There has to be a tacit agreement, in other words, that they are prepared to accept that something else is about to unfold before their eyes. Some of the best theatre manages to dissolve the separation between actor and audience so that one enters into the life, dilemmas and joys of the character – that is, we empathize with a character, feel that ache in our own heart or the rage in our own belly. In effect, we are allowed, invited, challenged at times, to let go of who we are, our own separateness in fact, and to join and merge with this person before us and to engage with the story they are portraying. An amateur actor friend of mine once told me of a young woman who, utterly enthralled by the performance she had just witnessed, came rushing up to the cast at the end of the show. She demanded to know what she had just seen. He gave her the title of the play. She looked puzzled and asked again what she had seen. It took a while for him to realize that this woman had never seen a play before! There is a sadness and a poignancy with this story. It was extraordinary that she had never experienced a play, yet her joy at discovering that such a thing existed in the world was like that of a young child's wonder in seeing magic. I imagine this was not the last play she went to see.

So the term 'play', as well as being a spontaneous activity that emerges between two people, can also be a prepared event that an audience attends at the theatre. Its prevalence and diversity make play so difficult to define. Besides being so utterly common in everyday language, it is also the subject of a great many specialisms, such as in education, psychology, anthropology and ethology, each staking their claim and with their own theoretical and ethical presumptions about play, and often these assumptions are contradictory to one another. As Spariosu says, play transcends all disciplines, if not all discipline, and yet each discipline must still try to find its own meaning for play.[30] It is as if we can only view one piece of the jigsaw at any one time. Add to this idea the image that the jigsaw is not two-dimensional, not even three-dimensional, but rather a moving hologram of a jigsaw, and we can begin to grasp the tremendous challenge in finding one all-encompassing definition for this elusive and evasive process. Play is as fluid as water that cannot be grasped and held by the hands; perhaps it is even more fluid than water, like air. Play is a trickster – slippery and fleeting. Using words, then, to define play is possible; however, as Sutton-Smith illustrates, it results in a complex, incomplete and circuitous description:[31]

> Play, as a unique form of adaptive variability, instigates an imagined but equilibrial reality within which disequilibrial exigencies can be paradoxically stimulated and give rise to the pleasurable effects of excitement and optimism. The genres of play are humor, skill, pretense, fantasy, risk, contest, and celebrations, all of which are selective stimulations of paradoxical variability.[32]

Although Sutton-Smith's definition is dense, he identifies important aspects of play: there is nothing else like it; it has a flexible diversity (anything is possible in play); it happens in, and provokes, a different reality to that of the everyday; yet play has its own stability and in fluctuating situations can be animated. Play generates enjoyment; play feeds on the energy, the willingness and courage of its players. Play has an intrinsic role in religious and secular events, and, as noted, can also be present in high-level competitions.

Although it can manifest and disappear in an instant, play can be invited to stay with consent and mutual agreement from all parties involved. It can reveal its presence through a physical form, becoming what is referred to as a transitional object such as a poem, a play, a piece of music, a sculpture, but there may not be a final product – for example, as in improvisation – for play is first and foremost a process, a transitional phenomenon. As its nature is transitory, so too is our relationship to it. So a play, although it may be written down on a page, will never be the same twice. It cannot be identically replicated because it lives in a particular moment, and once that moment has gone it can never exist again, except in the memories of those present and perhaps the stories they tell. A play comes alive through the relationship between the playwright's words, the director, set designers, actors and the audiences who witness it.

In order to play, we need to experience and cross a threshold from linear or objective reality and invite others into another reality. This can be lengthy and complex, as in actors preparing for their audience and the audience entering the theatre, purchasing tickets, taking their seats and the lights dimming as the curtain opens, or it can be instantaneous as a wink, a certain tone of voice, even a pause.

> To prepare for play is to begin to play; to ready for play is already to be at play. In all play, there is an instant or an interval that separates what has not been from what will soon be play.[33]

Earlier we posed the question: Can it only be play when participants have an awareness or consciousness of it not being reality? Theatre director Peter Brook[34] reminds us that 'reality' is a word that has many meanings.[35] Sam Harris engages with the mysterious subject of consciousness and, drawing on the writing of philosopher Thomas Nagel, suggests that 'consciousness is first and foremost, subjective – for it is simply the fact of subjectivity itself'.[36] In other words, unless we are able to actually *be* the cat chasing the leaf across the lawn, or a baby with the transitional object of the soft toy bear, we really cannot know the level of consciousness present. We can have our observations, of course, but then these are open to our own subjective interpretations based on our own levels of consciousness. Harris concludes that 'whether something *seems* conscious from the outside is never quite the point'.[37]

Whatever one's view of consciousness, mostly there is a consensus between the development of complex beings and an emerging consciousness. This is reflected in our more sophisticated forms of play that evolve later and do require more elaborate understanding and awareness (as well as many other qualities such as courage, commitment, decisiveness, tenacity, resilience, skill and trust). Play has a pivotal role in the development of this understanding and awareness (and these other qualities too).

Despite play's immense ambiguity, Scott Eberle has arrived at a working model he describes as the Elements of Play:

Play = Anticipation + Surprise + Pleasure + Understanding + Strength + Poise

Reading the Play Elements Chart

The columns in this chart represent the six basic elements of play. Each is present every time you play fully.

Read downward to see how the elements grow more powerful as you play. Scan across the rows to see how play unfolds as you go. Note how each element of play is in itself a reward. Think about how you play and how your feelings fit these elements.

	Anticipation	Surprise	Pleasure	Understanding	Strength	Poise
	interest	appreciation	satisfaction	tolerance	stamina	dignity
	openness	awakening	buoyancy	empathy	vitality	grace
	readiness	stimulation	gratification	knowledge	devotion	composure
	expectation	excitement	joy	skill	ingenuity	ease
	curiosity	discovery	happiness	insight	wit	contentment
	desire	arousal	delight	mutuality	drive	fulfilment
	exuberance	thrill	glee	sensitivity	passion	spontaneity
	wonderment	astonishment	fun	mastery	creativity	balance
Play Elements	To infinity! And beyond! Buzz Lightyear Spaceman	Playfully challenging the limitations of a science, an art or a technology just to see what happens is one of the most common ways in which novel ideas are born. Robert and Michele Root-Bernstein Contemporary American physiologist; historian	Men do not quit playing because they grow old; they grow old because they quit playing. Oliver Wendell Holmes American physician 1809–1894	Learning through play means trying things this way and that, staying loose, changing your perspective, and trying the intuitive instead of the logical. Stuart Brown, M.D. Contemporary American psychiatrist	A child loves his play, not because it's easy, but because it's hard. Benjamin Spock American paediatrician 1903–1998	Play grows from our sense of freedom, it produces strength and skill for the players, stimulates the imagination, and encourages agility and self-confidence. Joseph W. Meeker Contemporary American human ecologist

Figure 1 The Play Elements Chart
Source: Copyright © The Strong. Reproduced with permission from The Strong. All rights reserved.

What draws me to this model in particular is that each of the elements – anticipation, surprise, pleasure, understanding, strength, poise – has its own continuum. For example, anticipation ranges from interest that is necessary for primary engagement through to openness, readiness, expectation, curiosity (which Eberle seems to regard as a more intense 'expression' compared with interest), desire and exuberance, culminating in wonderment. In the model, there has to be a spark of interest, a willingness to engage before any play can begin, whether that is a sudden wink of the eye, a raised eyebrow or the long preparations for an entrance on the stage, or art gallery or tennis court.

Surprise follows anticipation. Eberle comments, 'A game of peekaboo is front loaded with the pleasures of anticipation and surprise.'[38] Again and again the child will demand a repeat performance even though he knows just what is coming; each time he laughs as if for the first time until his need for surprise is exhausted. Eberle notes the apparent paradoxical nature of being surprised by something we have readied ourselves to receive, like the audience waiting for the punch line of a joke. He adds that the perceived paradox simply highlights the relationship between anticipation and surprise: '[M]emory and prediction share a neural substrate, [so] players in a state of anticipation may be "remembering" a future pleasure.'[39] Surprise is rewarding in itself and so players will perpetuate the play for as long as possible. Pleasure, as we have previously noted, is an essential aspect of play, both as a stimulus to play and a motivation to continue playing. According to Eberle, if pleasure is not present (albeit fleetingly), then it simply is not play. Pleasure is not only imbued in satisfaction, happiness and fun; it is also there in exuberance, vitality, contentment and empathy. If we are fortunate enough, Eberle says, we will experience poise in play from a sense of dignity to contentment and balance – again, all pleasurable feelings. The last three elements of play – understanding, strength and poise – relate to physical, intellectual and social pleasures. There are other means of gaining these skills and developing our capacities; however, as Eberle suggests, there are none quite as enjoyable as play.

The table of elements can also be understood horizontally so that desire can lead to arousal which stimulates delight, generating mutuality, developing drive and culminating in fulfilment. This process can be seen in forms of play ranging from a young child playing peekaboo to the discovery of penicillin to two people falling in love. Once again, we return to the aspect of fun:

> We play because it is fun, to be sure, but we reap short- and long-term benefits thereby mostly unknowingly.[40]

Eberle offers a word of caution, though, when using the table:

> We should not reify these elements, taking them as things in themselves. Instead, we should read the elements as conveniences, as manners of speaking, and above all, as moving images more akin to concepts in aesthetics and philosophy.[41]

Humans have a tendency to want to fix and solidify, to make the subjective into the objective, and this is what Eberle is expressly advising against.

Those whose lives, especially in early childhood, have not been conducive to supporting the natural development of play may indeed suffer a double calamity being denied arguably the most profound medium for healing. In a later scene, we will explore the extraordinary power play possesses for the transformation of suffering. In this way, play is the vehicle for psychological healing and in the cultivation of the spiritual dimension. Yet play is not only a defence against a frightening or dangerous world. It is fundamentally a way of creatively engaging with the world. For a neglected and/or abused child or adult, an inability to fully engage in play not only robs him or her of a means of healing, but also denies access to great joy and pleasure.

> Play is one of those things, like dreaming, that seems superfluous but that we cannot seem to live without it. Like dreams, play is driven by desire. It is a naturally arising, spontaneous expression of the self's need to negotiate all kinds of threatening situations, situations that throw a person into a confrontation with his own aloneness... [S]uccessful play reveals both the truth and the falseness of these threats – they become trauma only when there is no way out...[42]

Play, like dreaming, inhabits an internal, intrapsychic threshold between the subjective/personal and non-personal/collective aspects to which each of us has access, whether we realize it or not. Where Winnicott made reference to the theoretical line between subjective and objectively perceived reality – the horizontal – we now address another dimension to play, introducing a further threshold between the personal and the collective; between what we believe ourselves to be – the I/cloak – and our connection to something beyond the cloak[43] – the vertical. The cosmic play of *līlā, duende, athyrma* – the manifestation of the divine, whatever that means to us – pertains to this dimension of play. In the previous scene, we looked at a commonly held fear of being 'a puppet to the gods' rather than having control over our own being. If we refer back to Shakespeare's Jacques and his observation that we are all players on the stage of life, it is possible to imagine some Great Director orchestrating our actions, thoughts, emotions. I ask you, when you play, where do those images and ideas come from? Why were you born when you were, where and to the parents you have? Why do you fall in love with one person and not another? Just how much free will do you actually have? I have no answers, of course, but I am open to the enquiry all the same.

Jonathan Kay offers a very playful (and often extremely serious) way of engaging in this enquiry. Working through the archetype of the Fool, Kay invites his participants to open to this deeper ground of play. In the medieval court, the Fool traditionally spoke the truth that no one else dared, but because s/he spoke from the paradoxical place of play, it was possible for others to hear and heed the words of the Fool (if they wanted to) without punishment.[44] Kay recognizes the Fool's playful engagement with the uncensored, thereby accessing something bigger than our own separate selves. Indeed, given free rein, the Fool can shine through the illusion of the cloak, our defences, with such shocking luminosity that participants have been known to experience disorientation and confusion not unlike Manjushri's monk. It has always been my experience that Kay's practice originates from a place of love and compassion. This is a crucial factor. Having attended several of Kay's workshops, I was intrigued to learn more of his approach and his understanding of the different aspects of play, and so we met.

Jonathan Kay talks about *a play*, *play* and *The Play* (I have added the italics). For him, a play is very specific. It could literally be a theatrical play, or a story someone is retelling of their own life experience conveyed through their own subjective lens, a book, or an individual life itself. Again we can see the holographic nature of play. Material from play and The Play influence a play, so that a play, every play, is a merging of the other two elements – as Kay describes, 'they combust in your imagination to create something utterly individual called *a* play...*a* play is just a residue of play and the play – an interpretation'. This is the cloak as I understand it. Again we can see the holographic nature of play. He goes on to say how it would be for a person to live only in play – he or she would be unable to create a coherent narrative. This corresponds with my understanding of the cloak as a necessary requirement for life on earth. Alternatively, for a person who lives *only* in a play, everything is already sorted so there is no need to explore anything.

Jonathan Kay often speaks in what seems like koans – a way of speech originating from Zen Buddhism in which a paradoxical anecdote or riddle is asked of a student without there being a solution. Koans are used to demonstrate the limitations of rational reasoning and to encourage awakening. Kay certainly does this! In effect, he and I are each attempting to define phenomena ultimately undefinable in words.

Kay understands there to be a fundamental conflict between play and a play, and this is what he describes as the Twin Effect. He uses the archetypal story of Cain and Abel, sons of Eve and Adam found in Christianity, Islam and Judaism, to illustrate his understanding.[45] Abel being closer to God provokes the jealousy and wrath of his brother. Cain, despite trying hard to win the approval of God, is driven to such extremes of envy by his brother's closeness to Him for simply just *being*. The story culminates in Cain killing off Abel. Kay equates a play to Cain – the doer who is ambitious and egotistic – and play to Abel. This reminds me of Rob Burbea's words of caution against labelling any image, for, in so doing, in effect we kill it. 'Nailing' something seems to be Cain's domain.

In this enquiry with Kay, I find myself making sense of this new material through consideration of what I already knew. I have found that the Twin Effect resonates strongly with my training in Buddhist psychotherapy. Franklyn Sills, Director of the Karuna Institute and author of the book *Being and Becoming*, introduces the concept of Source–Being–self. Source, also known as Emptiness, gives rise to Being or our intrinsic/buddha nature, which is inherently whole. Being corresponds to Abel, whereas our self – what we are describing as the cloak – relates to Cain. Our Being nature, like Abel, is closer to the Source or, in Christian, Islamic or Judaic terms, to God or Allah.

God/Allah	Abel	Cain
Source	Being	self (Sills)
The Play	play	a play (Kay)

We will explore Sills' paradigm more fully in subsequent scenes in this book.

Kay's model can also be applied to other concepts:

| The Word | word | a word |
| The Life | life | a life |

Kay was keen to stress that the conflict between Cain (self/a play/ the cloak) and Abel (Being/play) is constant. You must *real-eyes* this struggle is going on all the time, he tells me.

The archetypal Fool seems able to traverse the planes between The Play, play and a play, bringing 'mind-blowing' revelations for us to hear or to ignore as we wish. The Fool also understands words as spells, deciphering them as Joseph interpreted the pharaoh's dreams and solved his riddles in the Old Testament. It was said that Joseph had the spirit of God. Perhaps the Fool embodies the spirit of Source? The Fool, seeing with a third eye and listening with a third ear, hears the Foolish meaning of words, such as *real-eyes*, thus seeing beyond the reasoned and the rational.[46]

Attempting to describe Jonathan Kay's work is immediately doomed. I am using words (Cain's medium) to describe Abel's world. Abel does not use words, and, according to Kay, has never learned to write. The archetypal story of Cain and Abel is a metaphor Kay employs to approximate his practice. He generally does not talk *about* his work; rather he guides people through it in an embodied, experiential way. Having experienced the Twin Effect directly myself, I can relay just how profound it is to have my *real-eyes* opened. Kay uses the medium of play – improvisation, storytelling, spontaneous movement – to enquire into this realm. You, the reader, would need to experience Jonathan Kay's work first-hand rather than taking my word for it. He certainly challenges and, as one participant noted, there is no hiding from him. Yet his ground is love; of that I am in no doubt.

THE CLOAK

From heaven they go forth simply-clad, like you,
But, as years pass, they let the whirring brain
Weave no thoughts but of self-glory and self-gain.
These, though not visibly to their mortal view,
Become a cloak, a richly-patterned cloak...[1]

The patchwork quilt of who we are derives from many sources: what
others have told us, how people respond to us, how we relate to solitude.[2]

Donald Winnicott spoke about there being no such thing as an infant as a separate entity. The infant is always in relationship to another.[3] The human infant is completely dependent upon the other in order to survive, and usually the other (though not necessarily) is the mother.

The Illusion of Separateness

In Buddhism, there are considered to be two forms of truths or realities – absolute and relative. Conventionally, we perceive the world and all it contains, including ourselves, as separate and distinct objects. This is relative truth or reality. Here I am sitting, writing, at my kitchen table. In relative reality, it is undeniable that the table and I are separate. I know this because the table is wooden and I am made of flesh, blood and the like. I can get up and move around whereas the table stays put. I experience this difference, between myself and the table, through my senses and my body. My brain uses the language of distinction and separation, the table *is* and I *am*. My body, though, is made up of atoms – oxygen, nitrogen, carbon and iron, to name a few. Where did these elements come from? Our infant universe was once made up almost entirely of hydrogen. It has been, and continues to be, the action of stars that through their reactions cause hydrogen atoms to be forced together to make heavier and more complex elements, releasing energy in the process. Einstein said that energy can be neither created nor destroyed. It can only be changed from one form to another. So it is that our solar system, our planet earth, and the tree that grew this wood which was used to make my kitchen table and my own body, are made up of elements that have been made by stars. This is absolute reality. Everything is connected.

Historian Carl Kerényi, drawing on the ideas of Greek philosopher Plotinus, knows this life force as *zoë*. *Zoë* is understood to be life before it orients into *a* life, whether that individual life becomes a human being, a tree or something else. In contrast to *zoë*, there is the individual life, known as *bios*. From *bios* we have biography, the story of an individual life, a cloak. Kerényi describes their relationship thus: 'zoë is the thread upon which every individual bios is strung like a bead, and which, in contrast to bios, can be conceived of only as endless'.[4] Plotinus called *zoë* 'the time of the soul', and that through rebirth the soul moves from one *bios* to another. Although I can offer no view on the subject of rebirth, I wanted to make reference to *zoë* and *bios* as we will return to these in Act 3 and their manifestations in art forms.

For now, I am breathing. Taking in oxygen and exhaling carbon dioxide (taken in by leaves through the process of photosynthesis in return for oxygen). I also need to take in food in exchange for matter my body cannot use. Every living organism metabolizes. Everything is, in one way or another, an exchange of energy. I am both separate from and indistinct from my kitchen table. Furthermore, my understanding of truth and reality can only be perceived through my own subjective experience. If I am fortunate, others will share my reality sufficiently to give it validity.

The human body contains ten times as many microbial cells as human cells, and without these benign organisms we simply would not survive. A.L. Kennedy wrote the following on this subject entitled 'How do you do?' It includes the lines:

> What is human in our bodies is outnumbered by trillions of strangers…you're like a wild island, a forgotten rainforest and so am I. And we're not just ambulant hotels, we're communities with gatekeepers, janitors, nurses, farmers, builders, drones. Our newborn

safety, our chemical balance, our ability to eat, it all relies on our tiny collaborators, their happy accommodation, their ability to reproduce in us...and to know that we are both as wonderful and as crowded as we sometimes feel. How do you do?[5]

Stephan Harding, resident ecologist at Schumacher College in Dartington, Devon, adds:

We are both a community and in-community. So what you thought of as 'yourself' is actually something much vaster, more grand, than you ever dared imagine...you are connected with every living being – every rock, every little fragment of atmosphere, every speck of water.[6]

Dr Winnicott's observation related to an infant in the context of another human being; however, it is apparent that our interrelations go much further than this. The artist Grayson Perry reminds us that this interrelatedness continues throughout our lives to help us construct our sense of who we are, for it is only through relationships that we can understand how and where we fit in.[7]

In order for us to survive and reproduce, we need to develop in ways that are seemingly contrary, at odds with this fundamental interconnectedness. We need to assert ourselves as separate from one another – creating boundaries between me-and-the-world, between me-and-you. For me to be in relationship with you, I have to separate myself physically, emotionally, psychically. I also need to create and maintain a workable level of stability and predictability in this system I call 'me'. Finally, I need to be able to recognize what will support my life and what will threaten it. As my well-being is dependent on others, this prey/predator mentality is also highly relevant to this system.

This separate self, then, is an illusion, but a necessary one. As Stephan Harding describes it, a 'provisional identity', or, as philosopher Julian Baggini refers to it, 'practical identity',[8] which, within the context of this book, we are using the metaphor of the cloak to describe: those aspects that define our earthly existence, who we are, the parts we learn to play in this drama we call life. So, the cloak, the self, the ego, whatever we choose to call it, is an illusion, and, as Baggini describes it, a trick. Neuroscientist and Zen practitioner Susan Blackmore, interviewed by Baggini, adds, 'I think that is what the Buddha was saying – not that there is no such self...but that the self is not what [it] seems to be.'[9]

Our unique, individual cloaks have their origins long before we are born. The cloak comprises our genetic threads passed on to us most immediately by our parents and all our ancestors before them. We do not choose which threads we are given, nor the time or location where we come into form (at least not consciously).

The staging instructions for Clifford Bax's play refer to a highly embroidered, elaborately decorated garment that shrouds and protects its wearer. Let us explore the symbolism of the cloak as it relates to our own identity – what is its nature, its fabric and texture, the weft and the weave – and ask the question: Is this cloak, then, all that we are? Is there more or, as Bax's deceased character believed, are we really nothing without it?

The cloak is both conditioned by, and conditioning of, its environment, meaning that it is directly responsive to and affected by the external world and has agency in that world. At birth, we each bring with us our own unique potentialities – dormant qualities – that need certain conditions in order to be realized. The cloak's qualities are determined by our gender, sexuality, nationality, physical health and appearance, demography, education, family, religion, beliefs, nurturing, achievements, losses and abilities, and, in turn, it influences these too. The cloak is influenced by the expectations projected on to us by others. It is our identity: a rich, dynamic tapestry that, despite its invisibility to 'their mortal view',[10] conveys to the world who we are, described by Grayson Perry as possibly our most successful artistic/creative endeavour. In his television series *Who Are You?* Perry made visible and tangible aspects of his subjects' identities. He interviewed a range of individuals and groups, and, from the information received and his own intuitive sense and creativity, he made pieces of art which included tapestries, one of his distinctive vases and a silk screen-printed burka.

The cloak offers us protection against the world. Sigmund Freud used the image of a shield rather than a cloak to describe our defence system, guarding against harm and shrouding our vulnerabilities.[11] Personally, I prefer the metaphor of a cloak because it can potentially cover the entire body, it is perhaps more than our defence system and, unlike a shield, the texture of a cloak can vary greatly. The cloak is multilayered, holographic, dynamic, changing and changeable. It holds unconscious and conscious patterning: implicit and explicit layers consisting of subtle aspects of body-mind and specific thoughts, concepts and language respectively. It has a psychological continuity that for us as individuals undergoing the many changes we experience over our lifetimes still maintains the sense of 'I'. Baggini describes 'I' as really being a verb in the guise of a noun.[12] In his book *The Ego Trick*, Baggini sets out to explore the nature of self and personal identity, asking the question, 'What are we and on what does our continued existence over time depend?'[13] According to Baggini, many philosophers 'have argued that we are constituted by a psychologically continuous web of thoughts, feelings, beliefs and memories'.[14] Derek Parfit describes this as 'overlapping chains of psychological connectedness'.[15] Chains, however, suggest a rigidity and hardness. I much prefer the ideas of threads. The threads making up each of our unique cloaks include our individual temperaments, and upon encountering the world these will be woven together with our beliefs, expectations and intentions.

The cloak may be an illusion, but it is not nothing. It is absolutely necessary for this embodied, earthly existence. In Bax's play, the Dead character is clear in her understanding of her cloak when the Unborn Spirit tries to convince her it is merely a garment – 'No, – much more! It is the personality that I wore so long – my memories – all that I have been',[16] and for the still living, this is crucial. Degenerative conditions such as dementia and Alzheimer's are stark reminders of what happens to human beings and those caring for them when the cloak begins to unravel and fray. There is no question that, during our earthly existence, the cloak is needed, and a coherent cloak at that.

One of the most obvious, yet profound, ways we define ourselves is by our name. Our name is, in effect, a label. How often do we think about the name we have, the name we were given and by whom, and what our thoughts and feelings are towards that name? I am curious when an unborn child is named, even more curious when parents change a child's name after several months because 'it just doesn't feel right', and I am intrigued when an individual adapts or changes his name entirely at some stage in his life, and by traditions and cultures in which renaming is a common practice. Our name is, as poet and novelist Carol Rifka Brunt suggests, something akin to a sanctuary and a construct that holds the dead/unliving.

A Name is an Anchor and a Coffin

Here are the names of the dogs I might have one day:
Sir Galahad, Barnaby, AngelEyes,
Pancake, Kimchi, Basketcase,
Slowburn, Nowhere Man, Jackson, Sharpie
Pigeon, Megatron
Or maybe I would go literary:
Holden, Boo, Ahab, Madame Bovary
To show my quirkiness, my sense of the absurd
Or historical:
Marie Antoinette, Catherine De Medici, Octavian VIII
To showcase my intelligence.
I have been storing these names for a long time
But so far I have only been the inheritor of named animals
'A name is all they have when they lose their home'
That's what I've been told.
'It isn't right to take it away.'
So I have Supercat and Mojo.
Upon introduction, I make sure to mention
I did not name them

It is a lot to assume
That because a name
Is all that nails you
To your old life
It is a good and necessary thing.
I would like a name that is disposable
A paper plate, candy wrapper name
Tossable, replaceable
I would like a name that feels more liquid
Than solid
I am full of holes
A fluid name could leak away
I would like to know what it is like
To walk the world as a
Charlotte or a Deborah or a Bonnie-Jo
A name is a coffin
And an anchor

I have heard of places
With no names at all
In these places
You have to touch a person
Gently on the shoulder
Or make them look
Into your eyes
To get their attention
To gossip
First you have to describe –
Her with the red hair and the dead husband
Him with the three fingers on one hand and the twin girls
The one who used to dance ballet

It has been observed
That this is a place of little gossip
Most people
Upon conjuring the details
Of another's life
Find that
In the end
They have nothing to say at all.[17]

Names are strongly identified with places, people and time. They are intrinsically linked to religions, beliefs and personal experience. They could be linked to the position a child holds within the sibling group (fifth son, for instance, called Quentin), or determined by the state as they were in France, where there was an approved list of names that could be given to a newborn. Personal circumstances are sometimes communicated in a name: parents who were told would never conceive calling their much-wanted child Hope or Faith. Sometimes we acquire a name when we come of age or go through a rite of passage – Catholic confirmation, for instance, or Buddhist ordination. Names are special, secretive and unique. They provide us with our unique identity. The way to dehumanize a person is to refer to him not by his name but by a number, as the Nazis did with concentration camp prisoners during the Second World War, or, as in the harrowing autobiographical account of David Pelzer, to refer to someone as 'It'.[18] Pelzer wrote a sequel to this book entitled *A Man Named Dave*,[19] thereby reclaiming his sense of self as he reclaimed his name. Our name goes before us as people make associations with other people they have known with that name. Names are not neutral. They carry meanings and associations, often unconsciously.

How would we manage without names? How would we define ourselves? We might emphasize our appearance ('the tall/short/ stocky man') or experiences ('the woman who walked around the world') or location ('the woman who lives in the woods'), our profession/occupation ('the judge', 'the drug dealer'), the qualities we are known by ('she's so intelligent') or our relationships ('the one with three black cats and the teenage boy'). We do already do this, of course, when we perhaps don't know or can't recall the person's name, but imagine there being no name to remember at all. We would need to change the definition often if our circumstances changed. It is also true that these descriptions can be just as confining as a name – a person, say, with Down's syndrome would rather, I imagine, be known as Claire than 'the woman with Down's syndrome'.

Conversely, how would you not define yourself? 'The one who is not a gardener and does not enjoy the countryside and animal smells'? Is this also a transient description, or might you be open to reviewing your position on gardens, the countryside and its aromas?

Our names are personal to us and yet they have been given, just like the threads with which we weave our cloaks. There are some people in my life who rarely call me Di, much preferring Dianne. I also have unique names that only certain individuals use at specific times. In the exercise 'The Story of Your Name', a group participant reconnected to her long-dead beloved grandmother who had been the only person to call her this one particular name – her 'pet name'. In recalling this name, she conjured up her dear relative and relived herself as a small child being told stories and drinking dandelion and burdock in her grandmother's garden. Remembrance of the name brought with it a treasured narrative that was both enriching and nostalgic. The converse, of course, is also possible.

In addition to our first names, we also have our family names, or surnames, connecting us to one or both parents and their parents and their parents before them. Many are fascinated by the opportunity to explore their ancestral heritage, uncovering generations going back centuries, and this is only made possible because we have the names that connect us through time. We pick up and follow those threads that lead us into unknown territories. It is not uncommon for the woman in many cultures to give up her own name and take on her husband's name at marriage. As a consequence, tracing the female ancestral line is more challenging than the male. The psychological repercussions for this are complex. Other cultures prefer to combine both the female and male surnames at marriage, but then may end up with a long string of names forever increasing with each generation.

We also know that people come to identify themselves with the names/labels they may be given. The most obvious ones are 'good' and 'bad', and many children, even babies, are frequently described using these terms. Awareness of this influence is vital and can be used for better or for ill. Social psychologist and Emeritus Professor at Stanford University Philip Zimbardo recognizes the value of skilful projections. He believes that labelling people in a particular way can motivate behaviour, and Dr Zimbardo is best placed to know this. He was principal researcher and acting prison superintendent in the infamous and hugely influential Stanford Prison Experiment in 1971.[20]

The cloak may also hold unlived, and thus only imagined, experiences. These may engender longing, fear, regret or intention. Sometimes the things we most fear may reside in our imaginations. Mark Twain allegedly said some of the worst experiences of his life never happened.

The cloak reflects our learning from our families and friends, culture and society. Less visible are those aspects we have learned (often with much suffering) that are less desirable and even unacceptable to others. We are faced with a choice: reveal and risk isolation (rejection) or conceal in favour of relationships (connection). Inevitably, in order to preserve our connection to others (safeguarding our survival), we understand that it is better to keep some behaviours, impulses, feelings, beliefs and thoughts hidden. This is what Carl Jung describes as the shadow.[21] These aspects are relegated to the darkness, split off and repressed so that instead we might present only what we believe from experience will court approval and thus maintain relationship with others. Shame and humiliation are often the sentinels at the gateway to the shadow realm, guarding against any breakout and its possible outcomes. It is important to say that what is repressed into the shadows is not innately or necessarily bad or evil. What is deemed shadowy material is largely culturally subjective. Furthermore, its potency is magnified because it has been hidden from the light, giving our fears, worries and anxieties much to feast upon. We will return to this important subject later in the book when we explore the power of play in casting light into the shadowy realm.

The essence of the cloak is a very necessary requirement for healthy, functional relating as human beings. This may appear contrary to many spiritual traditions (recalling the old monk in the Prologue dropping his 'whole defensive organization' and the disorientation that ensued). I avoided Buddhism for a long time as it seemed to undermine my own experience and purpose as a therapist. Much therapeutic work focuses on the painstaking work of co-creating cloaks which function adequately in different circumstances, particularly in instances when clients have experienced impingements such as non-responsiveness, misattunement, intrusions and worse in pregnancy, infancy and childhood. Many people who seek therapy sense a deficit in day-to-day functioning. In such cases, we might imagine cloaks that are threadbare in parts, rigid like armour in other parts, fragile and brittle. As relational beings, we need our cloaks to meet and engage with this material world, to navigate our way through it as skilfully as we can. The cloak is not the enemy, yet it can block or disrupt our vital energy and connection to life, just as a cloak that is woven too densely or inflexibly, precariously or inconsistently is unlikely to offer enough protection or the right sort of protection against the elements. The question, then, is not whether the cloak is necessary but whether it is serving its true purpose.

Epstein, in his reflection on the Zen story, described our defensive organization against the world. This may feel quite an embattled description of identity as if life is a struggle and we are at war and fighting for our survival. Although there are undoubtedly occasions when this is so for each of us, some more than others, perhaps a more enveloping description is one borrowed from Ron Kurtz. Kurtz founded the Hakomi Method.[22] Kurtz offers a simpler, more inclusive and reflective proposal in place of defences. He describes the process as 'the way we manage our life experiences'.[23] Within a therapeutic context, describing a client's behaviours as 'defences', Kurtz suggests, reveals our own attitudes to force and authority, and implies that the client is in opposition to the therapist. Appreciating a person's need to manage their life experiences – in other words, to grow and maintain their cloak – engenders a sense of safety and control for the person. This alleviates the combative aspect of the cloak and gives validation to the cloak's complexity and necessity. We all need to find ways of managing our life experiences, after all – even the most wonderful and joyful ones. Working from this nonviolent stance gives the opportunity to enquire and explore the texture and patterns within the cloak together with what it is protecting. To respect the cloak conveys an important message to its wearer.

Jungian analyst Donald Kalsched's description of the 'self care system', which 'performs the self-regulatory and inner/outer mediational function',[24] is another way of understanding the cloak and its purpose. Kalsched makes the important point that where there has been trauma, especially in the early period of its creation, the cloak is organized in such a way as to act as a screen defending against further trauma and becomes a 'major resistance to all unguarded spontaneous expressions of self in the world. The person survives but cannot live creatively.'[25] Thus, the cloak has the capacity not only to protect but also to imprison its wearer inadvertently through the act of protecting. The nature of the cloak is dynamic and fluid, yet it has some stability to it; otherwise we would be reforming ourselves quite drastically on a day-to-day basis, or even moment-to-moment.

The Dead character in Bax's play certainly believed her cloak was all that she was. However, the Angel makes claim to the contrary: 'And having worn it (on the earth) so long, they will not cast it by, but think they are the garment which they wear.'[26] It is a play and Bax a playwright, yet he invites the enquiry: If the cloak is not all of who we are, what else are we? What lies beneath the cloak? What is it hiding and protecting? According to the Angel, the cloak hides our true selves 'as a flame in smoke'. Maintaining the view that the cloak *is* all of who we are potentially generates much fear in the living – the fear of being nothing, of being no one. No wonder the Dead character battled to keep hold of hers. Why on earth (or heaven or non-earth) wouldn't she?

Baggini, searching for something fixed at the centre, beneath what we are calling the cloak, whether called a soul or something else, says this:

> In all my years of reading and thinking about soul and self, I've yet to come across a single argument that is left standing after even a little serious scrutiny. As an idea, the immaterial soul is dead, and it's time we buried it, along with any other dreams we might have had about finding a pearl at the heart of our identity.[27]

Baggini is concerned with finding a soul that has a sense of continuity of identity and that this could only be possible if consciousness also continues. Baggini presents us with a paradoxical, circular statement that invites enquiry but does not provide a resolution, strongly resonant of a koan: 'We are no more than, but more than just, matter.'[28] He follows this with another koan-style statement: 'We seem to be wholly physical yet oddly not essentially physical at all.'[29] Perhaps Baggini would agree on this point with Franklyn Sills? Baggini is in no doubt of our physicality (we, of course, inhabit this relative reality) and yet he concedes that 'we do not yet fully understand [how the Ego Trick works]...we may *never* understand'.[30] As a philosopher, he is intent on proving or disproving the existence of a soul or a spirit or whatever we call that aspect of ourselves (and maybe we cannot even refer to it as belonging to ourselves) that exists in addition to the ego/cloak.

As a philosopher addressing the question 'Who am I?' from an intellectual perspective, is Baggini seeking Abel through Cain's eyes? He uses his senses and his honed rationale in an attempt to seek answers. By his own acknowledgement, he reads, thinks about, argues and scrutinizes. This, however valuable in so many endeavours for philosophical truths, may not support *this* particular enquiry. Sometimes we can try to dissect something which, frankly, is beyond dissection. I am reminded of lines from Keats' poem 'Lamia':

> In the dull catalogue of common things
> Philosophy will clip an Angel's wings,
> Conquer all mysteries by rule and line,
> Empty the haunted air and gnomèd mine –
> Unweave a rainbow...[31]

Bax's Angel makes the point of men (and women) living their lives as if only dust and raises the question: How would we live *if* we were more than just dust? Would we live our lives any differently? What if there is something beneath the 'I'? In his *A Map of Days*, a huge visual statement incorporating all aspects of himself denoted as an aerial map of a walled village, with rivers cascading, roads weaving and intricate buildings, Grayson Perry has at the centre a lone figure kicking around a tin can. This image gives the impression of the core self. There seems to be an emptiness about the small, almost insignificant figure in contrast to the busyness of his milieu. The juxtaposition of this emptiness with such form is intriguing.

For now, can we loosen our own busyness, relax intellectual capacities, soften our gaze and find another way to listen to what may lie beneath the smoke, cloud or wave? To pay attention in the way Byrd Baylor and Peter Parnall[32] invite us to do in their book *The Other Way to Listen*. This simply illustrated and poetically written children's book tells the story of an eager and frustrated young child begging an old wise soul, a grandfather figure, to teach him how to hear corn singing, wildflower seeds bursting open underground or the murmurings of the trees. The old man advises the boy to cultivate patience, humility and stillness. He shares with him that sitting in a tree is the most important thing he has ever done. Over time, the boy grows into a man. He has heeded the grandfather's words and cultivated his own practice of being present, of softening and gently listening, rather than trying to grasp and struggling to hear. One day, out in the hills, he realizes that the sounds that once evaded him now surround him – the oldest sounds in the world – and what he realizes is how completely natural this is. Is the old man showing the boy how to listen with the third ear? To listen as the Fool listens?

The old man's recollection of the tree reminds me of Siddhartha Guatama's awakening under the Bodhi tree where he came to realize the root of all suffering and henceforth became recognized as the Buddha, the Awakened One. There are no objective measures here, no verifiable outcomes, no categorical certainties. The Buddha says that you have to know these experiences for yourself; it is down to you. Like the boy in the story, we are invited to cultivate this open, gentle stillness. The sounds are already present but we can't hear because of all the noise going on in our own heads.

There are many images or analogies used to help us understand the quality of the separate self besides the cloak – Perry's can-kicking figure; smoke as referred to by the Angel in Bax's play; clouds; foaming white horses that appear on the tips of waves in the sea. All these appear to have solidity and shape, yet upon closer inspection you see the illusion and the transitory nature of these substances. Surely we humans are more permanent than mere vapour? But if we recall Baggini's wise words about the 'I' being a verb masquerading as a noun and now consider cloak and cloud not as nouns, as tangible objects, but rather as verbs, to cloak or to cloud, we open up a different path of enquiry...

In the previous scene, I introduced Franklyn Sills in relation to Jonathan Kay's concept of play, The Play and a play. One of the most significant contributions Franklyn Sills has made to my understanding is that he regards life as essentially spiritual in nature, and it is on this foundation that Sills and his co-founder of Karuna, Maura Sills, spent many years practising and developing Core Process psychotherapy. Together they established the Karuna Institute in the heart of wild Dartmoor in Devon, offering in-depth training on psychospiritual psychotherapy. For Sills, the enquiry is not an intellectual and philosophical exercise; rather, it is directly applied to the field of healing, to alleviating the suffering of people.

Sills offers us a model for understanding the origins of selfhood, describing three areas – *Source, Being* and *self* – which I touched briefly upon earlier. These are terms drawn from the Buddhist concepts of *bodhicitta*, defined as the already awakened ground state; *citta*, the manifestation of *bodhicitta* as the core of human existence; and *atta*, the self that evolves in relationship to life. Sills is careful to note that these three territories are not separate to one another; rather, they are 'holographically enfolded and spontaneously co-arise' just as the foam atop the wave is not separate to the ocean that lies beneath it.[33]

In Sills' terms, self directly corresponds to the cloak, as it is 'the conditioned form that develops as being meets the world of contingencies'.[34] Sills explains how self's nature can seem solid and stable, yet is really an 'ephemeral, contingent process in which any particular form or identity has only momentary existence',[35] equating self as a spinning wheel where the wheel hub is our Being nature. Note that he describes self as a process rather than a product, just as Baggini describes 'I' as a verb rather than a noun.

In some forms of Buddhism, there is the belief that the personal self is a hindrance to awakening and so must be overcome or disposed of if one is to have any possibility of becoming enlightened – the goal of no-self, as *anattā* was originally understood to mean. As mentioned earlier, this was my initial experience of Buddhism, which certainly contributed to my avoidance of it for several years. The Buddha's teaching, however, is commonly referred to as 'the middle way', and so, contrary to this view of rejecting the personal self, the Buddha recognized the necessity for relative truth within the context of absolute truth. As Sills might say, we are spiritual in nature, living within a material world. Stephen Batchelor, author of *Buddhism without Beliefs* and renowned Buddhist teacher, believes the term not-self more accurately represents *anattā*. This has fundamental significance in how we comprehend and practise, personally and collectively, the process of awakening. In Buddhism, there is an unequivocal acknowledgement that the self/cloak is not all of who we are, and, indeed, attachment to it, as if that is all of who we are, is understood as the origin of suffering in the Four Noble Truths. The self, the cloak, is an illusion, a fabrication, created for existence in the relative world, and we need to weave this cloak with care. The Buddha said, 'Well-makers lead the water (wherever they like); fletchers bend the arrow; carpenters bend a log of wood; *wise people fashion themselves.*'[36] The self/cloak, like a name, is definitely an anchor in this world, but it does not have to become a coffin.

We will return to the Four Noble Truths. For now, let us continue to explore Sills' paradigm to learn of Source and Being that simultaneously underlie and enfold this illusional self. Where self or the cloak defines, distinguishes and separates one person from another, Being is intrinsically connected to all other beings. It arises from Source — absolute truth — from what Carl Jung describes as the archetypal, numinous realm.[37] In Buddhism, Source is understood to be *dharmakaya*, one of the three *kayas*, referred to in Scene 1. *Dharmakaya* is inherent emptiness, a naturally awakened, primordial state, and is sometimes referred to as God, or Goddess, Infinity, The Truth, Tao, or Sacred Unity. Being, emanating from Source, is understood to be 'a locus, or coalescence, of awareness and meaning, the still centre in the midst of self-conditions',[38] and is the context for Source's development in the relational world. As the self or cloak mediates Being's relationship to the world, Being develops a 'way of being'[39] — self is essential for Being to manifest in the world:

> Being is experienced as I-am, while self filters that experience as I-am-this. Thus the context for Being is self and the context for self is a world of meaning, and Being and self are mutually interactive. Being needs self in order to manifest in the relational world of form, and self needs Being as a fulcrum for the cohesive I-am experience.[40]

Where Sills describes self and Being's encounter as 'interactive', Jonathan Kay would describe Cain and Abel's encounter as 'conflictual'. Being, unlike self/the cloak, is unaffected by worldly encounters. Rather, it is a stable presence, *citta*, described by the Buddha as inherently luminous and free, yet its brilliance[41] is cloaked by experiences in the relational world, just as smoke masks the flame. Jung makes the distinction between self/cloak/ego as the intermediary and Self as the unifying principle of life.[42] Jung understood Self as inhabiting the archetypal space between self and the divine, or within Sills' paradigm, between self and Source.

Sills has been inspired by the German philosopher Husserl, by Husserl's enquiry into the essential nature of Being and by Husserl's belief that through the process of gently paying attention to this Being-ness it will naturally reveal itself. This gentle approach requires a softening non-judgment, a capacity to accept whatever is arising without imposing our own will or meaning on to it. This is the central tenet of the healing process in Core Process psychotherapy. When *citta* is liberated, said the Buddha, Source is recognized.

Source is the realm of absolute truth or non-separateness. As previously mentioned, Source goes by many different names; however, the meaning of Source is unique to each individual. Names, as I have argued, are arbitrary labels, approximations of something we are attempting to define, and we have to accept the human limitations as we try to encapsulate the expansive, primordial essence of what we are calling Source. Primordial exists outside our understanding of time and space and transcends the causal conditions that subject and object experience. Lui Hsu Chi advises, 'The name that can be named is not the eternal name.'[43] Source is often understood as emptiness in Buddhism, but it is an emptiness that is full of, or pregnant with, potential.

The presence of Source can be sensed; we can cultivate the environment and the conditions that allow us to experience Source, but it can never be grasped. The felt-sense, or direct experience of Source, can be explored by cultivating the Brahma Viharas. The Brahma Viharas, known as the Illimitable or Immeasurable Minds because they are infinite and boundless, are transpersonal qualities known as the Four Great Catalysts of Awakening. They are loving-kindness, compassion, sympathetic joy and equanimity. As the conditions necessary for awakening, we will explore the Brahma Viharas fully later in the book.

When Being arises from Source and meets the material world, unobstructed, there is a 'continuity of being'.[44] This can only happen when the newborn infant experiences a holding environment created by the other that truly sees and serves the child and his needs. In the following scene, we will explore the part that play has in the creation of the holding environment – in the weaving of the cloak.

Scene 4

PLAY THE WEAVER

There was a child went forth every day;
And the first object he look'd upon, that object he became;
And that object became part of him for the day, or a certain part of the
day, or for many
years, or stretching cycles of years.
. . .
His own parents,
He that had father'd him, and she that had conceiv'd him in her womb,
and birth'd him,
They gave this child more of themselves than that;
They gave him afterward every day – they became part of him.
. . .
The horizon's edge, the flying sea-crow, the fragrance of salt marsh and
shore mud;
These became part of that child who went forth every day, and who
now goes, and will always go forth every day.[1]

This necessity of the human mind to dramatize the elements of its
environment that it perceives, in order to be able to emotionally
assimilate them, is a characteristic that runs throughout the whole
fabric of human life.[2]

In this scene, we will explore a child's first years from the perspective of
play, in particular, using the developmental play paradigm comprising
embodiment, projection and role play (EPR). The EPR model has
been substantially developed by play therapist and dramatherapist Sue
Jennings,[3] based on the earlier work of pioneering drama practitioner
Peter Slade.[4] At the core of Slade's understanding of personality
growth – that is, the formation of the cloak – is the postulation of

two forms of play seen in the child – personal and projected. Personal play encompasses anything relating to the body – movement, voice, physical activity, the child becoming an object or a character. This is in contrast to projected play wherein the child transfers their imaginative energies on to objects outside the self, including dolls, cars and other recognizable toys, but also the creation of written stories, painting and design. Slade, in recognizing the crucial part dramatic play has in the process of becoming, laid the foundation for Jennings' later model of EPR. Embodiment, also known as sensory or pre-play, is akin to the early stages of Slade's personal play. Embodiment play relates to the physical body and engages the senses. It also incorporates movement, sounds, facial expressions and imitation. Projection corresponds to Slade's projected play, wherein the imaginative energy is directed outwards on to toys, objects, puppets and stories (established or created by the child). Jennings' final mode, role play, relates to the later stages of Slade's personal play in which the child can be seen taking on different characters using costume and props.

Jennings suggests that by the time a child has reached the age of seven he will be fully competent in all forms of play and be able to use them with ease. We never cease engaging in EPR throughout life as these processes take on a holographic quality, and we can at times find ourselves employing all three modes simultaneously. The EPR model is germane to the child's development as it directly emulates the processes at work in the early months and years of the child's life. Indeed, as Jennings states, 'competence in EPR creates the core of the attachment between the mother and infant'.[5] Before we explore the paradigm, however, let us first take time to consider where the infant comes from prior to conception.

Pre-form

'But *where* did I come from?' implores the three-year-old child. If the parent were religious, spiritual in any way or drawn towards metaphysical poetry, they might perhaps respond with lines from Wordsworth's 'Intimations of Immortality':

...trailing clouds of glory do we come
    From God, who is our home;
Heaven lies about us in our infancy![6]

Or they may answer simply, 'Well, I wonder...', and encourage the child to wonder too.

Our place of origin has long been a fascination to many three-year-olds and to poets, playwrights, theologians, philosophers and scientists alike. Where were we before we were born? What happens to us when we die? Myths and stories of creation abound in all the world's religions in response to these questions.

Some years ago, I heard a story enacted by a Jewish theatre company, the Besht Tellers, which captured my imagination and has been echoed several times in my clients' stories. This creation myth tells of the angel Lila and her task to transplant a soul from the Garden of Eden at the precise moment of conception and to embed it into the womb. In that second and until the moment of birth, the growing child is encircled in a brilliant white light while Lila whispers into the child's ear all that life on earth will hold for her. When the child is born, the light is quenched and she forgets *everything*. The child's life then becomes a journey of remembering all that she once knew. A version of this myth is also told by Jungian psychologist Gerhard Adler:

> God orders the angel in charge of the souls living in the Beyond to initiate this soul into all the mysteries of that other world...in such manner the soul experiences all the secrets of the world Beyond. At the moment of birth, when the soul comes to earth, the angel extinguishes the light of knowledge burning above it, and the soul, enclosed in its earthly envelope, enters this world, having forgotten its lofty wisdom, but always seeking to regain it.[7]

I wonder if this fate befalls the Unborn Spirit in Bax's play and whether this 'earthly envelope' that encloses each of us is, in fact, the intimation of the cloak itself contributing to our forgetting?

On the subject of our innate 'lofty' wisdom that Adler speaks of, perhaps this corresponds with the archetypal Wise One that resides in every one of us without exception and is a powerful ally in the healing process. In Jungian psychology and dramatherapy, the Wise One within the client is conjured and welcomed into the space for the purpose of aiding at times of great suffering and uncertainty. Could it be that, although we might consciously forget our deeper wisdom, in effect, it never leaves us? Rather, it is obscured by the layers of 'life' that happen to all of us?

Philosophers such as Baggini, discussed in the previous scene, have struggled with the question of continuity beyond the cloak and whether there is something that exists beyond this earthly form – a soul perhaps, or a spirit. This is the meat of almost every religion, if not every religion. The Bible proclaims that we humans are made up of two distinct elements – physical and spiritual – and that humankind possesses an immortal nature ('the dust returneth to the earth as it was, and the spirit returneth unto God who gave it'[8]). Baggini concedes to this in his own words: '[W]e are no more than, but more than just matter.'[9] In Franklyn Sills' model, explored in Scene 3, he identified the territories of Source, Being and self based on the Buddhist concepts of *bodhicitta*, *citta* and *atta*, and invited us to explore the idea that we each arise from this already awakened ground.

In Bax's play, the Angel proposes the idea: What if man (and woman) chose to live their lives on the basis of being something more than just dust; what would this kind of life look like?

Should a person choose to believe she or he were just matter – in other words, that the cloak is all we are, that there is nothing before birth and nothing after birth, that there is no continuity of *anything* – that is their choice, of course. Perhaps, though, with curiosity, we might ask: How does this understanding manifest in their day-to-day life in the world and their relationships with others? Furthermore, how does this perspective influence their outlook on death and dying?

It is apparent that our understanding of our origin is not an abstract concept that only becomes applicable at times of death (though admittedly this is the key moment). Religious traditions including Christians, Muslims, Buddhists, Sikhs and Sufis cultivate and celebrate an ongoing, dynamic relationship with their Truth. Holding this as background, let's return to the cloak, for it is during the time of childhood, the 'period of maximum creativity', according to anthropologist Ashley Montagu, that

> the child weaves his multiple experiences into a pattern which becomes himself. This self-creative process derives from a variety of experiences available to him in his encounter with and response to the environment, the wordless dialectic between himself and the world of his earliest days and years.[10]

The cloak begins to be woven in earnest, and it is play that significantly contributes to this weaving. The infant is formed not only by the sperm and egg but by the multitude of imaginings of his parents. Even before he comes into physical form, he may be called by them, longed for, dreamt of and anticipated. These future parents project their wishes, hopes and expectations upon the foetus, and perhaps even their fears. All the while, he grows in his liquid nest, feeling the intimacy of his mother's body as he lengthens, stretches and pushes. He vibrates with his mother's as well as his own heartbeat, can hear his mother's muffled voice through the sap-filled sac. He is encircled and held – in body, in mind and in heart. His whole body is a sense organ, receptive to every movement, every noise, every poke and prod. A finger or a fist may locate a mouth or arms wrap around soft, malleable legs. He may somersault, twisting and knotting his life line as he does so. His mother, acutely aware of this alien gymnast, will marvel at the strange other lying within while the world around her continues unaware of the miracle she is carrying. She knows the appointed day will arrive when this child will rotate, direct his perfectly formed body deep into the cavernous mouth of her cervix and push and squeeze, arrow-headed, out into the cold, dry world, and she, the mother, must do her courageous part in abetting his release. Only then will she see with her own eyes the stranger that she loves beyond any love she has experienced. This, of course, is the ideal.

Rob Burbea[11] suggests that it is the imaginal reality full of dancing light, contrasting shapes, intense aromas and moving air around him that first engages the infant and invites him into the world. Here is an extract from Daniel Stern's seminal book *Diary of a Baby*, illustrating the unfolding world through the eyes of a newborn, describing his experience as he awakens and watches a patch of sunlight as it falls on the wall beside his cot.

> A space glows over there,
> A gentle magnet pulls to capture.
> The space is growing warmer and coming to life.
> Inside it, forces start to turn around one another in a slow dance.
> The dance comes closer and closer.
> Everything rises to meet it.
> It keeps coming. But it never arrives.
> The thrill ebbs away.[12]

This sense organ of the tiny, intricately formed body must now begin to navigate the vastness of his environment and to start his journey to becoming an 'I'. He is naked, uncloaked literally and metaphorically, when he enters the world, and from this fragile place the threads start to coalesce and the cloak actively begins to be woven much like the neuron 'threads' in his brain beginning to make connections and neural pathways. A newborn baby fresh from his mother's body has no sense of 'I'. He has only the rich threads of DNA and RNA that he carries from his ancestors and a readiness to begin weaving. The baby, however, is no blank screen upon which others' projections might land, although these will indeed have great consequence for him in the shaping of his identity. He is an emptiness full of potential, eager to come into form. He is the quiddity of *sambhogakaya*. He is a pure manifestation of the life force entering the physical world, open and vulnerable to the vicissitudes of human existence, having a tendency towards expression and form.

As the baby grows, he will encounter different ways of engaging with his environment and with himself within the environment. Stern[13] describes these different ways as 'worlds', beginning with the World of Feelings. I would like also to add Sensations here as the baby first experiences happenings in his body – tingling, quivers, throbs, constrictions, warmth, agitations – which are subsequently recognized as feelings of excitement, trepidation, fear, comfort and discomfort.[14] Sensations, and subsequently feelings, generally fall into three types – pleasurable, painful and ones that we are indifferent to. Buddhist teacher Martine Batchelor explores the qualities of pleasant, unpleasant and neutral in what she describes as 'feeling tones'. She encourages open enquiry of immediate feeling tones, urging the individual to creatively engage in this enquiry so as to recognize the deeper habitual feeling 'streams' of sadness, anger or anxiety.[15] I refer to her work here for two reasons.

First, to illustrate the multilayered nature of feelings that weave together to create what Damasio defines as 'the bedrock of our minds'.[16]

Clinical psychologist David Wallin writes:

Emotions...are the processes by which we viscerally appraise the goodness and badness of the experiences we encounter – and it is largely on the basis of such appraisals that we decide (consciously or unconsciously) how we act.[17]

Our emotions act as a kind of barometer throughout our lives, enabling us to ascribe meaning to experiences from which choices are made.[18]

The second reason for including Martine Batchelor here is because she writes from the perspective that feelings, *all* feelings, are habitual states. Therefore, with practice, it is possible to change any feeling, however deeply ingrained it may be.

The newborn, experiencing his environment with such immediate intensity, is likely to be drawn towards situations which create pleasurable feelings and want to avoid ones that cause uncomfortable feelings, rather than towards indifference, except at times of over-stimulation.

Stern explores four further developmental processes that unfold in the infant's early years: the Immediate Social World, the World of Mindscapes, the World of Words and the World of Stories. Stern emphasizes, however, that the baby never leaves behind earlier worlds; rather, each supplementary world overlays the previous one. This is how the cloak is formed – layer upon layer of experience, each informing and forming subsequent ones, and acting holographically, determining the child's and then the adult's relationship to himself and to his environment. The layers interplay, influencing the vibrancy of human experience. It is, however, the World of Feelings and the regulation of them that underpins an overall coherent sense of self – in other words, a functional cloak.

The First World of Feelings (and Sensations)

Having tasted the amniotic fluid, the newborn infant can discern his own mother's milk from that of another mother from birth.[19] He is drawn to her face, particularly her eyes, watching their animation intently, listening to the musical rhythm and timbre and resonance of her words, a voice so familiar from the womb. She is his world, his universe. She makes his existence possible. She holds him in her arms, her voice, her gaze. She holds him with her presence, enveloping him in her own cloak that is now reshaping to accommodate this new and all-consuming role of Mother (even if she has previously experienced motherhood, she has never before mothered *this* infant). She provides the boundary and containment he needs. In her absence or misattunement to him, his delicately nascent sense of self begins to fragment and fall apart. He instinctively calls out for her and hopefully she will hear his call and return. In these early days, he is utterly dependent upon her for his survival. Encountering the world through his feelings and sensations, he senses a gnawing emptiness within, a panic that quickly arises, a fear of annihilation when he is hungry. Only she can quell that fear; can calm, reassure and fill the void. There is, as Stern says, 'an exquisite regulation most mothers do without a thought'.[20]

One aspect of the holding environment identified by Winnicott as being particularly noteworthy is 'object presentation'.[21] He stresses the importance of the mother's sensitivity towards her baby, especially in the earliest days, beginning with the activity of feeding. A baby will start to feel the first hint of hunger in his belly. When the emptiness is of a specific intensity, he can imagine the breast full of milk. At that precise moment, the breast appears and the baby experiences a sense of having created the breast through his own volition. In this way, Winnicott notes, 'the baby's legitimate experience of omnipotence is not violated'[22] and the baby is able to accept and use the object (in this case, the breast) satisfactorily. Conversely, if the breast is presented to the baby too soon, he will not have the sense of summoning it himself. He can feel invaded by repeatedly being forced to take the nipple when he does not have enough of the experience of hunger. If the breast is given too late and his anguish has reached such a crescendo, she will first need to gather him up, envelop him in her love and calm his agitation to a level whereby he can allow himself to attach to the nipple and feed. His experience of omnipotence will have been challenged in both cases. Repeated instances in too-early or too-late object presentation, especially for a newborn infant, will create a sense of mistrust in the environment and, by default, within himself. Object presentation relates directly to a child's capacity to trust his own creative impulse.

At birth, the baby's reptilian brain, already well formed, activates instinctive behaviour related to survival, so that when a baby is born he is already primed to breathe, to experience hunger, to feed and to digest his food. All his essential bodily functions necessary for life are stimulated by this ancient, core brain. From birth, the baby's voracious higher brain begins to take shape in relation to others. The lower, reptilian and mammalian or emotional parts of the brain are already quite well formed; however, it is the higher brain, also known as frontal lobes, that crucially needs human-to-human interaction in order to develop.[23] The infant's brain is a social organ and is designed to grow in relationship with others. Murray and Andrews[24] show how babies as young as three weeks old can, in their calmer moments, demonstrate an ability to reach and gesture. The eyes are one of the baby's crucial sense organs, and all (sighted)[25] infants are especially responsive to movement within their peripheral vision while their middle vision focuses on form. Babies are predisposed to seek out human faces, and experiments have shown that a newborn will turn his head towards a circle with two black shapes at the top and one below in the middle (emulating the human face) as opposed to one black shape on top and two below.[26]

The baby's mammalian or emotional brain, although quite well developed at birth, grows rapidly once in direct external relationship with the other. It helps to control the primitive fight-or-flight impulses, initiating powerful feelings such as rage and fear with the aim of bringing the other back into relationship. This management of the baby's emotions determines the integrity of the cloak, for, as neuroscientist Allan Schore advises, 'the core of the self lies in patterns of affect regulation'.[26] The mammalian brain activates separation anxiety in the infant to alert the empathic other to respond quickly so as to alleviate the fear. Thus, the infant's attachment to the other and her attachment to him are the key determinants in his survival.

We have learned through the early work of John Bowlby[28] and Mary Ainsworth[29] that babies attach to their primary carer in order to survive. Usually, the mother/maternal figure serves as a secure base in which the baby can feel held and received, physically, emotionally, psychologically and socially. There is consistency, stability and a growing predictability in the baby's world. This is secure attachment. There are three recognizable insecure attachment patterns – anxious-avoidant, anxious-ambivalent and disorganized. Anxious-avoidant is understood as a basic 'flight' response. An anxious-ambivalently attached child actively seeks the attention of his mother on her return but will simultaneously fight her by perhaps kicking or punching. He is unable to trust his mother's attention wholeheartedly.

Donald Winnicott introduced the concept of 'good-enough mothering' in recognition that no child experiences *absolute* secure attachment with their primary carer.[30] There will be elements of insecurity present because the mother cannot be present and available for the baby all the time. She is, however, 'one who makes active adaptation to the infant's needs…that gradually lessens, according to the infant's growing ability to account for failure of adaption and to tolerate the results of frustration'.[31] By introducing this concept, Winnicott is acknowledging the human frailty in the primary carer and reassures all of us that as long as the 'holding environment'[32] is good enough, the human infant will survive and grow. The cloak will have an integrated and harmonious weave. With such a cloak, a child will build emotional resilience, described by van der Kolk as:

> learn[ing] to trust both what they feel and how they understand the world. This allows them to rely both on their emotions and thoughts to react to any given situation. Their experience of feeling understood provides them with the confidence that they are capable of making good things happen, and that if they do not know how to deal with difficult situations they can find people who can help them find a solution.[33]

The third category of disorganized attachment was later recognized by Ainsworth and her team.[34] It applies to a very small yet critical percentage of children. Disorganized attachment can include either or both aspects of avoidant and ambivalent patterns of behaviour, usually in extreme form, together with notably disturbed behaviour such as head-banging or rocking. A child with disorganized attachments is likely to have experienced substantial relationship ruptures in his early life. His primary carers are liable to have been repeatedly unpredictable, with prolonged periods of physical and psychological unavailability. This child will most certainly have lacked the necessary holding environment providing sufficient embodiment and, by contrast, his cloak might be imagined as tenuous and punctured in parts where the threads have broken, and tangled in other places where the threads have snarled and snagged. Here we are in the realm of complex or developmental trauma which describes 'the experience of multiple and/or chronic and prolonged, developmentally adverse traumatic events, most often of an interpersonal nature and early-life onset'.[35] The causes and the effects of trauma and therapeutic interventions for trauma will be explored in Acts 2 and 3 respectively.

These attachment relationships are the primary milieu in which the infant learns about emotions – to have his emotions recognized, validated and regulated. In this way, parents, in effect, are the conduit for the baby to his inner environment as well as his external environment; they are the principal others who help to create meaning for and to manage the baby's world.

As previously mentioned, attachment patterns can be complex, although babies usually demonstrate recognizable tendencies. It is also the case that an insecurely attached individual *can* learn secure attachment beyond his early years.[36] As a psychotherapist working with children who have experienced early childhood neglect, abuse and breakdowns in subsequent relationships, I hold the hope that it is possible for secure attachments to grow. If I did not, then I would question whether I ought to be doing this work. It is, however, often a long, arduous and risky journey for the individual concerned, who has to unlearn that the whole world holds only danger, disappointment and desolation; that no one, not even he himself, can be trusted. Within the hard work, though, there are moments of grace. We will explore some of these journeys and these exquisite moments later in the book. For now, let us return to the baby who is fortunate to have good-enough parenting/caring and explore how he learns about himself and his world. The elemental medium through which this learning takes place is the interactive medium of play.

The Immediate Social World

In the days and weeks that follow birth, the baby starts to anticipate outcomes. When he is distressed, and he calls his primary carer, she appears and comforts him. When he is hungry, she feeds him. When he is wet, soiled or in other ways uncomfortable, she relieves his discomfort. These are the ideal. Patterns are beginning to be laid down in their relationship. The infant needs that special one who claims him, who embodies him in mind, loves and receives love from him. We are *object-seeking*[37] and our most basic anxiety is that of separation: 'the dread of the loss of the other, on whom our physical and psychological survival depends'.[38]

Setting the Stage – the Potential Space

As well as a psychoanalyst, Donald Winnicott was for many years a paediatrician, observing thousands of infants entering the world and coming into physical relationship with their carers. It has been

Winnicott's radical ideas on the importance of play in the field of child psychological development that have underpinned the understanding of play in this book.[39]

The space that opens up now both physically and psychically between the infant and his primary carers carries great relevance. It is the 'potential space',[40] that transitory, paradoxical space of play that was explored in Scene 2. That space belonging neither to external, objective reality nor to the infant's inner subjective world, yet belonging to both. It is an intermediate space in which the infant encounters his primary object, his mother-figure. The word 'potential' is exactly fitting to the quest. The infant now embarks on what is sometimes called 'the heroic journey of the ego'.[41] Gradually, he awakens to the realization that he is separate to her: begins to make this discovery (initially very shocking) that she is not, and therefore no one is, a part of him. They are different. And he is ultimately alone. This is the realization of relative truth. Contemplate this for a moment. Put yourself in the infant's place. We have all been there. We still are all there. This is the core existential terror we all have to live with if we dare to acknowledge it. And yet…

Although the infant will continue to remain under his mother's protective cloak for some time to come, in this potential space full of latent possibility he is now beginning to weave his own cloak. This space is also known as the transitional space for it is a place of change, growth and becoming. It is, of course, the place of play – the infant's, the mother's and the overlap of the two.[42]

Play inhabits the thresholds of transition between the two:

Infant ────────────────────────────→ Mother-figure
External potential space between

Figure 2

Yet this space is not of uniform quality. Rather it is a continuum, looking more like Figure 3. (Although there is not this equality where infant and mother-figure are concerned due to the power imbalance between the two. The infant is, of course, far more susceptible to conditioning than the adult. In all encounters between two individuals there will be a degree of imbalance.)

'Objective' reality

Figure 3

Play also inhabits the threshold of transition between the infant's Being (Sills) and emerging self/cloak:

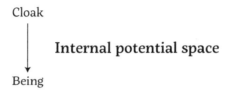

Figure 4

What Winnicott is exemplifying here is how the infant – every infant – engages in this process of becoming separate from and in relation to others, and that this fluctuating, dynamic and incredible journey begins within the space that exists between the two beings. The task is to shift from the position of omnipotence or illusion for the infant, where all external 'objects' are not yet separate, to a position of what Winnicott calls 'disillusionment',[43] wherein there is an increasing tolerance for frustration and a growing capacity to relate to objectively perceived objects and to accept that others are not under the infant's control. Since inhabiting this transitory space, play is itself a transitional phenomenon and any object (animate or inanimate) within this potential space becomes a transitional object in respect of its changeable meaning. It is fluid and impermanent, lending itself to the process of becoming in the development of an individual identity.

Weaving of the cloak

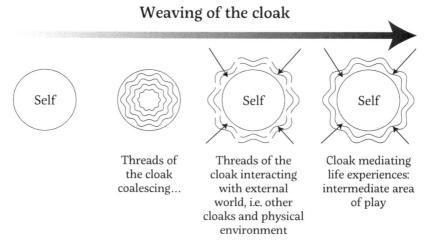

| Threads of the cloak coalescing... | Threads of the cloak interacting with external world, i.e. other cloaks and physical environment | Cloak mediating life experiences: intermediate area of play |

Relational world

Figure 5

This can only happen through the realization of separateness from the other and the emergence of an 'I–you' relationship. Becoming separate from, enduring the loss of that blissful state of merger and realizing one's ultimate aloneness in this world is, frankly, unbearable, or would be, except for the presence of play. I believe that Nietzsche's comment 'We have art [play] in order not to perish by the truth'[44] encapsulates the essential role of play in helping us to manage this discovery. Play mediates this truth and makes it tolerable. The process of disillusionment is ongoing throughout the life-span, so it makes sense that play, too, can continue to mediate this process for the duration. Disillusionment also means to awaken to something new, to have one's eyes opened and to see the reality of something. It *can* be a keenly exciting, stimulating time.

We see this intense animation, the purest of joys, in the ever-changing interactions between infants and their parents, referred to continually as play and interplay between the two.[45] This primary form of play initially takes place through the senses of sight, smell, touch, taste and hearing. These senses mediate the baby's world and most especially in his dynamic encounters with his loved ones. This is the stage of embodiment and is a vital time for the child in the beginning of body-self awareness as the cloak begins to be woven. In the infant's early life, he encounters the world primarily through his senses: the texture of the breast, the warmth of the milk, the sting of a wet nappy, a comforting hand. Anything – the family cat, the tiny threads of a rug, the bars of his cot, the sunlight falling upon a wall – is a legitimate plaything for the inquisitive baby. What he is *most* interested in, though, is the human face. From birth, as long as he is not experiencing the after effects of pain-relieving drugs, a newborn is ready to engage, showing an astonishing capacity to mirror the other's face by mouthing shapes and sticking out his tongue. In time, he will widen his eyes in response to the other, wait in anticipation, express surprise and gurgle with delight. In successive weeks, he will enjoy the pleasure of the game of peek-a-boo, believed to be played with newborns around the world. Tom Stafford[46] cites the significance of this universal game, believing it 'can help show us the foundations on which adult human thought is built'. As Eberle explains, peek-a-boo is 'front loaded' with pleasure and surprise.[47] Pleasure is key.

Provided the infant experiences enough reliable embodiment, the next stage of play, projective play, will naturally arise wherein he makes his own meaning from the objects inhabiting his space. Here, Winnicott describes the 'first possession' – the first 'not-me' objects – and we are likely to see intense interest being shown to a blanket or a soft toy, especially something that offers the infant comfort and reassurance at the time of going to sleep in the absence of the real mother. Many are familiar with the idea of the 'transitional object' that is adopted by the child, sometimes for years, which is imbued with special meaning and value. Its smell, appearance, taste, touch and, perhaps, the noise it makes are vitally important to the child, protecting against the anxiety of separation and aloneness. Winnicott is very explicit and detailed about the qualities and characteristics of the transitional object and the infant's relationship to it. Essentially, the object, its meaning and sensory qualities belong to the child and therefore they must never be changed by anyone other than the child.[48] The object must be able to survive extreme loving, hating and, if necessary, aggression. The object must give warmth and comfort to the child and it must do something that appears to show it has a vitality of its own. For the observer, the transitional object originates from external reality; this is not the child's experience. Paradoxically, it does not originate from the child either (i.e. it has a physical presence in external reality and is not a hallucination); thus, it exists in the space in between, the potential space of play. Ultimately, the transitional object loses its meaning to the child. As it becomes 'decathected', it is neither forgotten nor mourned. Winnicott's reason for this occurring is due to the transitional phenomena becoming spread across the 'whole cultural field'[49] rather than remaining intensely focused on one single object.

In the early months, the infant is beginning to form a mental model of his mother. He creates this picture, or rather pictures, of her from the many and varied interactions they share. He will have a 'soothing' mother, a 'playful' mother, an 'over-stimulating' mother, a 'disengaged' or 'preoccupied' mother. As the baby's brain is a social organ, he is programmed to adapt to his own environment – whatever that may be like. If his mother is preoccupied, he learns very quickly that he has to work extremely hard to generate her interest in him. The mental pictures of his mother form in conjunction with the growing mental pictures he is forming of himself. Winnicott said about the infant, 'When I look I am seen, so I exist',[50] meaning that the infant recognizes his sense of being and becoming through the eyes of the other. If he is nurtured and loved, he will adapt to living in a loving and nurturing world where he can take his mother's attention for granted and, over time, he will grow within himself a sense of being lovable. If he adapts to a mother who is anxious, he will learn to be fearful; he will grow to understand the world is a dangerous place and that nothing, no one, including himself, can be trusted. Human beings are extraordinarily adaptive and creative and we will do anything within our power to survive. A child brought up in fear will grow to become an anxious, hypervigilant, defensive individual with a well-developed reptilian brain, necessary for fight or flight in order to maximize the chance of survival.

Object Relations

Object relations is a psychological theory proposed by, among others, child psychoanalysts Melanie Klein,[51] W.R.D. Fairbairn[52] and Donald Winnicott.[53] The theory is based on the premise that the infant is an 'open system in constant relationship to the external world'.[54] Each of us, beginning with the primary relationship, has developed/ is developing an internal world made up of every significant object (person) we encounter in our lives. This is a dynamic and evolving internal world, changing with each new experience, although the earliest are regarded as the most influential, as it is in infancy and early childhood that the cloak begins to be woven into its defining patterns and shapes. Winnicott says, 'Sooner or later in an infant's development there comes a tendency on the part of the infant to weave other-than-me objects into the personal pattern.'[55]

In classical object relations theory, when the baby's needs are met he can experience the 'good' breast, and when his needs are withheld it is the failing of the 'bad' breast. The 'good' and 'bad' breasts are polarized part-objects of the mother, and, according to the theory, in order to manage this anxiety, the infant must split and perceive as separate these two aspects; otherwise, the persecutory bad breast may threaten to annihilate the nurturing good breast in the same way as it threatens to annihilate the baby. This act of splitting is one of the first defence mechanisms employed. Its function is essential in helping to distinguish our enemies from our friends most especially at times of threat.

It is important to note that what also becomes intertwined with these aspects of the mother-object are the emerging aspects of the infant himself in relation to her. So what we have appearing in the cloak in relationship to the 'good mother' is a 'good baby', not necessarily a baby who sleeps and eats well (often the term used for a baby displaying such behaviour); rather, here we are referring to a baby who is growing a positive self-image – he is experiencing himself as comforted, fed, held, loved. This loved-enough baby will, over time, become a 'lovable' baby. In contrast, we also have the baby who experiences the world as a hostile, dangerous, persecutory and unloving place. The persecuted baby does not feel loved and so, in time, an 'unlovable' baby emerges. These two are held in a precarious balance, within the same baby, like the foundations and scaffolding around a house, influencing all future development of the cloak. Although the baby brings with him his own characteristics, which of these are nurtured or thwarted will depend on his relationships with others. The more a baby embodies the sense of being lovable, the more likely reciprocal threads will be projected on to him from others (see Figure 4) – so, in theory, the more loved a child, the more lovable he becomes and the more loved he will be. Sadly, the converse also happens. The more a child experiences withholding of his needs, the more persecuted and unloved he will feel and the more others will be challenged to generate love for the child.

This, of course, is an oversimplified explanation of object relations theory. It must be remembered that the mother-object is not an object in the general sense of the term, but a subject in her own right. She will carry within her her own complex and multifaceted experiences of having been a baby, child, adolescent, adult. She will draw upon her own internal map, her own cloak, to guide her and influence her role of being mother. As long as the parenting is good enough, then these 'good' and 'bad' objects (the good mother and loved child and the bad mother and unloved child) will eventually become integrated, woven together within the cloak where the good can assuage the bad. This consolidation corresponds with our ability to tolerate ambiguity, not only in relationship. It also involves being able to accommodate both the good and the bad, whatever that may mean, in oneself and other but also more generally in meeting the world. Such tolerance allows us to appreciate difference without immediately feeling threatened by it, similarity without becoming merged with it. Crucially, an ability to tolerate ambiguity maintains the overall flexibility and adaptability of the cloak itself. If these inchoate threads hold too much tension, they will twist the garment out of shape. If they are threadbare, they may leave gaping holes offering little or no protection at all.

Object relations theory is profoundly dramatic in nature. It is a means of understanding how roles (like theatrical roles) begin to take form, helping to define us as our cloaks are woven. Yet this enquiry is not restricted to the psychological domain. American poet Walt Whitman's epic poem 'There Was a Child Went Forth', which opens this scene predates most of the psychoanalytic writing on the subject of object relations. We, like Whitman's child, embody significant others – parents, siblings, teachers, friends and our own versions of the horizon's edge or the fragrance of salt marsh and shore mud – and all are woven intricately into the cloak, together with those corresponding qualities in ourselves: the dominated child, the rebellious teenager, the longing-to-be-free self and the delighted-in-nature self.

> The process of identification, whereby an infant – or anyone – feels like and acts like another person, and makes that person, in a sense, part of himself, is fascinating.[56]

From as young as four months old, a baby is learning what it is to be a social being, interacting with others and making sense of their behaviour in ways that will underpin his ways of relating for the rest of his life. The baby's higher brain, as previously mentioned, grows in direct response to all his social interactions and will eventually make up around 85 per cent of the total brain. The higher brain envelops the reptilian and mammalian brains, and is responsible for capacities such as imagination and creativity, empathy and compassion, reasoning and reflection, and increasing self-awareness. It is often described as the rational brain[57] in contrast to the emotional and instinctive lower brains; however, despite the need for the higher brain to skilfully manage these less sophisticated parts, it nevertheless needs their input to produce an intellectually and emotionally balanced human being.

Besides realizing the sense of agency he has in the relationships with his mother and others, the infant is now also recognizing more and more the control he can exert within his own body. He is discovering that the arm, once flailing, moves under his volition. He notices that he experiences such movements in his own muscles. He is becoming an *actor*,[58] the 'I' upon this stage of life, creating his own unique cloak that encapsulates his memories of himself and others. Here is Stern again referring to attachment:

> So much of attachment consists of the memories and mental models of what happens between you and that other person: How you feel with them. What they can make you experience that others cannot. What you can permit yourself to do or feel or think or wish or dare – but only in their presence. What you can accomplish with their support. What parts, or view, of yourself need their eyes and ears as nourishment.[59]

We are relational beings, and it is through our cloaks that relationships are formed.

Let's return to Stern's Worlds.

The World of Mindscapes

The year-old baby has progressed from an inability to move his own body through space, to discovering his own hands and feet, holding his head, turning over, crawling and finally walking. He sees the world from a very different perspective now, from many different perspectives. The physical shift in changing perspective supports the baby's growing capacity to imagine another's perspective. This is the beginning of the child's lifelong development of empathic imagining. With a growing sense of 'I', we begin to 'weave a coherent story of our lived experience'.[60]

While sheltered by her cloak, he is grappling with the realization that he is separate to her. He has his own body and now he begins to understand that he has his own mind, his own feelings and intentions. Furthermore, this World of Mindscapes opens up the gateway, as Stern writes, to the world of mutual mindscapes, to 'intersubjectivity'.[61] Others, the child learns, can not only know about his feelings and intentions but can also share them with him. He also learns that they may not be aware of his feelings and intentions, or that they can misread them and come to conclusions and act in ways that are incongruent to how he is feeling.

Through their faces, bodies and voices, they engage in this dance of mutual conversation. Through play – not simple imitation by the mother being a mirror, rather by an attuned, dynamic vocal and visual exchange – the child will *know* that she really knows what it feels like to be him in that moment. As Stern notes, faithful imitation at these times will not satisfy the child's need to be understood. She magnifies, amplifies, vocalizes, translates into her own facial expression what she intuits is happening for her child, thereby creating an *analogue* rather than a copy of his experience. She is recreating and expressing his inner world experience, showing him he is not psychically alone in the world. This fundamental experience is woven deeply into his cloak and will act as a blueprint for all other human encounters throughout his life. This weaving of the cloak, this shaping of the child by his mother, his father and significant others, happens *from the inside*.[62]

The World of Words

The child at 20 months will now begin to play out events – that is, engage in role play – past, present or future – *on the stage of the mind*,[63] although for many months now he will have been experimenting with materials such as water (in the bath or basin), puddles, food, soil, perhaps paint, sand, basically anything he has been allowed to handle (aspects of embodiment play).

> Beginning now, Joey may observe someone do something he himself has never done before, such as dial a telephone or pour milk into a cup. Later that same day, or several days later, Joey will imitate the dialling or pouring for the first time in his life.[64]

Joey is going forth each day.

The child can even imagine and practise events without encountering them directly in reality because he is able to translate and expand one experience from another, such as feeding his soft toy as he himself has been fed. This is called 'deferred imitation' and arises around the same time as language acquisition.

The child's 'transitional object' mentioned earlier now lays the ground for future symbolism, and this is evident in his expanding repertoire of play and developing mastery of language. The word 'ball' represents the round object he plays with in the garden; the small four-wheeled toy he keeps in his pocket represents the vehicle he travels in with his parents and is represented by the word 'car'. In the absence of the ball or the car, he can imagine them in his mind; he can refer to them and ask for them. He is able to do this from the many months of creating his own internal picture of his mother and father and other significant others in his external world. Moreover, the child has found symbols that can represent himself – he will have learned his own name and he will know the pronouns of 'me, my and mine'. He will be able to express his sense of possession and relationship – 'my ball', 'my daddy', 'my mummy'. In the process of language acquisition, Stern draws upon Winnicott's concept of 'object presentation' mentioned earlier. Stern observes how a child first 'unlocks' a word, releasing its meaning. The meaning is given to the child by another, yet, simultaneously, the child discovers and creates the word for himself.[65]

In infancy, we spend our time in the immediacy of the present moment. Through life and living, we acquire memories of past experiences that are readily available to us, which are often so powerful and captivating that it is practically inevitable that they will permeate the present moment, impacting upon the here-and-now experience. Stern writes:

> As a result, our subjective experience of the present is impure: a cloth of many colours whose weft is threads from the past and expectations for the future, its warp threads from the here and now.[66]

Associations, usually out of awareness, structure present experience.

> To weave such a subjective tapestry, Joey must be able to associate one experience with another, across space and time.[67]

The World of Stories

All children between the ages of approximately two and a half and four years old begin to create narratives about themselves and their own lives. At four years old, a child's view of the world, themselves and the language they use to express themselves is rich and immediate; emotions are felt intensely and passed through like storm clouds scuttling across a vast sky. Crucially, at this age the child is now able to 'weave together an autobiographical narrative'.[68] The 'I' is the centre of the narrative and will remain so hereafter.

> These stories are made up of actors who have desires and motives directed toward goals, and they take place in a historical context and physical setting that help to interpret the plot. Also, each story has a dramatic line, with beginning, middle and end.[69]

Adults from all cultures use story-making and storytelling to express their histories, and their values, beliefs and practices. There is an innate human need to externalize and dramatize our experiences so that we might make and communicate meaning. Culturally, stories have significance in that they join together groups whether family, tribe or nation. These stories are the glue of our collective identity.

> The human mind needs to select meaningful details out of this disarray and pull them together into the most coherent, comprehensive, consistent, commonsensical, and simple organization possible.[70]

All imaginary events have some root in actual lived experience. Threads, if they are not recalled and rewoven into the cloak, become less significant and gradually fade from the overall patterns created in the cloak. Threads that carry particular emotional charge, however, can abide. This is especially so with regard to overwhelming, unbearable experiences. This is the nature of trauma.

The stories we tell ourselves about who we are are self-perpetuating. As a result of the harm we have experienced, such stories will be damaging and damning. For instance, if a small child is viewed as and told she is evil by her mother, what choice does she have but to become evil? The story she will tell herself is that she is dangerous and, if she has a particular character, she will create such conditions to avoid contact with others. We will meet such a young woman later in the book. Suffice to say that stories can perpetuate inflexible and deeply woven patterns even in young cloaks.

Dissociation

As we have seen, the highly adaptive, developing child has a basic need to stay in relationship with his caregivers, whatever the cost to his own integrity. He is very vulnerable to misrepresentation by those in positions of power in his life. He can be subject to an array of inaccurate projections by others without having the means to challenge them. His default position is to absorb their understanding of him, distorted or not. In order to maintain relationship, the child learns quickly that his behaviour and the motivation attributed to it is unwelcome, wrong or evil. He has no option but to find a way of repressing these so-experienced wrong parts of himself; as Stern adds sombrely, 'the failure of intersubjectivity can introduce a lifelong distortion'.[71] Language, too, has its part to play in creating a schism in the young child that is both confusing and sometimes painful as he has to maintain, for the first time in his young life, two differing versions of the same event: 'the simple wholeness of experience has been broken'.[72]

At times of misattunement, intersubjectivity and intrasubjectivity, the threads in the child's cloak may be dropped like a stitch in knitting. He experiences a fracture within himself. This is understood to be dissociation, a withdrawal from injury. Dissociation is described by Jungian psychoanalyst Donald Kalsched as:

> a trick the psyche plays on itself...allowing life to go on by dividing up the unbearable experience and distributing it to different compartments of the body and mind.[73]

The effects of dissociation include fragmentation, discontinuity, lack of integration between affect, sensation and behaviour, lack of connection between body and mind, and lack of a coherent narrative. The cloak, then, just like the memory of one's life, 'has holes in it'.[74] Dissociation is an effective defence mechanism ensuring survival, but the sacrifice is great. It is, as Kalsched notes, a violent affair.

In Act 2 we will discover that dissociation – or, as it will be referred to henceforth, *falling asleep* – is a continuum, and not a single human being is exempt from it.

ACT 2

FALLING ASLEEP

...the native honesty which so curiously starts in full bloom in the infant, then ripens to a bud.[1]

Our birth is but a sleep and a forgetting:

...

Not in entire forgetfulness,
And not in utter nakedness,

...

Shades of the prison-house begin to close
   Upon the growing boy.[2]

Wordsworth's poem has uncanny resonance with the themes we find in Bax's play: 'not in entire forgetfulness, not in utter nakedness', yet how quickly that nakedness and vulnerability are cloaked, hidden from the world; how swiftly we forget our origin. We fall asleep to our true nature; forgetting that each of us has a connection to Source, we close ourselves to this infinite reserve (denying the opportunity to re-Source ourselves). This happens because of our tendency to identify with our own individual cloaks and all that that entails.

Is this process of closing up, falling asleep and forgetting inevitable? If so, why? And are there degrees of falling asleep? What might be the benefits or the risks? Are there certain experiences which influence this process? These are some of the questions we will be exploring in this scene.

Poets, it seems, have long been aware of our tendency to close up to Source. In the epic book *The Marriage of Heaven and Hell*, William Blake provides us with both an observation of human behaviour and the antidote to it:

If the doors of perception were cleansed everything would appear to man as Infinite. For man has closed himself up, till he sees all things through narrow chinks of his cavern.[3]

Being born is a compromise (*birth contracts the sky-large mind*, says Bax's Angel). In order to function and have any chance of survival in this relational world, we each need to become separate and independent from others. We need to create and maintain our own cloaks. The world is an unstable, unpredictable and seemingly unjust place, where bad things happen to good people, and our cloaks, the things that distinguish and protect us from everyone else, conceal our vulnerability. Besides the conflict, famine, poverty and war which humanity inflicts upon itself (*yet most men squander life in fooleries or the stirring up of strife*, as Bax's Newly Dead character soberly reminds us), there are also natural disasters such as hurricanes, earthquakes, volcanoes and tsunamis. We have accidents. We have illnesses and diseases, we age and we will die. Those we love will also suffer. As we grow and experience life, with all its dissatisfactions, disappointments and unfulfilled dreams, there is a tendency to fall asleep, understood by psychotherapist Kalsched as 'psyche's natural anaesthetic'.[4] The psychic numbing is our most powerful way of protecting ourselves from the stark realities of the world. We could be hyperactive, busy with this project or that task, and actually *still be asleep*. It isn't a literal meaning, of course. Falling asleep within this context is when we are not alive to the present moment.

In the first of the Four Noble Truths, the Buddha states that *there is suffering* – not that the whole of life is suffering, but that suffering is an aspect of the human condition. The Buddha counsels that we need to understand the root of our suffering so that we might liberate ourselves from it.

Being born, we enter the material, tangible world of relative reality which appears separate to absolute reality. The baby is expelled from that blissful state of merger with his mother, and the harsh realization hits him that she is not part of him. Where there was one, now there are two – I and thou, the separation between self and other. We each need to separate from mother, the umbilical cord has to be severed; otherwise, we cannot become an individual, we cannot individuate. In my experience, this process of individuation goes on throughout life and it has many stages.

Other separations occur between body and mind and between soul (or spirit) and body. Metaphysical poet Andrew Marvell's poem 'A Dialogue between the Soul and Body' portrays the passionately conflictual relationship between the immortal and the mortal aspects of a human being.[5] The Soul experiences the Body as a prison, describing its confinement within:

Soul

O Who shall, from this Dungeon, raise
A Soul enslav'd so many ways?
With bolts of Bones, that fetter'd stands
In Feet; and manacled in Hands.
Here blinded with an Eye; and there
Deaf with the drumming of an Ear.
A Soul hung up, as 'twere, in Chains
Of Nerves, and Arteries, and Veins.
Tortur'd, besides each other part,
In a vain Head, and double Heart.

The Body responds, believing itself to be possessed:

Body

O who shall me deliver whole,
From bonds of this Tyrannic Soul?
Which, stretcht upright, impales me so,
That mine own Precipice I go;
And warms and moves this needless Frame:
(A Fever could but do the same.)
And, wanting where its spight to try,
Has made me live to let me dye.
A Body that could never rest,
Since this ill Spirit it possest.

Besides suffering ill-health, ageing and death, the Body also has to tolerate additional suffering that is incurable: emotional pain. In the lines that follow, the Body describes the torture of experiencing hope, fear, love, hatred, joy and madness, regarding love as a pestilence, an all-consuming emotion that can break the mightiest human being and turn them into an irrational, jabbering wreck. Hate is equated to a 'hidden ulcer' that festers deep within, malevolent and brewing.

Not only must the Body endure these emotions but, thanks to the Soul's hold, the Body is literally encoded with the memories and so is unable ever to forget them.

Yet the Body's greatest grievance is still to come:

What but a soul could have the wit
To build me up for sin so fit?

Here the Body makes the claim that it is the Soul leading it, unwittingly, into committing sin, for it is a short step from feeling the intensity of gnawing hatred to perpetrating an act of violence against another being.

In the final lines, the Body draws on a metaphor of architects and trees:

So Architects do square and hew
Green Trees that in the Forest grew.

Just as architects cut down and shape trees to their own design, so a Soul acts upon an innocent and powerless Body in its state of blissful ignorance and renders it human for the Soul's own benefit and entertainment. A tragic poem indeed.

Reflecting on Marvell's poem in relation to the Besht Tellers' myth, where the angel Lila is tasked with extracting resistant souls from paradise and transplanting the unhappy things into impregnated wombs, raises the question: Does the soul also reside in this place of utopian ignorance as well as the body and relish just as little the prospect of an earthly existence? If each could recognize the other's suffering, perhaps for different reasons, then they could console one another and realize that nothing is possible without the other – spirit needs to be embodied, and body needs to be inspired. Perhaps with this realization they could celebrate the union. Instead, they are set up in opposition, vying for acknowledgement and understanding of their own private hell.

Transpersonal psychologist Michael Washburn identifies other dualisms – between thought and feeling, logic and creativity, will and spontaneity, and, in particular, between the cloak and Source (or, in his terms, between the ego and the Dynamic Ground). Just as the child must assert his independence from his mother (primal alienation), so too must he disconnect himself from the original source of his being.[6] The developing cloak (ego) has a choice between *regression* or *repression*.

This choice is costly. It is, however, the only choice that is consistent with continued development.[7]

So the Dynamic Ground/Source becomes obscured. Washburn identifies ego first as a body ego, and this fits with observers of infant development such as Murray and Andrews whose work was discussed in the last scene. As the child develops, the ego becomes concentrated in the head – hence the separation between body and mind. We also learn from Washburn, and this corresponds with the Four Noble Truths, that once the ego/cloak is 'seaworthy',[8] it no longer needs to be separated from the Source.

Washburn differentiates between primal repression of the Dynamic Ground and primal alienation from the mother (which also includes the archetypal Mother); however, both result in the experience of separation. It would seem that in order for each of us to grow and develop a functional cloak that can navigate the vicissitudes of life and relations, we must make this fundamental sacrifice. This is the root of falling asleep and it creates much suffering. Like many of the concepts explored in this book, falling asleep is also a continuum, one that incorporates aspects which seem inevitable and to which all humanity is subjected, given that each one of us needs to develop as a unique human being. There are, however, traits that the Buddha recognized as being preventable, and ultimately all forms of suffering, according to the Four Noble Truths, are surmountable. We each have the possibility to awaken.

The second of the Four Noble Truths tells us that *there is a root to suffering and it must be understood.* The root to suffering is attachment or clinging to the illusion of solidity of identity. In other words, to the cloak, which was not news to Bax's Angel:

And having worn it (on the earth) so long, they will not cast it by,
but think they are the garment which they wear.

The cloak has a strong preference for certainty, as opposed to the uncertainty of ambiguity. In our relational nature, we need to know who we are, who we are not and where we stand in relation to others: comparing, weighing up, judging as better than, worse than, making choices, decisions, and with a deep, ingrained propensity to regard someone or something as this way or that. The cloak's *raison d'être* is to survive, and under threat it will quickly resort to fight or flight.

Certainty creates a sense of safety and security, and in a world that is intrinsically unpredictable, such a confidence is more than welcome. Although an illusion, it is nonetheless a compelling one.

In the previous scene, we looked at our very first days in this physical form, even before we are born, how we are subjected to other people's projections and how we absorb their meanings about us and create our identities in response to them. We may decide, in time, to reject their projections by holding an oppositional position – 'I will not be who you want me to be' – yet our identity is still formed and informed by another's meaning. These are the conditioning and conditioned aspects of self, the cloak, and, as Grayson Perry observes, these are constantly being shaped by things beyond our control.[9]

Most of us come to believe that this is who we are and how the world is, and that that is the end of the story. Franklyn Sills describes this (over)identification with the cloak as a 'tragedy of human life'[10] wherein our true nature – what Sills terms our Being or Buddha Nature – becomes obscured, cloaked, together with our true connection to other beings.

> That hides their true selves as a flame in smoke.[11]

However much the cloak reflects a person's splendid achievements and astonishing accomplishments, it is still only an aspect of that person, her identity, and a 'provisional identity' at that. To live one's life as if the cloak were all is to amplify the suffering experienced.

> The common suffering is the alienation from oneself, from one's fellow man, and from nature, the awareness that life runs out of one's hands like sand and that one will die without having lived; that one lives in the midst of plenty and yet is joyless.[12]

When children are born, they are usually open and receptive to their world. If they are to evolve into coherent beings, they have to be open to whatever is around them. Something happens as the innocence of childhood is left behind. That open vulnerability and curiosity to explore is so often replaced by hesitation and scepticism as the roles we experiment with are adopted and concretized. The cloak gives the illusion of being fixed and we learn to define ourselves as 'I am this' and 'I am not that' – in other words, 'shades of the prison-house begin to close upon the growing boy'. The growth of a coherent self that holds a system of ideas about the world, a collection of beliefs and views, is a functional necessity; however, if we hold on to these rigidly regardless, we are creating what Hanson describes as 'bars of an invisible cage'.[13]

Donald Winnicott first introduced us to the concepts of True and False selves.[14] The False self/selves defend/s the True Self, just as the cloak protects our true or Buddha Nature. Although our defences may be necessary in order to navigate the less than perfect relational world (anticipating significant others' demands, complying with them in order to stay in relationship), we have to recognize we are more, much more, than them. Winnicott noted how empowering it is for a child to develop confidence, curiosity and calmness in their learning without the need to invest precious energy into building defences.

The cloak's disposition towards duality together with its drive to survive means that we will view the world and its contents, including each other, as generally good or bad. The parts we regard as indifferent will not draw very much interest. This splitting arises from a basic intolerance of ambiguity. For many thousands of years, in order to survive, our ancestors needed to make swift decisions on this front: Is this situation safe or dangerous? Is this tribe friendly or hostile? Without this mechanism, we wouldn't be here now. In many societies today and in most of the world, this ability to categorize as good or bad may not be so critical. Rarely might we find ourselves in a life or death situation. That said, we still need to be able to discern what is potentially harmful, whether it be a physical or psychological threat, so I am not advocating switching off this survival mechanism (even if we could).

In psychology, that tendency to see only the good in another (despite contradictory information) is known as the 'halo' effect.[15] Contradictory information that challenges our opinion is ignored, and any additional information that reinforces our view is sought. Alternatively, when we feel aversion for a person (the 'horn' effect), we will look for further evidence to prove our view is 'right'. Frequently, in an argument or dispute, parties may resort to the 'and-another-thing' practice, illustrating a whole catalogue of misdemeanours that have been stockpiled waiting for the moment to be summoned. Human beings struggle with ambiguity. When over-identified with the cloak, we have great difficulty holding two conflicting positions, whether they are about ourselves, another person, a decision or a choice. Our default position is: this or that. Once that decision has been made, many of us will do whatever we can to defend that decision or idea. Here is a playful example that illustrates this point from the cartoon of Snoopy. Linus and Lucy are walking across a lawn when she spots something yellow sitting on the grass. She is so excited, believing it to be a rare, yellow butterfly that has flown in all the way from Brazil. Upon closer inspection, Linus tells her that it is a potato chip. Lucy replies, so how did it get here from Brazil? Like Lucy, in our cloaked-selves, we have a tendency to hold on to information in order to maintain a fixed idea, despite new and contradictory information.

Cathy Haynes,[16] discussing a 17th-century engraving of the moon by the astronomer Giovanni Cassini (which can be found in the British Library), is drawn to the engraving because it offers, as all maps offer, a clear, unambiguous image of its subject. Maps give us certainty. You know where you are, literally, when you have a map. As Haynes says, 'maps edit and order the tangled chaos of reality'.[17] There is, though, something extremely peculiar about Cassini's moon. Upon closer inspection, by the edge of the Sea of Rains, instead of finding the Cliffs of Heraclides promontory, there is a minute but unmistakable image of a woman's head. Cassini makes no mention of it anywhere. Haynes asks, 'Why is there a miniature fiction inside this picture of what seems to be perfect fact?' She observes how the map now holds two things simultaneously – certainty and ambiguity. Haynes concludes that perhaps Cassini is reminding us that both co-exist and somehow we need to be able to embrace both. I believe, if all we can tolerate is certainty, needing something to be right or wrong, good or bad, we close down any further enquiry. In other words, we fall asleep.

The continuum of falling asleep is essentially one of disconnection. Another way of describing this state is dissociation. As introduced in the previous scene, dissociation, though a highly effective and formidable mechanism for protection, is ultimately costly to the integrity of the individual.[18] The earliest dissociation experienced by all is that of primal repression from the Dynamic Ground. Subsequent dissociations occur on different levels, depending on the nature, intensity and duration of the injury and the time it happens in relation to the development of the cloak. It is also affected by the capacity and quality of repair in relationship following the injury. Although dissociation ensures survival, there is significant harm to the continuity of being and the integration of feeling, sensation, cognition and behaviour. It is a desperate response to a perceived act of violence.

An event or situation is experienced as traumatic when there is a physical and/or psychological threat towards oneself and/or towards another. A traumatic event 'overwhelms the ordinary systems of care that give people a sense of control, connection, and meaning'.[19]

It is only in relatively recent times that the psychological world has begun to recognize the nature of trauma in a coherent way.[20] It has, as psychiatrist Judith Herman keenly remarks, 'a curious history – one of episodic amnesia'.[21] She believes the reason for this is that the study of psychological trauma takes us into the territory of our own profound frailty and humanity's propensity to commit evil. Studying trauma, especially trauma inflicted upon a human being by another human being, compels the witness to engage emotionally and morally. It demands of the observer to empathize with the suffering when that suffering is already overwhelming to the victim. Herman cites Leo Eitinger, a psychiatrist who studied Nazi concentration camp survivors, saying, 'War and victims are something the community wants to forget; a veil of oblivion is drawn over everything painful and unpleasant.'[22] It is not only survivors of concentration camps that are overlooked; it is the sexually abused child, the beaten woman, the raped woman, the male survivor of physical and sexual abuse from his boarding school teacher, the victims of sexual abuse perpetrated by Catholic priests or gangs of taxi drivers; it is the small child killed by his mother and her boyfriend after years of torture. Trauma generates intense terror and helplessness. It is understandable that we want to fall asleep around trauma; however, in doing so we abandon the traumatized. By turning our backs, our inaction gives silent endorsement to the perpetrators. Waking up is a risk, though, because it puts us in danger of becoming traumatized and it means we have to do something.

In Act 1, we explored the earliest days of existence, from conception through to gestation, birth and the first years of life. The image portrayed was one of the ideal, a situation that cannot exist in reality. Perhaps, in the beginning, the developing foetus has a sense of unconditional bliss in utero, but very soon the space becomes cramped, and free and fluid movement a faint memory. Babies' senses, we now know, are well developed within the womb, and a baby is acutely sensitive to the mother's emotional state. The baby's heart rate will mirror the mother's, and cortisol, a hormone released by the mother's adrenalin glands at times of stress, passes directly into the baby's blood stream across the placenta.[23] So too do many of the substances taken by the mother during pregnancy, including alcohol and many drugs.[24] Intergenerational trauma including addiction is also believed to imprint on the infant's DNA. It is only in the 21st century that scientists have begun providing the evidence to support the understanding of such intergenerational trauma. Many unborn children are subjected to domestic abuse.[25] Many are subjected to invasive medical procedures carried out during pregnancy.

Then there is the birth itself. The best birth would be one in which the baby passes through the expanded neck of the cervix, down the birth canal and out into low light and soft sounds. Even then, the assault on the baby is immense. Even the gentlest of births[26] incurs elements of trauma. How the infant is received, held and loved in those first hours has a deep and lasting impact on his developing sense of self. How an individual experiences being welcomed into the world will form the foundation of the cloak that will protect him for the rest of his life.

Although scientists are now beginning to research the neuro-biological and physiological phenomena of intergenerational trauma, the discipline of psychoanalysis has long been aware of it. In the 1970s, Alice Miller woke up the world (or those who would/could hear) with her pronouncement that we are all, to a greater or lesser degree, traumatized and asleep to the fact. She understood that trauma has at its core the misuse of power. Almost every culture, if not every culture, is ignorant to its tendency to misuse power, and those who are most helpless to resist this practice are the youngest. Misuse of power and its far-reaching consequences are the norm. When those who are traumatized are unable to know it for what it is, then recreating those same patterns are inevitably going to be passed on to the next generation. In this way, Miller recognized not only the prevalence of trauma but also the existence of both intergenerational trauma and dissociation. Through her own commitment to waken up to this reality, she realized what was necessary: the vital need to acknowledge one's own suffering. Only then would it be possible to hear the suffering of others. She concluded that the responsibility for the next generation lay with every adult of the previous one. It is those adults who will create either compassionate human beings or monsters.[27]

Psychiatrist and Buddhist practitioner Mark Epstein wholly concurs with this view:

> Trauma is an indivisible part of human existence. It takes many forms but spares no one... It is simply a fact of life.[28]

It is understandable that we should wish to deny or ignore the nature and prevalence of trauma in our societies. What would it mean to waken up to this? Besides which, the pervasive effects of trauma can render us ignorant to the effects and perpetration of trauma. The very defence mechanisms we resort to in order to protect us from the fear and helplessness we experience cause us to fall asleep.

The impact of trauma on the newborn is devastating – the fragility of an evolving sense of control, connection and meaning can be easily fractured with far-reaching consequences. To some degree, this happens to all of us. If we are fortunate, we will have caregivers who are good enough and can ameliorate the impact of trauma. Loved ones who despite their human failings will persist in efforts to repair the wounding and continually endeavour to create meaning. Although I wholeheartedly agree with Judith Herman when she cautions against grading the severity of traumatic events on a single dimension and to guard against attempts to oversimplify the impact of trauma, prolonged trauma experienced in the earliest days, weeks and months of life, when those who are meant to love and protect instead subject us to neglect, cruelty and abuse, are the deepest and most profound woundings.

Trauma is pervasive and deep-rooted. Trauma creates in us a sense of *disconnection* and *disempowerment* that undermine the very fabric of what it means to be human and to have humanity. This disconnection (from Source, self and other) is ubiquitous in almost every society and in almost every institution created by human beings, from family, education, healthcare, governments, business and the military. It is evident in how we care for the vulnerable and how we treat the natural world. Below I share an example of the proliferation of trauma and societal dissociation within the British education system and the cost to individual children. This is not in any way an attempt to undermine those individuals in the teaching profession. I believe many governments and education ministers have succeeded in that.

Three days into secondary school, Holly returned home, ashen-faced and silent. She stood in the kitchen with her mother, Becky, and nine-year-old brother, Leo. Becky asked her how her day had gone but she said, 'I can't talk about it here, Mum, not with Leo around.' Leo was happy to vacate the room and watch television with his usual after-school snack. Holly spoke. 'Mum, we were learning about child soldiers in Sierra Leone.[29] Kids younger than me, some younger than Leo, taking their neighbours, people they had lived with all their lives, out into the fields...and...' At this point, Holly became tearful, red-faced. She could not speak. Becky held her daughter on her knee and stroked her hair. She knew just what Holly was trying to say because there had been many stories in the recent news of child 'soldiers' committing unspeakable atrocities. After a time, Holly's sobs subsided. 'Mum, how can they do that? I don't understand.' It was beyond an 11-year-old's comprehension. Beyond the comprehension of her mother was why the teaching staff in an English department believed it acceptable to introduce this subject to children who were still orientating themselves to a major life transition – still finding their way, learning teachers' and other children's names. In response, the Head of English explained, 'These atrocities happened to babies!', implying 11-year-olds should be able to bear this knowledge. Fortunately, Becky is a play therapist and she was able to discuss the wisdom of introducing such material to newcomers. The staff team removed it from the Year 7 curriculum. In addition, she was able to support Holly and help her make some sense of this disturbing material.

Just like the vulnerable infant and the need for the caregiver to protect with the illusion of omnipotence, the innocence of childhood also needs to be sheltered from becoming prematurely aware of the evil acts perpetrated by human beings on each other.[30] The fact that cruelty is inflicted upon babies does not mean an 11-year-old will not be traumatized by that information. I recently found a very helpful quote on social media from someone called Dr Phil.[31] He suggested two rules for children: do not ask them to deal with adult issues and do not burden them with situations they cannot control. In order for adults to protect children, those adults must be awake – to the child within as well as the child in front of them.

Here is another everyday example of adults' dissociation experienced by my psychotherapy client Phillipa.

> I had taken my 13-year-old son to his swimming club. I cringed when I overheard a father talking about 'toughening up his daughter' so she might survive as 'the world is an aggressive place', then I heard another girl shout out, 'I win!' I then saw the coach crouch down towards my son. He looked up into her face from the water as she shook her head. I saw the shame and humiliation as his cheeks reddened. I felt my chest contract and heat rise into my own face. Does it really have to be this way?

Although the father may argue he is wide awake and savvy to the workings of the world and he is adamant his daughter will not fall prey to the injustices, there is a disconnect between the logical outcome that the more we harden, even brutalize, our children, the more aggressive a place the world *will* be. It becomes then a vicious cycle. The more aggressive the world, the more our children have to fight to survive. Pema Chödrön adds this thought:

> The most fundamental aggression to ourselves, the most fundamental harm we can do to ourselves, is to remain ignorant by not having the courage and the respect to look at ourselves honestly and gently.[32]

Falling asleep is when we can't hear our own cries of suffering, or those of other people. It does not have to be this way if we can waken up to the realization that, although our cloaks are necessary, they are not all of who we are.

Philosophers, academics, politicians and writers have explored the role of education in many societies and its part in contributing to our collective amnesia. In *Pedagogy of the Oppressed*, Paulo Friere challenged the view of the student being seen as an empty receptacle waiting to be filled with knowledge, urging instead a more interactive and co-created process of learning.[33] He rejected the notion of education which he termed 'banking' on the basis that it produces a state of *dehumanization* of both teacher and student, the perfect ground for, as Alice Miller warned, a dangerous misuse of power. Nachmanovitch makes a clear distinction between education (arising from the verb 'educe', meaning to bring out something potential or latent) as opposed to training which produces children 'to feed the marketplace with workers, with managers, with consumers'.[34]

The ways in which a society prioritizes individual material gain and intellectual success above creativity, free-thinking and the collective has a profound and corrupting effect on everyone:

> ...the creative artist and poet and saint must fight the actual (as opposed to the ideal) gods of our society – the god of conformism as well as the gods of apathy, material success and exploitative power. These are the 'idols' of our society that are worshipped by multitudes of people.[35]

Existential psychotherapist Rollo May cautioned against the conformism in our society which he regarded as the antithesis of courage. My friend Vicki, herself a mother, was both moved and disturbed by the poignancy of a piece of writing she came across on the side of a telephone box in London's Covent Garden. It read:

> When you're a kid, you colour with reckless abandon. You colour outside the lines. You colour however you feel. Blue elephants, purple trees, red bears, green oceans...it's all good. As you get older, though, everyone tells you to stay inside the lines, to colour everything just as you see it. You end up painting by numbers...whether you actually paint or whether you write or sing or dance or act or direct. I think you should create what you feel. Create outside the lines. I want to watch green oceans and red bears. I'd love to listen to purple trees. And I long to read blue elephants.[36]

Nachmanovitch talks of the child's mind as being the 'original mind in action, the purest form of Zen'.[37] A child's mind is open and hungry for new experiences. Often unintentionally, a teacher can convey the primacy of right and wrong above anything else, engendering within the child the belief that *she* the child (as opposed to what she is doing) is flawed. We are in the realm here of Jonathan Kay's Cain encountered in Act 1. To believe oneself to be wrong, especially for a young child still in the early stages of weaving her cloak, can generate degrees of shame and humiliation that can permeate the cloak with lasting toxicity. The title of the next scene, *The Day of the Square Yellow Sun*, is taken directly from a comment made by psychotherapy client Trudy, a woman in her fifties who was still suffering from the ridicule by a teacher she had experienced as a seven-year-old. She is not the only client I have worked with in this area of trauma. In my view, it is never justifiable to deride a child, whether in school or in the home environment. Nachmanovitch warns that 'adventures, difficulties and even suffering inherent in growing up can serve to develop or educe our original voice, but more often they bury it'.[38] These traumatic memories are just as potent decades later, as we will see when we meet Trudy in the next scene.

There is another form of dissociation which is important to note in the context of awakening, and that is 'spiritual bypassing', defined by John Welwood as 'the tendency to sidestep or avoid facing unresolved emotional issues, psychological wounds and unfinished developmental tasks'.[39] Welwood recognizes that this form of dissociation is a particular risk to those seeking spiritual awakening. While acknowledging that, in the greater sense, absolute and relative realities are intrinsically interwoven and non-separate, he identifies in spiritual bypassing the tendency to disconnect from relative reality relating to the physical, psychological, emotional and social in preference to absolute reality, resulting in a withdrawal from authentic engagement with others. As with any form of dissociation, spiritual bypassing is a consequence of wounding in relationship, and so a shift away from personal relationship to the impersonal prevents any possibility of healing. This is spiritual practice employed as a defence rather than as an integrated, embodied aspect of functional living. Welwood also explores the dangers of meditation used as a way of avoiding difficult and unresolved issues, when it can increase indifference and disengagement from the world. Welwood voices concern that many Western Buddhists, rather than practising non-attachment, are instead avoiding attachment. Far from it being a freedom from attachment, it is a 'form of clinging, a clinging to the denial of one's human attachment needs'. Welwood stresses:

> We are not just humans learning to become buddhas, but also buddhas waking up in human form, learning to become fully human.[40]

Marshall Rosenberg, originator of Nonviolent Communication, defines its purpose as helping us do what we already know how to do…something we have forgotten because we've been educated to forget. He adds, 'When we play the game of "who's right?" everyone loses.'[41] This 'game' is dependent on a system based on punishment and reward. If we seek to be rewarded by others (or avoid being punished), especially by those more powerful than ourselves, then we are being robbed of that precious connection to our inner life – which chooses to do things because they enrich life per se rather than to court praise or avoid criticism or castigation. Winnicott's False selves have developed in response to the individual and collective environments of fear that many, if not all, of us have grown up in. I do not want to get into blaming or shaming anyone in particular here because I would simply be perpetuating the same violence. Instead, I am urging a new paradigm – to waken up!

The Dead character in Bax's play strikes alarm in the heart of the innocent Unborn Spirit:

> The Dead: That if you will not wear
> Some garment to impress your fellows there,
> You will go wretchedly to your dying day,
> For every man will push you from his way.
> The Unborn: Do men not help each other?
> The Dead: Can you be
> So ignorant, and yet would counsel **me**?
> For you the world will prove a bitter school
> I warn you, and men count you but a fool.

The Dead Woman thinks the Unborn Spirit a naïve fool for holding the view that humanity is innately life-seeking and enriching, not only towards one another, but towards all sentient beings and to the earth that we inhabit. One thing we know, though, is that 'violence begets violence'.[42] The more aggressive we train our children to be in the world, the more aggressive the world will be. If we are not awake to our own child within and to our own feeling, we will inadvertently perpetuate unnecessary suffering. I do not believe the child 'soldiers' (I have chosen to put the word in quotation marks as the definition of a soldier, as I understand it, is a brave, a warrior, fighter, *man*-of-arms or fighting *man* – or woman) have the capacity, freedom or intellectual understanding to consciously make a choice to fight. These children are victims of abuse, and many of them have experienced profound trauma including the massacre and rape of their parents and siblings and destruction of their homes.

Why is so much of what we do violent? Marshall Rosenberg's work began with this enquiry. He wanted to know why some people enjoy other people's suffering, making violence and the punishment of others deemed 'bad' enjoyable, while other people in the same society get their joy by contributing to people's well-being. He saw a fundamental difference in the language used between these groups of people. His enquiry into what he terms violent and nonviolent language has been the focus of his work for over half a century. Rosenberg believed that it has not always been the case that societies were characterized by domination structures, where the few have sought to gain power over others through religions, material wealth, land ownership, intellectual 'superiority' and fear. Domination structures – again, think of Jonathan Kay's metaphor of Cain and his annihilation of his brother, Abel – are dualistic in nature (royalty vs commoners, rich vs poor, normal vs abnormal, friend vs enemy) and use the language of labels. These may be gender-based or religious – Protestantism, Catholicism or Islamic, for example, and within these are further divisions such as Sunni and Shia. At times of threat, human beings, when we are identified with our cloaks as if this is who and only who we are, generally resort to the defence of splitting. Us and them. When we experience the world as dangerous, we will seek out allies and resist enemies. In one of his first interviews following the 9/11 attack on the Twin Towers in New York, President George W. Bush said, 'You are either with us or against us, there's no in between.' This event, in which almost 3000 people (of many different nationalities and religions) lost their lives, was traumatic on a scale unprecedented on American soil, an unbearable tragedy. In the ensuing 'war against terrorism', approximately half a million Iraqis have lost their lives. An unbearable tragedy.

When we compete against one another for apparently finite resources, we set ourselves up against each other, and there is a fundamental disconnection between us. There is also an inherent disconnection within ourselves. Rosenberg believed all we are ever trying to do is to have our needs met and that in reality all human needs are basic and universal. Once we realize this and learn to speak the language of compassionate communication, we will no longer perpetuate violence. Violence towards others and *towards ourselves.* One tribal chief in Nigeria, who engaged in mediation with an enemy tribe facilitated by Rosenberg, said, 'If we know how to speak this way, we don't need to kill each other.'[43] Perhaps with a deeper consciousness we could make the word *soldier* a thing of the past altogether...

If we are asleep, we perpetuate the old patterns. This could be on an individual or on a collective level – country against country, nation against nation, a government against its people, tribe against tribe.

If we are asleep, we will revert to old and, more than likely, violent patterns (abuse of power).

Counsellors and psychotherapists have known for some time that trauma itself is contagious.[44] Much has been studied on the nature of secondary, vicarious trauma, burnout and compassion fatigue[45] among professionals dealing with victims of abuse. The symptoms of vicarious trauma include a pervading sense of helplessness and hopelessness, a free-floating and easily triggered feeling of anger and irritation, sleeping difficulties, eating disorders, alcohol and/or drug abuse and exhaustion. It is not only those professionals who directly hear their victims' personal experiences of trauma that are susceptible to its impact. Human beings are relational beings. *We are all vulnerable.* When we read newspapers and watch or listen to the news, we are exposed to horrors we seem helpless to prevent or do anything about. The choice is to switch off or to become overwhelmed. It is my view that many people are experiencing completely unrecognized vicarious trauma. In response to apparent apathy from news audiences (what I understand to be overwhelm resulting from disempowerment), an approach called Constructive Journalism has evolved which seeks to ameliorate the harm caused by catastrophizing news stories.[46] This approach, backed by the United Nations, offers ways of resourcing ourselves that allow us to manage the challenges we face rather than turning our backs. It feels like early days but it is a collective contribution in allowing us to waken to the suffering experienced.

> The fragility of things is apparent to those who look, but if the mind can be taught to hold the instability with some measure of equanimity, a new kind of happiness reveals itself.[47]

Act 2
_____

Scene 2

THE DAY OF THE SQUARE YELLOW SUN – OBSTACLES TO PLAY

Pablo Picasso is reputed to have said that, although every child is an artist, our ability to hold on to our artistic identity is challenged when we grow up. In this scene we will further explore the idea that many adults struggle to engage in imaginative play and explore some of the reasons why this might be.

In their paper 'Pretend play as a life-span activity', Göncü and Perone identify how Western societies delineate between play and work, seeing play as appropriate for children and work as the valued activity for adults. Seen as essential for material and spiritual improvement, work was privileged over play and the latter considered a waste of precious time. As a consequence, the support and study of adult play and its relationship to other activities were significantly overlooked. This view is also reflected in the work of play theorists such as Piaget,[1] educationalists like Vygotsky[2] and even in the field of child psychology. Piaget regarded pretend play as the necessary means by which a preoperational child develops the skills to become concretely operational;[3] however, once a child achieves this maturity, pretend play evolves into games with rules and imaginative play becomes redundant. Sutton-Smith in his critique of Piaget says:

> His view that play is merely a buttress to an inadequate intelligence leads to the corollary that as that intelligence increases in efficiency and adequacy, play will cease to be important in the development of the mind.[4]

Sutton-Smith challenges Piaget's view, believing instead that 'rather than a decrease in the symbolic play function with age, what we actually find is a shift in the applications and the differentiation of this function'.[5] Piaget responds to Sutton-Smith's critique, clearly believing his theory on play to have been misunderstood. Piaget defends the view that 'symbolic play does not diminish but rather differentiates during the course of development', and, according to Piaget, in that differentiation the play 'becomes more and more adapted to *reality* (construction games, etc.)' (my italics).[6] Piaget does acknowledge that there is a diminishment in play if we understand the essential property of play to be (as Piaget also does) 'the deformation and subordination of reality to the desires of the self'. I find Piaget's language to describe the child alienating. The word 'operational' strikes me as more fitting to a description of a piece of machinery or equipment than to describe a unique human being. What does it mean for a child to become concretely operational? That they are somehow ready for use? For what use?

I struggle to see a clear distinction between Sutton-Smith's and Piaget's views. In Western societies, we can arguably witness a disconnection from the desires of the self, perhaps our true nature, and an increase in the more practical, technical, product-orientated uses of play. With the loss of spontaneous and free play that granted us the gift of changing reality and having it serve the longings of the self instead, the self becomes a servant of reality, twisting and distorting itself so as to fit in. But whose reality? The reality of conformism, consumerism and apathy?

Someone who could not be described as conformist is Charlie Todd. Todd is the co-author of *Causing a Scene* and founder of the New York-based collective Improv Everywhere, which describes its purpose as 'causing scenes of chaos and joy in public places'.[7] The mission of the Improv crew is to create a positive experience for members of the public and to give them a good story to tell. One of the criticisms they have faced is that the players 'have too much time on their hands'[8] and what they do is a waste of time. Todd reminds us, though, that thousands, if not millions, of people throughout the world regularly flock to sports events, an activity they would not regard as misspent. People play in a multitude of ways – with or without tangible outcomes. Sutton-Smith and Herron make this point by dedicating their book *Child's Play* to 'those who maintain that there is more than one way to play hopscotch'.[9]

As a direct consequence of what Göncü and Perone see as the prevalent view of human development, in which childhood is thought of as playful and exploratory and adulthood as rational and productive, they lament the 'void in the literature about adult play and its connection to childhood play'.[10]

Margaret Lowenfeld, a pioneer of child psychology and an influential proponent of children's play, recognizes the essential function of play in the evolution 'from immaturity to maturity'. Yet she too regards the child as the predominant figure in play, adding, 'Any individual without the opportunities for adequate play in early life will go on seeking them in the stuff of adult life.'[11] No one wants to be thought of as emotionally immature. Lowenfeld is the originator of the World Technique, a therapeutic approach in which the therapist invites a client to create a miniature world in a sand tray using a vast array of objects. The technique is highly adaptive to the client's age and circumstances (children as young as three and adults with no upper age limit can benefit from it), and so the view seems to run counter to Lowenfeld's own practice. Is she implying that all clients who make use of sand play are emotionally immature, having lacked opportunities for play in early life?

So it seems that either pretend/imaginary/symbolic play in adulthood is completely ignored or those adults partaking in it were deficient of it in childhood and emotionally immature. In her research into shame and her search for Wholehearted living, Brené Brown notes:

> Who has time for painting and scrapbooking and photography when the real work of achieving and accomplishing needs to be done?[12]

It appears that for societies to value the many different forms of play, not only must there be a tangible outcome, but that outcome must be of a standard set by others. Painting, scrapbooking or photography for oneself is often regarded as self-indulgent.

So many adults believe play to be irrelevant to them, and when the enquiry does open up, they often find themselves unable to play. With Lowenfeld's statement in mind, it has been my observation that adults who have lacked play in early life do not find it so easy to engage with it in adulthood. 'I can't draw/dance/sing/act/write' and 'I have no imagination' are statements I have heard countless times from therapy clients and students alike. Sadly, such statements are sometimes uttered by children too. Although a capacity for play is inherent to everyone, the gift is released and cultivated through relationship with other. If, as infants, we did not have that other who was reliable and dependable enough, then our capacity to play will be compromised. Winnicott recognized this when he described the 'deprived child'.[13] We might describe this child as one who has suffered from neglect and/or developmental trauma. They may still have developed ways of playing, but they may not be as free and spontaneous as they might have been. We will explore these darker forms of play in the next scene.

I think so many of us carry around the belief, often from childhood, that we are not creative, especially when we were told so by those of significance to us, usually our parents and teachers. We are taught to colour inside the lines and are chastised when we don't. In much teaching of the arts that I have seen, children are taught to replicate what they see in other people's work rather than create what they feel. This can give the far-reaching message that other people's ideas and how they express them are more prized than their own. I am not saying at all that we cannot learn from the 'great masters'. There is certainly a place for imitation, and many who become known as artists have spent many hours poring over the work of others, whether it be paintings, music or poetry. I understand the journey of apprenticeship, and what Will Gompertz[14] would say is that there is a need first to impersonate before finding one's own voice; however, I fear so many of our children's voices are silenced before they have a chance to be heard at all. I am saying let our education prioritize the child's individual expression and experimentation and support them in fulfilling their own potential. Agreed, it is a fine line at times, but my view is we have for too long overlooked the child's 'original mind'. At great cost to everyone.

When, as children, we do create something ourselves, it is often compared with the creations of others – siblings or classmates or our parents when they themselves were children. Marshall Rosenberg recommends a book entitled *How to Make Yourself Miserable* by humorist Dan Greenburg.[15] Greenburg highlights one of the most evasive and potent practices we employ that robs us of joy. It is the practice of comparing ourselves with others. As previously noted, comparison is a familiar aspect of the cloak's way of understanding and experiencing relationships, and our artistic and playful expressions are not spared the comparison treatment. As it is most often the product that is judged, many people abandon creative endeavours because they are told theirs are not good enough. What is lost is the experience of the process. Creating an end product, whether a painting, book, poem or photograph, from which one can stand back and say 'I made that', can be momentous, especially if one has dedicated time and effort. Easy to overlook, though, is the personal transformation undergone in the creator through the process of making. If we only value the product, we neglect something very precious.

In families, roles are frequently allocated to children – the creative one, the caring one or the rebel, for instance, as if creativity (care and rebellion too, for that matter) can only belong to one person. From a young age, we may also have learned that we are not 'the creative type' as if this was an explicit role we play or have designated to us. Picasso's words at the beginning of this scene voice the challenge to us all to hold on to what usually becomes the preserve of the minority. Allocation of one role to the exclusion of another role is an aspect related to falling asleep, as explored in the previous scene. From remarkably early ages, children become labelled as this or that, and resisting such typecasting requires resolute effort. Once classified as a creative/artist by others, there then follows implicit or explicit pressure to create *something*. A colleague reported that although she enjoyed drawing as a child, as soon as her father noticed and bought her an art folder to keep her artwork in, she instantly stopped drawing. Other people's expectations can threaten to crush our creativity. I suspect it is for this reason that that second book or album, after the acclaim of the first, is so difficult to create. Grayson Perry describes his own experience of trying to keep the playful spontaneity of childhood in the full glare of publicity and critical scrutiny.[16]

Twyla Tharp names all the distractions she faces when beginning a new project.[17] She cites her five big fears as humiliation, repeating something already done, being devoid of ideas, causing suffering to someone she loves and not being able to create in the world the idea that exists in her own mind. Tharp was a highly successful dancer for many years and then a much-acclaimed choreographer, yet still, with each new venture, she faces and has to overcome these fears.

Play is dangerous, especially for adults; going into the unknown is scary for the simple reason that we do not know what we will discover about ourselves.

> The play space/time is inherently dangerous because of its confusing, liminal character: it exists at the boundary between the vulnerable subjective self and the dangerous world of intractable objects and consequential actions. In play, nothing is what it seems.[18]

Free, spontaneous play has a habit of outwitting the cloak. It bypasses our well-established defences and exposes us to the outside world. No wonder so many adults want to box it in and reduce it to a measurable commodity. Perhaps children play so freely because they don't know any better? Once we become self-conscious and experience shame, we quietly collude with the banishment of free play. We pay homage to the artefacts when we visit the theatre or art gallery or pick up a poetry book, yet mostly our connection to the play behind that artefact or the play in our own lives is disregarded.

It takes enormous courage or perhaps foolishness for anyone to play whether in the creation of an end product or through something like improvisation. We put a part of ourselves out into the world for anyone to attack, reject, mock, destroy or steal. Worse still, as Malcolm Ross states, in play, nothing is what it seems, so what we believe we are conveying may not be what the other is receiving. Once out in the world, our creative endeavours cease being our property (if they ever were) and become available for anyone to project their own meaning on to. Makers, creators, players and artists surely hope for their work to be acknowledged by some kind of audience. Human beings have a need to find expression for their inner worlds, to articulate, dramatize or symbolically create with some material something of their own story. Hopefully, their offering will be received by others and understood sympathetically. How else can we counter our sense of aloneness? It would be hard to understand why anyone would go to such lengths not to have the work recognized somehow. There are exceptions. Take, for instance, the sand mandalas created by Tibetan Buddhist monks. These intricate circles meticulously divided into shapes and patterns that go back centuries can take many weeks to create, only to be dismantled almost immediately. The creation and destruction of the sand mandala is highly ritualistic and symbolizes the transitory nature of this material life. Afterwards, the sand is carefully carried and released into free-flowing water.

There are some artists who seem particularly mindful of their audience. Arundhati Roy, author of the much-acclaimed *The God of*

Small Things,[19] turned down a lucrative deal to have the book made into a film as she reputedly said 20 million people each had their own image of the story and she did not wish to shatter those by creating just one.

In our culture-hungry society, in order to be an artist one has to produce something artistic. Once labelled an artist, or novelist or dancer, one has to continue producing art in some form. Brené Brown addresses the link between 'our self-worth' and our 'net worth', and how we base our worthiness on 'our level of productivity'.[20] For many people, believing in their right to play and be creative without a goal is beyond their comprehension, preferring instead to leave that to 'the experts'. Even if we were able to acknowledge our right to play, we still frequently meet the obstacle of engaging in seemingly purposeless activities.

Our creative endeavours are frequently tied up with seeking approval, acceptance and love. One of my students, Cassie, was an accomplished pianist. She began learning to play the piano at the age of five. Both her parents were professional musicians and music teachers. Cassie's ear for music was recognized when she was still a baby and both parents invested great effort and time in coaching her. During the music therapy module in her training to be a creative arts therapist, Cassie realized a painful yet life-changing truth: she experienced no joy in playing the piano at all. There was no playful engagement between herself and the music she so ably played. On deeper exploration, she recognized that her motivation was simply to please her parents and to secure their love. This awareness was both heartbreaking and liberating for her. She stopped playing the piano and instead experimented with other ways of playing that were not encumbered with such emotional baggage. Cassie began to paint, first with watercolours, then oils, both of which she found didn't quite 'hit the spot'. Then she discovered finger painting with acrylics. It was as if her piano-key-trained fingers needed a freedom thus far denied them. She also began in her own therapy to address her deep-seated sense of worthlessness.

In contrast to Cassie, celebrated singer/songwriter Kate Bush gave special thanks to her father for always agreeing to listen to her compositions.[21] The pressure and expectations experienced by the player is a key factor in the process. Experienced as an impingement, it can shut down the creative impulse, yet too little can be equally detrimental to the process. The concept of object presentation was introduced earlier in relation to the newborn infant and the breast, the mother's sensitivity determining whether the infant experiences the presence of the breast as an encroachment or as sustenance. Winnicott understood object presentation as directly relating to a child's capacity to trust her own creative impulses. If, as an older child, the parental intervention is mistimed or misattuned, then the child's creative impulse is thwarted. This may have happened for Cassie with her piano playing. I think it is also noteworthy that Cassie was only ever encouraged to play other people's music. Kate Bush was given the creative freedom in her family to play at making her own compositions.

One might have considered Cassie fortunate to have been blessed with such a musical ability, but for her it was a 'blessed burden'. In contrast to Cassie's 'success', we might find we fail in our creative endeavours. The painting we create doesn't look as it should, the poem we're trying to write doesn't hang together, the dress we sew looks amateurish and we are embarrassed to wear it. When we fail, feelings of shame, worthlessness, humiliation and vulnerability are never far away.[22]

Returning to the idea of the cloak's purpose being to protect, it makes sense then that when pressurized to create, the cloak is likely going to contract, and far from creativity being a gateway to our Being nature, it becomes entangled and caught up in our conditioned selves. We tell ourselves we have been there before and it hurt like hell, and there is no way we are going there again.

The title of this chapter was inspired by my client Trudy. At the beginning of our working together, she expressed a feeling of discomfort as she felt she was expected to produce an image. She had attempted to draw a sun, but instead of being round, it was square. She commented, 'See, I can't even get that right!' It seems that established artists like Twyla Tharp and people who would never have imagined themselves as creators can be plagued by the same self-doubt. For Tharp, at least she can permit herself the idea, even though she still has to overcome the obstacle that it will never be as good out there as it is inside her mind. Trudy had first of all to allow herself the possibility of having a creative idea. Yet this in itself was fraught with torment. Trudy helped me to realize that *enough* emotional safety is not only a prerequisite in the relationship with the therapist, but it also has to be present within the client. If self-criticism and judgment accompany an image, thought, idea or feeling, then the situation clearly is not a safe one. The therapist has to work at creating a safe-enough holding environment. Trudy had an experience at the age of seven which she related to her blocked creative capacity. As mentioned earlier, she was publicly and repeatedly humiliated by her teacher. Whatever Trudy created, the teacher would single her out to show the class what she had done. Despite the shame, Trudy tried again and again to get it right. She described to the therapist how she had loved this teacher and wanted to please her. Wanted to make her smile at her in the way Trudy saw her smile at the other children. The torture went on for a whole academic year, unbeknown to Trudy's parents. In later years, Trudy persecuted herself with the way she had tried so hard to please this teacher. She berated herself for not standing up for herself.

Bessel van der Kolk describes the challenge traumatized people have in facing the shame over the way they behaved during traumatic experiences, whether it is a child soldier in Africa or a child placating her sex-abusing stepfather or appeasing her vindictive teacher:

> ...they despise themselves for how terrified, dependent, excited or enraged they felt.[23]

In his substantial work with war veterans, van der Kolk noticed something very particular in their ability to play. While undertaking a study with the veterans, van der Kolk introduced them to a Rorschach test and invited them to make spontaneous meanings from a sequence of ink blots. Around three-quarters of the men involved in the study showed a strong emotional reaction to the first card that contained colour. They were experiencing what van der Kolk later realized to be flashbacks: reliving their own private horrors from the war. As van der Kolk notes, 'they simply kept replaying an old reel';[24] stuck in the repetition of the first traumatic event, 'they were not displaying the mental flexibility that is the hallmark of imagination'. The men's ability to engage in free and spontaneous play through the use of their imagination had been completely hijacked by the traumatic experience and ongoing post-traumatic stress disorder (PTSD).[25] This is what I am describing as 'deadly play' and will be explored later in the book. For the remaining quarter of the men, van der Kolk witnessed reactions which he found even more disturbing. These men saw nothing other than splodges of ink. They had 'lost the capacity to let their minds play'.

Whether a small girl stuck in a classroom with a psychologically abusive teacher unable to speak to anyone about her living nightmare or a soldier caught in an ambush where he sees his comrades massacred, the impact that trauma has on the whole physiological and psychological system of the being is immense and widespread. It is almost impossible to play, certainly to play freely, when an organism is fighting for survival. The overwhelming and unbearable nature of trauma can lead to PTSD. The victim's whole life, including their creative capacities, is distorted by the unprocessed trauma. Sometimes it can take over the imagination; sometimes it can completely crush the imagination. Whichever outcome, imagination can no longer serve the health of the individual. As van der Kolk says, we lose the capacity to take respite from:

> the routine of everyday existence by fantasizing... [We lose] the opportunity to envision new possibilities...for making our hopes come true. It fires creativity, relieves boredom, alleviates our pain, enhances our pleasure, and enriches our most intimate relationships... Without imagination there is no hope, no chance to revision a better future, no place to go, no goal to reach.[26]

If we accept that spontaneous play in whatever form is potentially dangerous, as it takes us into unknown territory, then for a victim of PTSD the prospect must be terrifying. Furthermore, if we accept that each one of us occupies a place on the continuum of trauma, then it stands to reason that free play is, not surprisingly, something many people avoid. Psychotherapist and author Adam Phillips writes:

> If you let your mind wander, the question is where will it end? Therefore, people want games that have rules in them. Games with rules are like someone believing in god. Someone is containing the experience. Someone knows what the game is, knows there's a beginning, a middle and an end and play is actually something that does away with these categories. We don't know where it begins and we don't know where it will end.[27]

One of the greatest obstacles to play in many so-called developed societies is the precious commodity of time. Despite all our labour-saving devices, we never seem to have enough time, especially for such a seemingly pointless activity as play. There is barely time for children growing up in the Western world to 'pick a scab' as one play therapy colleague describes it. Educationalist David Elkind warns of the immense pressure today's young people are subjected to in meeting governmental targets. Yet these children are among the most fortunate. There are a staggering 230 million children currently living in countries affected by war, and a further 20 million are refugees displaced from their homes, many of them living without their families.[28] There are children throughout the world suffering poverty and deprivation. In the context of this book, I cannot begin to address this issue. Children need to be safe, loved, protected, fed and educated. They also need to be able to play. How else will they be able to envision a different future?

As this scene was inspired by Trudy, I would like to give the final thought to her. Trudy, I am sure Picasso would have delighted in the emergence of a square sun; it may have given him an idea for future avenues to explore in his painting.

DEADLY PLAY

In this scene, I will be drawing on the term 'deadly', borrowed from theatre director Peter Brook's concept of Deadly Theatre,[1] and exploring its relevance to the field of play. Brook used the term in relation to the theatre; however, the deadly form could be broadened to describe any playful expression that is lacking in spontaneity and freedom, essentially alienated from the creative impulse. In the theatre (and all other art forms), this estrangement from the life force is most often a result of over-identification with a final product at the sacrifice of the process. It is formulaic and soulless. It depicts the loss of that capacity to play like a kid, as Grayson Perry notes, and instead to play to the gallery, the camera crew, insatiable collectors or the critics. As Brook warns, 'building a career and artistic development do not necessarily go hand in hand'.[2] I think it is the greatest challenge to any creator, especially when they have been met with critical acclaim, to keep their work fresh and open to new discoveries. Deadly art forms lack the spontaneous capacity to create and play with images that arise from the vitality of spirit that Jung recognized and held in such deference. At the extreme, deadly art, as Brook describes it, not only fails to elevate and instruct; it also rarely entertains. It fails to undermine or challenge everyday assumptions and jeopardizes any desire for curiosity. Deadly art is characterized by blandness, rigidity and a dull predictability. It is the territory of the so-called expert who seems to have arrived at how a play, a painting, a piece of music *should* be done. What underlies deadly art forms? I would suggest fear. Fear of loss – loss of status, loss of income, loss of reputation, loss of control – and fear blocks the creative impulse. Brook laments the deadly actor, fearful of letting go of their self-image that 'has hardened round an inner emptiness'.[3] There is a grasping, a craving, a solidifying, an attachment to something – an image, an idea, a way of doing something that resists any interference from outside.

What do Deadly Theatre and deadly art, then, have in common with play? Surely, according to the definition arrived at so far in this book, the term 'deadly play' must be an oxymoron? How can play that is rigid, lacking in spontaneity and predictable arguably be called play at all? Knowing too that the ambiguous nature of play lends itself to the subjective interpretation of the participants and audience/witness/spectator, who then determines whether the play is alive or dead? Peter Brook cautions that Deadly Theatre is extremely difficult to recognize; however, he says, 'but a child can smell it out'.[4] What is it that the child has that is no longer available to the adult? Perhaps he is referring here to that naïve innocence epitomized by the child in the fairy tale *The Emperor's New Clothes* who shouts out 'The Emperor is naked!' when all around are in a fearful stupor.

In order to explore deadly play, it is first necessary to look at the human tendency to develop habits, to become habituated, to become addicted. Alice Miller understands an addiction as a symptom of distress that needs to be understood.[5] According to Buddhist nun Pema Chödrön, our ego or self is simply just a collection of our addictions.[6] We create these addictions in attempts to shield ourselves from pain and suffering. American psychiatrist Gabor Maté concurs with this view. Maté, who works closely with some of Canada's most desperate drug addicts, describes his patients as inhabitants of the Hungry Ghost Realm. This realm, one of the six ways of being in human existence, is part of the Buddhist Wheel of Life. In this realm, 'we constantly seek something outside ourselves to curb an insatiable yearning for relief or fulfilment… We haunt our lives without being fully present.'[7] Although Maté's patients may live almost constantly in this realm, we all know it for ourselves, for all addictions, whether they be substance or behaviour, have suffering at their core. Most of us are trying to avoid the Hell Realm, whether we are conscious of it or not. Through the many dedicated years of work, Maté has recognized recurring themes 'like patterns in a tapestry' with addicts:

> The drug as an anaesthetic; as an antidote to a frightening feeling of emptiness; as a tonic against fatigue, boredom, alienation and a sense of personal inadequacy; as stress reliever and social lubricant.[8]

Practically all of these themes identified can be met in play, so it should not be too much of a surprise that we can also become addicted to the territory of play.

Addictive Play

One of the core qualities of play is a fundamental freedom to enter into it or choose not to. Where an individual is compelled to engage in an activity (whatever that is), it ceases to possess that quality; therefore, that activity, even if it began as play, essentially is no longer. This is the nature of addictive play. Perhaps one of the most obvious places we would expect to see addictive play is in the area of electronic games. Screens requiring dextrous manipulations of a handheld controller, in particular, seem to encourage this habit-forming, compulsive tendency. Anyone who has any doubt about this should try to distract a teenager (often a boy) when playing a racing or a shooting game. The allure of the game, especially online games that can be played between hundreds if not thousands of players simultaneously, is its potentially never-ending enthralment. Its financial cost is relatively low – another attraction, particularly for younger gamers. There appear to be many benefits for the player – a game can make the player feel powerful, in control; it can be an escape. In the words of an ex-addict, 'the world of the game was a private and unassailable refuge from a seemingly hostile world'.[9] Players of computer games are protected from consequences in day-to-day reality. If I shoot someone in a game, the police are not going to be hammering on my door to arrest me for murder. In a game, if I steal a car or buy weapons, I can safely step outside my own home and no one is going to hunt me down. I can give my fantasies expression, especially my darkest ones, and no one is going to think any less of me because 'it's just a game' and everyone I know is playing it. I can experience a freedom I may never have tasted in my everyday, mundane or fearful life. Sometimes this escape into a safer world reveals exceptional creative talents that can be cultivated and honed. I know of one such individual, Carl, who found not only solace in his computer games but an opportunity to develop his own ideas. Carl is now a well-known and highly respected film animator.

There have been concerns raised, for example, by parents, educators, psychologists and politicians, for players' behaviour that apparently replicates the violence witnessed on video games, without conclusive evidence in either direction. These debates are by no means linear. There are a multitude of factors involved. As Gabor Maté may say, a computer game does not make an addict. Content aside, what might be the harm of playing these games hour after hour? Some research suggests that extensive game playing can exacerbate poor concentration levels in other activities such as reading, human interaction when empathy is a desired quality, and self-stimulating playing.[10] One teacher in a Devon school in the UK conducted his own research and discovered that the children's sleepiness and inability to concentrate were due to playing video games for much of the night, unbeknown to their parents.[11] There also seems to be evidence emerging that physical harm, such as deep-vein thrombosis, can result from extensive periods of sitting still.[12]

In contrast, other research highlights the benefits of hand–eye coordination and reduced reaction times.[13] I can certainly imagine occasions when the need to think and act quickly and decisively could mean the difference between life and death. Game designer Jane McGonigal, whom we met in Act 1, extols the benefits of 'living gamefully' by applying the psychological gains developed through gaming to manage real-life difficulties such as disease, disabilities and changing unhelpful habits.[14] McGonigal invented a game to aid her recovery from a brain injury and ensuing depression which over half a million people have accessed and reportedly benefited from themselves.[15] The game, initially named Jane the Concussion-Slayer (renamed SuperBetter), allows the player to accrue 'power-ups' from achieving small, manageable steps, regaining a sense of control and empowerment in their life. For someone struck down with a physical and/or mental illness, that experience of empowerment played in their own home, especially when it can be transferred into real life, is of no small significance on the journey to recovery.

There are some phenomenal widespread gains from advances in electronic gaming and a game does not make someone into an addict. However, addiction to video games is increasing and there are specialist clinics to be found in the United States, Asia, the UK and other parts of Europe in response to the problem. At present this addiction is not recognized in the *Diagnostic and Statistical Manual of Mental Disorders*. As a therapist and a parent, I am particularly concerned for what is potentially lost by playing these electronic games (often in isolation) – namely, face-to-face human interaction. Here I am reminded of the lyrics from a Kate Bush song, the haunting 'Deeper Understanding', as the protagonist laments his growing isolation from humanity he seeks increasing solace from his computer.[16] Usually, the gamer is the last person to acknowledge they have an addiction, but perhaps in this respect an addict of video games is no different to a drug addict or an alcoholic.

There is often a subtle difference, however, between what we would define as 'true' play (possessing that quality of free choice) and addictive play. Nachmanovitch argues that the basic distinction is that addiction 'consumes energy and leads to slavery' whereas practice 'generates energy and leads to freedom'.[17] When we know or sense ourselves close to a discovery (say in science), a breakthrough in composing a piece of music or locating that vital quality of a character in drama, perhaps we find we cannot rest until the work is done. Usually, however, this compulsion is short-lived and that tension immediately abates when we reach the point of climax. Addictive play, by its very nature, is habitual and based on craving. There is no end. And with every climax, the addiction intensifies. A gambler, for instance, does not stop gambling when they have won. The winning buoys them up and fuels the activity. Etymologically, the term 'addiction' relates to the state of enslavement, and any addict will know intimately that experience of being a slave to their addiction.

Nachmanovitch advises that the 'creative processes of free play and concentrated practice can easily be derailed':

> spinning off into addiction or procrastination, into obsession or obstruction, leaving us, outside our own natural flow of activity, in states of confusion and self-doubt.[18]

He uses the term 'vicious cycles' to describe any activity, including play, that has been hijacked by an unconscious process that is urging repetition and lacking a capacity to stand back and reflect upon what has emerged. Pema Chödrön, in her exploration of addictive behaviour, describes it as weakening us because of this pull into the vicious cycle; succumbing to our addiction, whatever that may be, will offer only momentary relief before we are needing to feed it once again.

Resisting the temptation to look at play through a bivalent lens, so defining it as this or that, let's return to the continuum introduced in Act 1, Scene 2 of free play and depression:

Free play			Depression
Improvisation	Organized play, e.g. games and sports, the arts	Outcome-focused and compulsory work	Drudgery, enslavement, deadening 'work'

Deadly Theatre and other deadly art forms are likely to be outcome-focused but may not have a compulsory element. A video gamer in full flow might be in a heightened state of tension and agitation, so the image of deadening seems hardly an accurate description. And yet in both there is this 'vicious cycle' that seems unbreakable and unresolvable. There is another form of play that seems to embody many of the qualities of deadly play – having an addictive, obsessive, compulsive energy, this form of play seems to 'play the player'.

Traumatized Play

Child psychiatrist Lenore Terr identified what she termed post-traumatic play which is quite unlike 'the free and easy…bubbly and light-spirited' everyday play. Instead, post-traumatic play is 'grim and monotonous'.[19] Freud recognized this urge to repeat a traumatic event in his adult patients[20] and so it seems perfectly natural that children should show a compulsion to reproduce traumatic events from their own lives through their play. Terr's play therapy work was with children and young people who had suffered very obvious known traumatic events – in particular, the 26 Californian school children kidnapped from their school bus and buried alive in 1976. Astonishingly, all the children survived; however, their psychological suffering continued for several years. Her invaluable book has been dedicated to these kidnapped survivors of Chowchilla and the book's title, *Too Scared to Cry*, is a direct quote from Billy, one of the children. Although Terr's choice of the term 'post-traumatic play' is a fitting description as the event itself is over, I wonder whether the term 'traumatized play' may be more apposite? What we know about play is that it brings the then into the now and the there into the here, so, in effect, a child or young person replaying a traumatic event is literally reliving that event over and over again. In this respect, traumatized play displays many of the qualities of deadly forms of play mentioned above.

To the trained observer of traumatized play, it can seem that it is the play enslaving the player. There is a compulsion to play and replay painful and unresolved events, sometimes contained within a metaphor but mostly very literally shown. Winnicott says that extreme trauma cannot be held within the area of symbolic illusion or the child's omnipotence.[21] I would not necessarily agree with this statement as I believe I have seen children engaged in traumatized play using metaphor. With each playing, the trauma is carved deeper and deeper into the psyche. Deadly play perpetuates the trauma. As Epstein says, 'we do not play...we repeat'.[22] The question then arises: At what point does the therapist intervene to interrupt the cycle of traumatized play? This form of play is not easy to stop and it is not readily open to outside influence. In the children engaged in traumatized play, I have seen a dogged determination to play till the end of the sequence of events, again and again, yet there is no resolution, no happy ending. Deadly play can be seen in the traumatic play of a child, in the obsessive 'play' of an adult; it has a driven quality and lacks witness consciousness, perspective and spontaneity. It has a rigidity around the emotional content, it is emotionally charged and it has to be done in this particular way and no other way will do; however, the child/player does not always express the emotion that their play warrants. There can be an emotional dullness. Often there is an inconsistency between the content and/or language and the emotions accompanying the play. This is often also true when PTSD survivors speak about their trauma.

Deadly play does not only relate to past events. The content of this kind of play may well be the imagined future, the fear of something happening, and in this sense the play may serve the purpose of trying to equip or rehearse the player for fear of the event (re)occurring. The traumatized play resembles some macabre video game that repeatedly plays the same scenario, but rather than the hero or heroine triumphing over the evil, they are instead overwhelmed by the antagonist every time.

In the Challenge of Change Resilience programme,[23] one of the key factors identified as affecting an individual's capacity for resilience is rumination. Derek Roger defines rumination as 'the tendency to continue to churn over emotionally upsetting events that have either happened in the past, or might happen in the future'.[24] One example might be that you are driving down the motorway and as you take a bend you see a bank of red brake lights hurtling towards you. If you are fortunate, you will slam your feet on the brake and clutch and stop in time. When the traffic clears and you are back on the open road, you recognize what a close shave you had but are able to let go of the terror. The accident did not happen. Your body recovers. Alternatively – and this is what most of us tend to do – we ruminate about the experience. We play over and over in our mind the 'what ifs' and the 'if onlys'. What if I hadn't been able to stop? I could have been badly injured or dead, my children would be without a parent, I could have killed my children…if only I had been paying better attention/ not listening to the radio/thinking about my destination/replaced my brakes. A child is more likely to externalize their ruminative thoughts in play, whereas the process of rumination for most adults happens in our minds. We are in a vicious cycle. We may be verbal ruminators, so those around us will be very familiar with our repetition of the same stories. You might be familiar with the term 'stuck record'? At least verbal ruminators have this outlet, although for their friends and families there may be little relief.

In the example above with the brake lights and emergency stop, the body's flight-or-fight mechanism will react immediately (hopefully). Though always present, there will be a steep increase in the levels of the hormones adrenalin and cortisol as the body attempts to deal with the crisis on hand. After the event has passed, providing the individual does not go into rumination, the body will reabsorb the adrenalin and cortisol and they will return to their normal baseline levels. Each time we ruminate, however, the body does not make a distinction between the actual event and the memory that we bring back to life through the ruminative process. Again and again, we can activate this survival mechanism. This is what causes us to waken at four in the morning in a state of anxiety, sweating profusely with a pounding heart. Someone who is suffering from PTSD is living in a perpetual state of hyperarousal. Although the actual event may be in the past, the experience of it is still very much alive and our bodies will react accordingly. Our bodies, though, are not designed to sustain the fight-or-flight response. It is extremely costly and will take precedence over *every* other body function, including the manufacture of white blood cells needed to maintain a healthy immune system. There is strong evidence linking stress to illness as we will be less able to fight infections, especially if we are not sleeping well. Many play therapists have encountered this vicious cycle of play in the children they work with.

Let's look at some of the qualities of traumatized play in contrast to what we understand as free play:

Traumatized play	Free play
Reliving trauma	Working through trauma
Repetitive	Changeable
Compulsive/obsessive qualities	Voluntary
Predictable	Unpredictable
Fixed ending (certainly not happy or joyful)	Resolution
Resistant to outside intervention	Open to outside intervention from other players
Monotonous (though paradoxically can be highly charged)	Spontaneous
Difficult to stop mid-flow	Can be stopped (depending on stage of play)
Literal (mostly)	Available to metaphoric representation
Highly contagious	Other players much freer to join in or not
Lack of reflective capacity	Greater ability to transition between play and non-play
Dissociated	Awareness of connection to known events

A significant aspect of traumatized play is its disconnection to known events, even when the roles, actions and script seem unmistakably to belong to the traumatic incident(s). Freud notes that 'however often the patient repeated her obsessional action, she knew nothing of its being derived from the experience she had had'.[25] The traumatized individual has the urge to externalize the unconscious in an attempt to gain control and resolution, yet without awareness they seem destined to remain in this vicious cycle. Just as traumatized play can enslave the child, it can also enslave the therapist working with the child. Sometimes literally...

Nine-year-old Menna was a looked-after child who had recently been placed permanently in local authority care. Prior to this she and her two younger siblings had yo-yoed between their mother's home, grandparents' home and various residential settings. As with many children like Menna, professionals lacked a coherent sequence of events. It was known that she had suffered chronic neglect from infancy, there had been domestic violence against her mother from several partners and there had been alcohol and drug abuse in the home. It was Menna's disclosure of physical abuse against her four-year-old sister by the mother's current partner that had precipitated recent care proceedings. Although Menna had been interviewed by the police and a statement taken, the Crown Prosecution Service had deemed the case too weak to pursue in the courts. Separated from her siblings, Menna's behaviour was fast deteriorating and she had been referred to the play therapy service at her school. Newly qualified play therapist Leigh brought an audio recording of her latest session with Menna to supervision. The supervisor listened to the recording with rapidly growing horror. It sounded like a clip from *The Exorcist*. Menna had tied the therapist to a chair using scarves and lengths of material. Leigh was completely immobilized. Menna's voice had taken on a menacing growl as she explained in soft, slow tones how she was going to put on the kettle for a 'nice cup of tea', and when she had made her tea she would use the remaining boiling water to wash Leigh's 'filthy, grubby head'. Thankfully, there was no kettle in the therapy room. But there were scissors, and with these Menna threatened to cut off Leigh's 'disgusting hair'. She took the scissors and approached the therapist... 'Chop, chop, chop! I'm going to cut it all off! Ha! You stinking little shit!' A terrified Leigh tried to calm Menna, urging her to put down the scissors and untie her. Menna positioned her face close to Leigh's and demanded she open her eyes. 'Look at me, you little piece of shit!' She spat into Leigh's face. 'Now you can wash that shit off your face!' Leigh managed, using all her strength, to release her hands, then her arms (Leigh was undoubtedly in a state of fight or flight). All the time she spoke as gently as she could to Menna. Whether Menna could hear or not, Leigh didn't know, but she knew she wanted to stay as connected as she possibly could to this traumatized little girl. As Menna approached total hysteria, Leigh succeeded in freeing herself from the chair and grabbed the child, preventing her from launching herself out of the first-floor window. Leigh held Menna as she fought and struggled against her. Finally, the child collapsed, sobbing, in Leigh's shaking arms. Leigh also sobbed. As the recording concluded, both Leigh and her supervisor were also sobbing.

Had Menna shown Leigh something of her own experience? Yes, it transpired this child had regularly been tortured in this way by her mother and the mother's partner, and she had been forced to 'wash' her own siblings' hair and faces in the same manner. If she didn't, she would be beaten and locked in a cupboard. The play therapy sessions had revealed the true extent of the cruelty inflicted upon these children; however, it could so easily have ended in tragedy. During her training, Leigh had never been taught about deadly or traumatized play. As a child-centred play therapist, she believed it necessary to allow the child to do whatever she needed to do in order to express herself. Leigh was following Virginia Axline's eight basic principles of non-directive play therapy[26] in accepting Menna completely, not attempting to direct Menna's actions and trusting Menna to find her own resolution. Crucially, Leigh overlooked the eighth principle: 'the therapist establishes only those limits that are necessary to anchor the therapy to the world of reality and *to make the child aware of her responsibility in the relationship*'.[27] In traumatized play, the child typically lacks any awareness, and so in that moment it is impossible for her to summon any sense of responsibility to another person.

As Menna showed, in traumatized play it is not uncommon to see the child (or adult) identify with the perpetrator. For a victim of violence and cruelty, one way to ensure self-protection is to align with the abuser, thus becoming an abuser oneself. Agencies that recruit so-called child soldiers rely on this aspect of human behaviour, and this is why cycles of abuse are dangerously self-perpetuating unless they are interrupted.

It is extremely tempting for anyone working with a traumatized individual who has experienced profound disempowerment to give away their own power as Leigh did. In the 1990s, I had the good fortune to be working alongside Dr Anne Bannister[28] when I underwent the same initiation. I was co-facilitating a therapy group for women who had disclosed their own sexual abuse following disclosures made by their children. Despite several years of experience as a therapist, I found I lost my voice in this group. I felt small, insignificant, deskilled and completely disempowered. I also reneged on my responsibilities as a facilitator. Thankfully, my co-facilitator, Pat, was a very experienced therapist in Transactional Analysis, and from Pat and Anne, my supervisor, I learned a vital lesson: giving away my own power did not empower my clients. Rather, it created a deep lack of safety and consequent fear in them as I failed to hold and contain the group sufficiently for them to feel safe and able to explore their patterns of abuse. Although I could see that I was embodying, in the transference, the sense of disempowerment, it was *my disempowerment*. In supervision, I explored the likelihood of feeling guilty for what these women and their children had endured.[29] Even though I had played no part in the abuse, feeling a sense of responsibility to rescue the women and their children, and not being able to do so, left me feeling powerless. I also realized that guilt can mask many other emotions, and I discovered the depth of horror, rage, shock, sadness and overwhelm that were present for me with this group. With support, I was also able to see a positive function of guilt as a trigger to act productively. In that group, I realized the essential difference between 'power over' and 'empowerment from within'.

Deadly Play as the Near Enemy of Free Play

The question remains: Is deadly play actually play in the way so far defined in this book? It certainly seems to be lacking essential qualities such as choice and spontaneous discovery. Deadly play masquerades as free play, and yet when we begin to take a closer look, it appears obvious that this form of play bears little resemblance to the free and spontaneous play defined thus far. In Buddhism, there is a wealth of teaching on what are called the Brahma Viharas, which means 'abodes of brahma'.[30] These four virtues are known by many different names, including the Four Great Catalysts of Awakening and the Illimitable Minds. They are *metta* (loving-kindness), *karuna* (compassion), *mudita* (sympathetic joy) and *upekkha* (equanimity). We will explore the Brahma Viharas in Act 3, but for now let us look at what is understood to be the 'near enemy' of each of them. A near enemy is the traditional term used to identify something else – another quality or experience – that resembles the real thing. For example, attachment or grasping is regarded as the near enemy of loving-kindness (*metta*). Attachment can clearly look like loving-kindness but, unlike the bona fide quality, its near enemy, attachment, pertains to self. It is the difference between loving and wishing the best for someone in their life (which may mean that person chooses not to be in my life) and loving someone because they make me feel better about myself. We are so conditioned to see attachment as loving-kindness that most of the time, I believe, we don't make any distinction. Underneath every near enemy is fear: fear of loss, loss of control, loss of a sense of identity, the same fears that underlie deadly play. One very important quality, however, about the near enemies of the Brahma Viharas is that they exist on a continuum:

Brahma Vihara	near enemy	far enemy

They are not unrelated to each other. So, although deadly play may not be the spontaneous play that helps free us from suffering, it is nevertheless the psyche's attempt to seek understanding, to seek a resolution, to attempt to regain what has been lost and to stave off anxiety, fear and panic. For the most part, this is possible when the play space is held by an empathic, attuned other. Regaining what has been lost is not always available to us; however, it is possible to grieve what has been lost, which allows us to let go and to move on.

Dr Eliana Gil recognizes that a continuum exists between what she terms 'dynamic posttraumatic play' and 'stagnant posttraumatic play'.[31] The former is marked by the availability of energy for greater emotional expression, physical flexibility and a wider range of play forms. This type of play also involves freer interactions with the therapist, and openness to new elements including themes, objects and locations and, crucially, to different outcomes. Although dynamic post-traumatic play (DPTP) may begin with a rigidity, there is a discernible loosening over time. In contrast to DPTP, stagnant post-traumatic play is marked by constriction, repetition and stuckness. The energy is blocked. Using a combination of what Gil calls 'low-challenge/low-intrusion interventions' and 'high-challenge/high-intrusion interventions' within the context of the therapeutic relationship, the therapist supports the traumatized child in exploring her experiences *without* re-experiencing the disconnection and disempowerment felt at the time of the original trauma.

THE SHADOW SIDE OF PLAY

The shadow, first proposed by Jung,[1] has a subtle range of meaning; however, for those initiates electing to descend 'to the deep well' Jung warns the shadow is a 'tight passage, a narrow door…[a] painful constriction'.[2] There is no other way. Marie-Louise von Franz defines the shadow in plain terms as 'the whole unconscious'.[3] Primarily, it refers to those characteristics, qualities and aspects of ourselves that we have learned not to show to the outside world. It relates to those parts of the cloak that are buried deep in the recesses of our unconscious, hidden from the light of day but nevertheless potent in their covert manipulation of us. I found a greetings card which says, 'We never grow up, we just learn how to act in public.'[4] The photograph accompanying the text is of a little boy, maybe four years old, standing proudly in his underpants, hands on hips, wearing a yellow towel thrown around his shoulders as a cap and yellow swimming goggles. This card sits on the windowsill of my study reminding me every day to remember those anti-social, eccentric, sometimes exciting parts of myself that have a place in my life even if I do not show them to the world. Then there are the cruel, mean-spirited, shameful and rageful parts, to name a few. I fully accept there are parts of myself that I am still ignorant of, still repressing, even though I am not aware that I am repressing them. I am still learning who I am and I am reliant upon the other (family, friends, colleagues, therapist, supervisor) to act as mirrors, benign mirrors, reflecting back those shadowy aspects of myself, so that I might bring awareness to my blind spots.

Society requires all of us to 'grow up', and this process begins very, very early in childhood. In fact, the formation of the shadow is simultaneous with the formation of the cloak. It arises simultaneously with the cloak and the two are co-created. The light and the dark. And neither can exist without the other.

We learn from a young age those characteristics in us that endear us to others and those that are disapproved of. For our survival, we need to maintain connection with others and so it becomes necessary to hide away from view the less attractive parts of ourselves. These are still woven into the cloak but occupy the deeper, darker layers from which they are ever ready to jump out and express themselves in the world, much to our shame and the world's likely displeasure. As these aspects of ourselves are unacceptable to others, it follows they must be disagreeable to us too, so they must be cast deep into the dungeons of our minds, into the unconscious, with the hope, possibly, that they will just wither and die, leaving us without risk of rejection, disapproval and being unlovable.

The shadow's influence is far-reaching in our lives – in thought, belief and action – and yet we expend a great deal of energy attempting to deny its existence. In our negation of the shadow, we project those disowned aspects of ourselves on to others: 'since everything unconscious is projected, we encounter the shadow in projection'.[5] You may recall the process of projection in relation to Sue Jennings' developmental play model, EPR, in Act 1, Scene 4. In play, projection is the second of the three stages (between embodiment and role play) and describes the process of externalizing what is internal. In play, we project our own imaginative meaning on to toys, objects, puppets or stories. The projective process is, of course, not unique to the play realm. It is a continuous process in all human relations and we are all recipients of other people's projections. The more conscious we can become of our own inner worlds, most especially our shadow, through the engagement of the benign mirror, the less we will be predisposed to project our own material on to others and the more available we will be for authentic relating.

Jung made a distinction between the personal shadow and the collective/archetypal shadow. As the collective/archetypal is innate to humanity, it exists in the deeper layers and beneath the layers of the cloak (recalling that the cloak is not a separate, indistinct entity but a manifestation of our Being or Self in relationship).

The archetypal is impersonal, universal and cross-cultural, yet how the archetypal is realized in each human being will be dependent upon that individual's life experiences. The deeper layers of the cloak relate to the personal-in-group shadow which is learned from our cultural identity and from the collective/archetypal. The earliest personal shadow is woven into the cloak in infancy, and therefore there is no verbal language to encapsulate and communicate its nature. The shadow then is experienced through sensations, feelings, bodily reactions and behaviour. As the cognitive mind cannot fathom these mysterious signals, there is a tendency to dismiss them as irrational and irrelevant. This dismissing often means a disowning, and instead of the individual taking ownership of them, they are projected out on to someone else. What we cannot name, we cannot know.

The personal shadow is our own individual direct experience, whatever we have learned from our attachment figures to be undesirable in our immediate family culture. In some families/living groups, for instance, forthright communication in preference to sensitivity is valued; in some families, vulnerability and the demonstration of loving emotions are prized. In other families, physical expression of aggressive feelings is encouraged, in some families it is artistic endeavour, and in other families the generation of money is the key concern. We each learn from an early age the cultural system of laws that operate within our social unit. We may succumb to the system and in doing so repress more authentic aspects of ourselves (giving rise to False selves). We might reject the familial values, but we will still know what they are all the same.

The personal expands to our wider sphere of attachments beyond family to culture, tribe, society or nation. Gabor Maté advises, 'No society can understand itself without looking at its shadow side.'[6] Beyond the personal and cultural lies the archetypal shadow. As the collective/archetypal is innate to humanity, it exists beneath the layers of the cloak and is 'always present, ready to be reunited, sitting intimately among us as one of our most loyal friends'.[7]

As the impersonal aspect, the archetypal shadow is connected to the spiritual or transpersonal realm communicated in symbol, image and metaphor. The three aspects – personal, personal cultural and collective/archetypal – are not entirely separate and distinct from one another; rather, they can influence and merge as the threads of the universal are seamlessly woven into each individual cloak. Due to the multilayered nature of the shadow, its creation involves both unconscious and conscious processes.

> All the feelings and capacities that are rejected by the ego and exiled into the shadow contribute to the hidden power of the dark side of human nature.[8]

This 'hidden power of the dark side' is often referred to as 'evil'. As a general tendency, human beings fear what they do not know, and what we do not know are those aspects of ourselves that once threatened to alienate us from those we loved and depended upon for our survival. We were each required to split off and cast those parts into the darkness. It is understandable that we will not relish uncovering such material. We will be even less inclined to venture into shady regions (where angels fear to tread) if we have been brought up to believe that what lies therein is evil, demonic, overpoweringly destructive and will lead to catastrophic consequences. That we will open a Pandora's Box and release all manner of mayhem upon and about us. Yet our failure to realize these disowned parts may well render them more hostile and antagonistic, as a child denied love and acceptance might eventually wreak devastation upon the world.

Buddhist teachers have a different relationship to the shadow. Rob Preece says this:

> The forces of the Shadow are not inherently demonic and terrible. Light and dark, good and evil, creation and destruction are relative dualities that have no ultimate true nature. They are not absolutes. It is our ignorance and lack of insight that seeks out one and fears the other.[9]

A psychotherapist aims to support an individual who has been crippled by childhood experiences to find the language and a safe space in which to begin expressing the power the shadow has thus far exerted over them. In Act 1, Scene 4, I introduced a child who had learned from her mother that she was evil. Her name is Kim…

Fifteen-year-old Kim's first words to her therapist were: 'F*****g therapists! They do my f*****g head in!' The therapist knew instinctively that Kim would not be able to tolerate the intensity of sitting together in a room with a stranger, certainly one she already perceived as a threat. The therapist reassured her that this was not her intention and so suggested instead an outing to a local café. The arrangement of frequenting various cafés in the town continued for several months. The two talked about clothes, animals, the best banana milkshake. One day, Kim stared hard at the therapist and said, 'You don't want to get any closer to me if you know what's good for you.' The therapist gently enquired why this might be, to which Kim replied, 'I'm so evil. I hurt everyone who gets close to me. I even hurt my mum before I was born by kicking her so hard I injured her back.' The therapist thought about Kim's statement and was about to answer, 'No, you're not evil, Kim', and then thought better of it. Instead, she replied, 'Yes, Kim, but I don't believe that's all of who you are.' The hardness in Kim's eyes softened slightly as she visibly reflected on the possibility of another way of seeing herself.

What do we mean by evil? Evil is universally understood as the intentional act of causing harm (in particular, murder and serious injury). Across the world, each country has set its own age for an individual to be held criminally responsible for causing intentional harm to another human being. In 33 states in the USA, there is no minimum age, theoretically meaning that a child of any age could be sentenced to criminal penalty, although in most states a capacity-related test is applied.[10] In France too, there is no minimum age; however, a child will be considered to have 'discernment' between the ages of eight and ten. In Qatar and India, the minimum age is seven, whereas in Brazil it is 18. In Iran, the age of criminal responsibility is defined by the Civil Code as the time of puberty, which is 15 lunar years for boys and nine for girls. In effect, although there may be a common understanding as to the nature of evil, internationally we do not have any agreement as to the age at which an individual can be held responsible for committing such acts of evil. I would imagine, however, that no country would consider an unborn baby as intentionally causing harm to her mother, but what Kim's mother was projecting on to her daughter was by no means rational and logical. Like so many children, Kim was an easy target for scapegoating by a parent who, I would suggest, had not begun to look at her own shadow side.

The question of whether evil exists is arguably indisputable. Each one of us has been harmed by another and, if we are honest, caused harm to another, and we are all familiar with the horrors that are being perpetrated around the world every day. The degree of harm caused is significant, as is the intention to cause harm. At one extreme, history books and newspapers recount atrocities carried out by despotic leaders or the 'quiet loner' that no one suspected. If it is possible for a human to inflict some cruelty upon another, the chances are someone somewhere is doing it. If we are prepared to accept the existence of goodness in the world, then surely we need also accept that evil exists along the same continuum. The question is: Are human beings born evil or are they made evil? Personally, unlike psychiatrist Morgan Scott Peck,[11] I do not believe there is such a thing as an evil personality trait. I do not believe Kim was born evil, whatever her mother might claim, nor do I believe Kim's mother was born evil. I do not believe there is a gene for evilness, nor do I believe there is such a thing as an evil person. Forensic psychotherapist Jessica Williams Saunders,[12] who worked for a number of years in high-security psychiatric hospital Broadmoor, describes offenders not as evil but as humans 'with a capacity to carry out deeply disturbing, dark acts'.[13]

When we repress certain qualities, such as our murderous tendencies and fantasies, our envy, greed and lust, to the deepest reaches of our unconscious – to the dungeon or the labyrinth – they are not killed off. They do not wither away. Anger, in particular, when denied or avoided can easily turn into hatred. Hatred can fester, seethe and contort into monsters, beasts or devils that can commit the most appalling atrocities. Seeds of anger, hatred and resentment that are sown in early life germinate in the shadowy realms to break through with frightening voracity. Progress is made when we are able to own uncomfortable, difficult emotions. When we can acknowledge them without feeding them. When we can play with them.

Forensic psychologist Professor Joanna Clarke, who worked for many years with high-risk prisoners, concurs with this viewpoint of the early origins of evil, saying, 'In my experience every offender I have encountered has suffered serious psychological damage in childhood.'[14] It would be mighty convenient to believe some people are born evil. We could excuse ourselves of any commitment to enquire into these people's lives, incarcerating them (or, even better, executing them), and we need never be troubled with guilt or self-reproach. In my view, this stance is deeply flawed. It serves to support a split in each of us as well as in our societies and renders our own shadow unacknowledged. It is a sobering question to ask oneself: What if I had been subjected to the same experiences as this individual – could I truly say I would not have done what they did? Novelist Aleksandr Solzhenitsyn is reputed to have cautioned that the line dividing good and evil cuts through every human heart. To be sure, I am not suggesting that people who commit atrocities be condoned for their actions. Indeed, I think it is vital that they be facilitated in taking responsibility for the harm they have caused. Genuine remorse is one of the most effective agents against recidivism.

Where I do find myself agreeing with Scott Peck is in his view of scapegoating as a form of evil. The term originates from the book of Leviticus[15] in which a goat would be sent out into the wilderness to perish on Yom Kippur after the high priest had symbolically laid the sins of the people upon its head, thereby relieving everyone of their own wrongdoings. Scapegoating is a form of projection. It is unconscious by definition and relieves us of the disagreeable task of taking responsibility. Just like the individual, societies can scapegoat groups that are different, less powerful and in a minority. Scapegoating per se may not directly cause physical harm to an individual or to a group, and so is easy to ignore or avoid, but it can and frequently does lead to the perpetration of 'deeply disturbing, dark acts' that can easily be justified by the majority. These acts may be psychological in nature. Kim's mother scapegoated her daughter, creating in her a deeply held conviction of her own capacity to harm others and denying her the possibility of intimacy with another human being. I am sure her mother was in great pain too, for I believe the will to cause harm comes from a troubled and therefore troubling individual. I also concur with Scott Peck's view that '[w]e become evil by attempting to hide from ourselves'.[16]

Similarly, philosopher Martin Buber writes of '[t]he uncanny game of hide-and-seek in the obscurity of the soul, in which it, the single human soul, evades itself, avoids itself, hides from itself'.[17]

In Western societies, there is a general tendency to split between good/the light and evil/the shadow. In Buddhist traditions, the duality is not between good and evil but between wisdom and ignorance. Preece continues, 'While we remain ignorant and unconscious of the archetypal darkness of the Shadow, it has power to dominate us unconsciously.'[18] The antidote to ignorance is awareness, bringing light into the darkness.

> Modern man must rediscover a deeper source of his own spiritual life.
> To do this, he is obliged to struggle with evil, to confront his shadow,
> to integrate the devil. There is no other choice.[19]

According to Rollo May, the word 'devil' originates from the Greek
word *diabolos*, the strict meaning of which is 'to tear apart'. The word
'diabolic' is the antonym of symbolic, meaning 'to unite'. He writes:

> There lie in these two words tremendous implications with respect
> to ontology of good and evil. The symbolic is that which draws
> together, ties, integrates the individual in himself and with his group;
> the diabolic, in contrast, is that which disintegrates and tears apart.
> Both of these are present in the daimonic.[20]

You may recall Greek play therapists Vicky Zerva and Peter Vagiakakos
speaking of *daimon* in Act 1, Scene 1, and citing its meaning as *I
have deep knowledge*. This deep knowledge relates to oneself. Rather
than being something to fear and avoid, the *daimon* instead allows
us to learn and to understand who we are, providing we meet it with
awareness. It is the door to our self-knowledge, referred to by Jung
as the process of 'individuation',[21] wherein the many aspects of the
psyche may become integrated.

> The daimonic is any natural function which has the power to take
> over the whole person.[22]

This explains the ambiguity around *athyrma* that Zerva and Vagiakakos
have reclaimed for their play therapy programme in Athens. *Athyrma*
– the action of play – has the negative connotation of someone
possessed by a god rather than that person being empowered by
the energy of play. Likewise, daimonic energy can either take over
a person, causing them to carry out violent acts, or it can facilitate
tremendous change in the person. Historically, 'daimon possession' is
the name for psychosis.[23]

> Violence is the daimonic gone awry. It is 'demon possession' in its
> starkest form. Our age is one of transition, in which the normal
> channels for utilizing the daimonic are denied; and such ages tend
> to be times when the daimonic is expressed in its most destructive
> form.[24]

Denial of the shadow serves only to remove it from our awareness. The
energy of shadow can, and often does, cause us to act in apparently

irrational and unreasonable ways, and often we do not know why we are doing so. It may be in the form of an angry outburst, a physical 'lashing-out', or an acting-out behaviour that causes harm to ourselves and/or others. It is the action/behaviour that creates the outcome of evil.

Rollo May was writing in the 1960s and 1970s, times of great transition indeed. Yet every age is an age of transition, and each generation surely would benefit from creating healthy channels for utilizing the daimonic. One thing we know is that the daimonic is omnipresent within each of us.

The shadow can be seen in humour, jokes and slapstick antics. In December 2012, two Australian DJs, Mel Greig and Michael Christian, made a hoax call as part of a live radio stunt to a central London hospital. The Duchess of Cambridge had recently been admitted, and Greig and Christian, claiming to be calling from the royal household, rang the hospital switchboard. Instead of the rebuff from an irate receptionist they had apparently expected, the two found themselves speaking directly to a nurse caring for the Duchess. Three days later, the nurse, Jacintha Saldanha, hanged herself. One might suggest that the shame experienced by this nurse was too much to bear. Four years earlier, Jonathan Ross and Russell Brand faced heavy public criticism for the message they left on actor Andrew Sachs' answer phone, live on air, disclosing to millions Brand's sexual activities with Sachs' granddaughter. In this instance, nobody died as a consequence, although there was much human suffering caused as a result of the prank.

Unsuspecting members of the public, together with celebrity figures, have long been subjected to so-called 'ambush' radio and television over the years. In 1948, *Candid Camera* appeared on American television and audiences laughed wincingly with disbelief and relief (that it wasn't them) as they watched bewildered people look on while their cars were flattened or apparently normal people around them began behaving in unpredictable and outrageous ways. The idea caught on in the UK in 1960, seemingly even more popular among the British who have a long tradition of the trickster format. Most recently, the satirical *The Revolution Will Be Televised* shows two talented and convincing actors, Heydon Prowse and Jolyon Rubinstein, righting the wrongs of corruption, hypocrisy and greed by targeting politicians, bankers and gun supporters. Prank filming, however, is much more expensive than radio. In addition, permission of the individual being filmed is required (unless there is significant public interest in exposing them) and so radio hoaxes have become much more popular.

The two Australian DJs could not have foreseen the nurse's suicide; however, this tragedy has called into question the whole practice of this shadow side of play. Where is the line between entertainment and bullying, intimidation or harassment, and who determines the ethical boundaries? Not surprisingly, in this case, we could not reach a consensus. The DJs themselves both received death threats while others excused their actions, completely detaching their actions from the nurse's death. As the social media networks continue to spread across the world, it becomes all too easy to play to the audience and be drawn into acting without thinking of the consequences, as many who have faced lawsuits will attest.

Mark Lawson, writing on the subject of pranks, makes the suggestion that judgment should lie in whether the broadcast be deemed 'funny or clever enough to justify the discomfort'.[25] Again, who decides? We may urge Prowse and Rubinstein to accost 'greedy bankers' or 'corrupt politicians', believing such actions are justified and deserved. In some ways, they play the role of the court jester, speaking the truth on our behalf. And yet such public teasing can be extremely humiliating for those teased, and who is to say if it will not result in more tragic consequences?

Besides the obvious role of entertainer, one of the traditional roles of the circus clown or the fool has been to manifest aspects of the shadow, always playing on the cusp between what is shadow and acceptable *enough*, with the dangerous possibility of stepping over that threshold. We never really know with these characters how they will behave in public and so we can be both attracted to and reviled by their anarchic ways as they act out the impulses, urges and desires of our own shadow-selves.

> …the audience members may experience a vicarious pleasure in witnessing the clown behaving in ways in which they may wish to behave but which the constraints of society forbid.[26]

By their nature, clowns perform a disruptive role in their blatant disregard of the conventions of performance – that is, they interrupt and disrupt other acts and contravene the audience/performer boundary.

Indeed, according to mime artist Jacques Lecoq, the clown relies on his audience for his very existence: 'He comes to life by playing with the people who are looking at him.'[27] At times, the clown gently taunts audience members, perhaps someone with a balding head having a particularly ideal target for a water spray, yet there still remains an acceptable way of being for the clown, as Louise Peacock comments: 'The moment a member of the audience is singled out and soaked, the clown has found a way of extending the disruption beyond the limits of expectation and acceptability towards transgression.'[28] Most forms of clowning in Western societies are less transgressive than in other parts of the world. Peacock cites the feigned violence of the performers of the French circus Archaos created in 1986 by Pierrot Bidon. In the show *Metal Clown*, the audience is threatened with chainsaws and there is a feigned execution of a clown, with a female clown then using the severed head to simulate oral sex. Although in play, the acts are so shocking, Peacock questions the audience's capacity to remain in a play state. This is a very significant point. Once the audience decides this is no longer play, then the play no longer exists. Presumably, the audience members have some idea of the Archaos circus and consciously make a choice to attend a performance. Some, of course, may be ignorant and may choose to leave. Another theatrical group that plays with the blurred boundaries between performer and audience is the Spanish company La Fura dels Baus, founded in 1979. The 1985 show *Suz/O/Suz*, held in a London Docklands warehouse, was both exhilarating and terrifying for the audience, with performers mingling among the crowd and suddenly, without warning, launching into action. The *NME* (*New Musical Express*) review described the group's intention to 'create a kind of adult adventure playground of fun, danger, slapstick and fantasy'.[29] Here, one might question the difference between risk and danger. Would an audience unanimously choose to partake in a truly dangerous activity? In the 1990s, La Fura dels Baus widened its creative endeavours to include the opening ceremony at the 1992 Barcelona Olympics together with many other huge-scale corporate events. It seems, though, that the company never forgot its early roots and the 2000s saw a return to performance in the streets and many unconventional venues. Though not clowns, both these companies continually experiment with the unpredictable, often explosive play realm without clearly designated thresholds for the audience to benefit from some level of psychological or physical safety. Although I don't believe any member of the public, or any performer for that matter, has ever been injured during a show, the danger feels very real. I cannot help wondering what impact performing the show repeatedly and what effect seeing genuinely terrified members of the public have on the psychological state of the clowns and performers themselves?

Lecoq makes a distinction between clowns and bouffons, regarding the latter as 'people who believe in nothing and make fun of everything'.[30] Bouffonry play is more vicious and dangerous. Peacock adds another dimension to their threat: 'Whilst clowns may play alone, bouffons always appear as part of a gang.'[31] Lecoq notes the bouffon's purpose is to mock us, often to the point of spite, attacking our preciously held beliefs and values. The Lecoq-trained clown and founder of the circus training school Circomedia, Bim Mason, makes the proposal that bouffonry was adopted by street performers in response to having 'experienced prejudice towards the world of beggars, travellers and the disadvantaged and…excited by the use of comedy as a weapon'.[32] Perhaps bouffons, more than clowns, live closer to the shadow realm than their counterparts in their savviness and ability to 'confront the public with their own [self-imposed] limitations'.[33] The bouffon, like the court jester or medieval king's fool, presents us with truths about ourselves that we would much rather keep hidden.

The court fool or jester was a recognizable figure in 14th- and 15th-century England, Italy, Germany and France. The fool, with his (and occasionally her) physical and intellectual adeptness, sharp wit and courage (or foolishness) in speaking the truth, often risks his own life. According to Sandra Billington,[34] German fools of the 16th century were deeply enmeshed in religious polemics of the time and sometimes became the puppets of politicians who used the fools' freedom of expression to their own ends. Many court jesters are recorded in history, such as Henry VIII's jester Will Somers, who is reputed to have had a significant part in the downfall of Cardinal Wolsey.

Billington recognizes too the fool's purpose of 'providing a corrective to the pretentious vanity of officialdom'.[35] On the one hand, notes Peacock, the function of the fool could be 'as carnivalesque in providing an outlet for behaviour or views that would otherwise contribute to civil unrest';[36] on the other, the fool *can* actively contribute towards civil unrest. Some might say the political role of the fool has lessened over the centuries; however, this is debatable.

My view is that, being an archetypal figure, the fool is ever-present; it may simply alter its form of expression. You may even find yourself in a Fooling workshop with one called Jonathan Kay...

The trickster is another archetypal form that generally receives very bad press in most Western societies. The term seems analogous with an imposter, a rogue or a cheat. These are cultural values that have been applied to the archetype. An alternative view of the trickster is one who is acutely aware of the shadow, able to cross fluidly between the light and the dark. This image of the trickster is one who is highly skilful, ingenious and creative, and employs his talents to break the established orders of society and nature, to shake up everyday life and recreate a new order. The trickster is cross-cultural, appearing as Loki in Norse mythology, Hermes in Greek mythology, Mercury in Roman mythology, Anansi in West African mythology and Coyote in Ohlone Native American mythology. Although the trickster archetype is universal, it carries different meanings in different cultures. The archetype is at times seen as a catalyst, his pranks causing confusion and even ruin in others while he is left unchanged. Often those the trickster brings down are oppressors and perpetrators. In many native traditions, there is a strong affiliation to the sacred and to creation, showing a willingness to engage with the complexities and paradoxes of life. In this rapidly evolving cyber-world, the presence of the trickster has been suggested especially in relation to internet trolling. There is ongoing debate regarding the delineation between cyber-trickery and cyber-bullying, the former understood to be generally harmless and entertaining in contrast to the latter.

The challenge with defining the 'shadow side' of play is fundamentally that play serves as a significant vehicle for transforming the shadow, inhabiting as it does the space in between what is known/conscious and what is unknown/unconscious. Play's unique quality of paradox allows us the psychological safety to express seemingly unacceptable behaviours, attitudes, thoughts and feelings, without the danger of consequence, provided the play happens in a contained space with consenting players. However, play is often used to lend legitimacy to the acting out of sadistic and cruel behaviours – for instance, when the exposed playground bully attempts to excuse their aggressive behaviour by claiming it to be 'only playing'. At a recent seminar on the subject of social networking, the comment was made that 'electronic technology reveals the less acceptable aspects of ourselves'.[37] This is not surprising because, like play, electronic technology such as Twitter, Facebook, Snapchat and Instagram can hide the true identity of the 'player', thereby giving anonymity and freedom from responsibility. It also comes as no surprise that many of the dangers young people are experiencing today in the fast-evolving world of cyberspace constellate around sexual behaviour and attitudes.

When does play cease being fun and become coercive? When *any* of the players/individuals involved deem it so. It is necessary to explore the intention behind the play. However, if someone is experiencing harm, it can no longer be called play. When exploring the issue of play's shadow side, it may be helpful to ask the following questions: Who holds power and how do they hold it? What happens if/when their power is challenged? Crucially, is the play bound by the shadow rather than it being a vehicle for transforming the shadow? Status, control and choice are also fruitful territories for exploration. When play encompasses any form of activity that objectifies, dehumanizes or demonizes the other, its play status needs to be reviewed.

It has been my observation when introducing the subject of play that many people express trepidation, nervousness and even fear. From experience, I have come to realize that so many of us have negative associations with play. I asked workshop participants to identify their own direct experiences of the dark side of play. The findings include play masking acts of bullying, teasing, exclusion from the group, mimicry, torment, humiliation and emotional and sexual abuse ('we are *only* playing...'). Some children who have suffered sexual abuse have been grossly and grotesquely misled by the perpetrator claiming the 'activity' is play. Supporting such children to reclaim their own playful capacity in support of their healing can take a long time.

I have a small greetings card by my bedside with a self-portrait by the 18th-century novelist Charlotte Brontë, inscribed with her enquiring words 'We can in the creative state feel driven, possessed, taken over, inhabited by someone else, but what?' As we explore more deeply into the realm of play and creativity, we are faced with the same questions. Just how much individual autonomy do we have when we enter the creative state? Do human beings act as conduits for something greater than ourselves? Can we do so with awareness and presence? Can we be expected to take full responsibility for our creative endeavours?

Play transgresses the rules of everyday reality existing in the liminal space between the individual and other (external space) and the liminal space between the cloak and Self (internal space). Each of these territories can be dangerous in as much as they are frequently unexplored. In unknown territory, we are fundamentally unable to exercise the same levels of control we have in other parts of our lives. Play opens us up and catches us out because it has a habit of bypassing our well-established defences. It is this very condition of surrendering our habits of self-protection for a time that makes play so extraordinarily valuable to us. As drama specialist Malcolm Ross states, 'play is dangerous, and in its danger lies its usefulness'.[38] What is threatened by play is our sense of identity, and this may well call into question our integrity and self-worth. Play challenges our own sense of who we believe we are by dissolving our perceptions and certainties about ourselves and one another. Play is the ideal medium for conveying, expressing and engaging with the shadow.

Creating *enough* safety is imperative to enable us to enter into the world of play. Yet the experience of danger and where exactly we position ourselves on that spectrum of *safe enough* is, to a large degree, personal and subjective. In Act 2, Scene 2, we looked at the work of Charlie Todd and his company Improv Everywhere. In one prank, male members of the troupe are filmed individually boarding the Metro at successive stops minus their trousers. Eventually, a woman boards the train with a bag, selling trousers for a dollar each. In the secret filming, a young, unsuspecting woman is seen reading a book on rape. There is much hilarity as the footage is replayed to an appreciative audience. Ultimately, the female traveller realizes it is a frolic…but what if she hadn't? In Act 1, Scene 1, I recounted a visit I had made to a Welsh playground with a group of trainee play therapists. We were all in our child-selves, much to the consternation of the young mother also in the playground. Both these examples could be seen as being on the cusp of shadow play as neither member of the public had consented to taking part in the play activity and both showed a level of anxiety and trepidation.

When we are in play, including being an audience (with the possibility of becoming a participant), we are uniquely vulnerable. Our defences are dismantled. We are disrobed, and as such we are open to assault whether that is intended or not. Just how much 'duty of care' does a theatre company, a radio station or a television programme have for its audience? As play is inherently risky, often mischievous, in nature, it can easily be distorted for ill-intention and misuse. Clearly, such activities would not fit with the criteria we are applying here to define play, such as entering into the activity exercising free choice, mutuality, enjoyment and non-harm. Earlier in the book, I mentioned my cat chasing a leaf across the lawn. What if this had been a mouse that he was tossing around between his jaws and clawed paws? The cat might have been playing, but it would certainly have been no game for the creature about to be eaten.

What seems to be key here in the enquiry of play's shadow side is the intention behind the player's actions, the degree to which they are aware of this intention and their sensitivity to anyone else experiencing the action. Being able to bring awareness to our own shadow – for once we bring something out into the light, it no longer belongs in the shadow and it can no longer dictate our behaviour and actions.

One of the requirements or conditions of intentional play is that it happens through choice. No one can be forced to play. There has to be mutual agreement, and this is continually open to renegotiation so that players can withdraw their agreement at any time. The majority of the time, the threshold between non-play/reality and play is easily discernible; however, true to the natural ambiguity of play, sometimes that threshold is not at all clear. One example would be Invisible Theatre developed by theatre practitioner Augusto Boal in 1960s Argentina. Invisible Theatre takes place in a public place, such as a public square or street, and the public become an unwitting audience to a drama enacted by actors. Although people may not immediately realize they are watching a performance, it is usually the case that they are free to enter into the spirit of the drama, or not, and usually they catch on before too long. Sometimes, audience members are invited to participate in the drama (Spect-actors). This element of choice is an essential aspect of Invisible Theatre. Traditionally, its main purpose has been to highlight issues of abuse and oppression,[39] particularly on social and political themes, and so to force or manipulate another group of people would be incongruous with the cause. An Invisible Theatre troupe may, however, deliberately set out to provoke feelings of injustice in an unsuspecting audience understood to be more empowered so as to generate empathy for another less empowered group. This is a risky business. What may also be provoked are feelings of anger and humiliation at the sense of being duped. It takes a skilled group of actors to manage such a situation. Furthermore, if the unsuspecting audience is more captive, emotions are likely to become more intense. Generally, people react strongly to experiences where their sense of personal freedom and choice are compromised, and this is just as true in the realm of play as in the realm of non-play/reality.

The true nature of play, then, is fundamentally about freedom and choice so that the shadow can be played *with*, rather than the shadow playing us. Earlier in the book, we looked at the Play Elements table created by Scott Eberle. In the spirit of play, I have taken the table and experimented with the possible shadowy elements related to each of Eberle's qualities using near and far enemies. The concepts of near and far enemies have been borrowed from the Brahma Viharas – those infinite transpersonal attributes of loving-kindness, compassion, sympathetic joy and equanimity. We will revisit the Brahma Viharas in Act 3. Each one has an antithetic quality, the far enemy, and each has a near enemy that masquerades as the true attribute. What is noteworthy is that all reside along a continuum, so all are connected in some way to each other. With certain conditions, the near and even the far enemies can be transformed into the true attribute. This I believe to be so for shadow elements of play.

Near and far enemies of Eberle's play elements		
		Power over…I over you or you over me
anticipation	**fear**	**denial**
interest	fanaticism	boredom/indifference
openness	naïveté	cynicism
readiness	anxiety	unpreparedness
expectation	presumption	dread
curiosity	intrusiveness	lassitude/conformity
desire	craving	aversion
exuberance	exaggeration	lifelessness
wonderment	startle	disregard

surprise	shock/horror	monotony
appreciation	obligation	neglect
awakening	distraction	deadening
stimulation	agitation	stagnation
excitement	disturbance	repression
discovery	distraction	neglect/disregard
arousal	provocation	suppression
thrill	seduction	boredom/disappointment

pleasure	titillation	pain
satisfaction	craving	frustration/disappointment
buoyancy	denial	collapse
gratification	hedonism	asceticism
joy	mania	despair
happiness	ebullience	wretchedness
delight	ecstasy	anguish
glee	amusement	dismay
fun	distraction	woe

understanding	pity	misattunement
tolerance	fear/submission	prejudice/bigotry
empathy	insincerity/charm	cruelty/shame
knowledge	dogma/arrogance	ignorance
skill	cunning	impotence
insight	deception	superficiality
mutuality	collusion	hostility
sensitivity	sentimentality	apathy
mastery	domination	chaos/coercion

strength	bravado	fear
stamina	obstinacy	lethargy
vitality	audacity	collapse
devotion	obsession	violation
ingenuity	trickery	disorientation
wit	sarcasm	stupidity/monotony
drive	fixation	inertia
passion	rage	aloofness
creativity	distraction	destruction/conformity

poise	indifference	chaos/overwhelm
dignity	pride	disinhibition
grace	charisma	repulsion
composure	aloofness/forbearance	anxiety/agitation
ease	abandon	tension
contentment	resignation	disquiet/irritation
fulfilment	abdication/denial	disappointment/frustration
spontaneity	impulsiveness/recklessness	rigidity/freezing
balance	impassivity	overwhelm

The near and far enemies seem to have quite significant energetic differences. The near enemies feel much darker and more manipulative. The far enemies, in contrast, feel dead and dissociated.

Play is a unique medium for working with and transforming the shadow; contributing to that process of discovery and reconnection to the dissociated aspects of the self and to Source. Jungian analyst Liliane Frey-Rohn reminds us of the hidden treasures locked away in the shadow – our undeveloped child with all their gifts and talents lying in potential. The shadow, says Frey-Rohn, 'retains contact with the lost depths of the soul, with life and vitality'.[40] Winnicott reminds us, 'It is in playing and only in playing…that the individual discovers the self.'[41] So many of play's qualities previously mentioned allow us to come into relationship with those repressed, denied, feared aspects of ourselves and to do so with enough psychological safety to permit a softening and loosening of the fixed and often stuck patterns embedded into our cloaks. Were this psychological safety to be lacking, we would simply shore up the cloak's enfoldment further. The paradoxical nature of play gives us a freedom to ask, *What if? I wonder…and perhaps…* Such freedom grants the player what dramatherapist Robert Landy terms 'aesthetic distance',[42] which supports both cognitive and emotional engagement and prevents overwhelm. Whether we believe the images and symbols arise within us from the archetypal realm, or we hold some other explanation as to their origin, we as individuals still maintain, as Jung described, 'the autonomous and sovereign manipulation of these images'.[43] We make them our own. We play with them and, in creating the dialogue, we uncover forgotten aspects of ourselves. However long ago those parts of us were abandoned, we find we have opportunity to welcome them back into the present time, no longer 'haunting our lives without being fully present', as Maté observes in his patients with addictions, rather living an integrated and present life in this moment.

How do you find a lion that has swallowed you?[44]

Jung's comment is like a koan. It is echoed by Einstein's sentiment that we cannot solve our problems with the same thinking we used when we created them. We need a different way. Maté speaks of adults' 'envy of the open-hearted and open-minded explorations of children; seeing their joy and curiosity, we pine for our own lost capacity for wide-eyed wonder'.[45] The play realm is paradoxical, oblique, irrational, non-linear and without goals, and it is awaiting discovery whatever age we are.

ACT 3

Act 3

Scene I

THE CALL FROM
THE GREAT BELOW –
ASPIRATION TO AWAKEN

Men are afraid to forget their minds, fearing to fall through the Void with nothing to stay their fall. They do not know that the Void is not really void, but the realm of the real Dharma.[1]

Shades of the prison-house begin to close
*   Upon the growing boy.*
But he beholds the light, and whence it flows,
*   He sees it in his joy.[2]*

In this scene we will define awakening and ask the question: Why awaken? We will explore the nature of awakening; whether it is a process or a product, or both, and we will look at what is it that calls someone on to this path and why and how they might hear that call. We will deepen our enquiry into the Brahma Viharas, the Four Great Catalysts of Awakening, and discover why these universal, transpersonal qualities are also called the necessary conditions for awakening. Finally, we will examine how a myth, an ancient form of play, can support this journey towards awakening and recapitulate some of play's unique qualities that make it so well placed to promote self-awareness and discovery.

A buddha is a spiritually awakened person, someone whose wisdom has been completely unveiled.[3] Awakening is a multifarious process and, as such, challenges any single, reductive definition. Awakening is, at one end of the continuum, the total disintegration of one's identity as a separate self – to use the metaphor thus far used, becoming cloakless. In Bax's play, the Newly Dead Woman does eventually relinquish her cloak and *dis-covers* a previously unknown or forgotten freedom and interconnectedness with all beings. What I am about to say may counter many spiritual writings; however, it is my view that while we live and breathe and hold this bodily form, we still *need* our cloaks to enable us to function and relate to one another. For me, awakening means recognizing that the cloaks we wear are not all of who we are. Once we truly acknowledge this, then our lives are irrevocably changed and we become active, empowered beings in all aspects of our lives. Pema Chödrön describes a fully enlightened being as someone who is completely fearless and stays open to all that arises.[4] Awakening is understanding and practising the Four Noble Truths – that there is suffering, there is a cause of suffering, there is freedom from the cause of suffering and there is a path to that freedom. The Four Noble Truths, Batchelor reminds us, are not four separate, esoteric or intellectual ideas or concepts, they are the 'four phases within the process of awakening itself'.[5]

In the Prologue of this book, an elderly Chinese monk sets out on an onerous journey in search of enlightenment. He encountered the bodhisattva Manjushri. In learning of the monk's quest, Manjushri dropped the bundle of sticks he was carrying and the elderly monk was instantly and profoundly enlightened. The monk's experience was tumultuous and unsettling, and we learn he was left to manage his own fate as Manjushri retrieved his sticks and continued on his way. Some people do experience this sudden 'spiritual awakening' that literally can break them open, or break them down. A distinction is sometimes made between 'enlightenment' and 'awakening', the former being a sudden shift in consciousness or a sudden expansion that is usually quite dramatic in nature,[6] as the monk experienced. Psychiatrist John Nelson addresses this particular point and observes: 'Nothing in my medical training prepared me to distinguish profound breakthroughs of higher consciousness from malignant psychotic regressions that permanently submerge the self in primitive areas of the psyche.'[7] These spiritual emergencies are potentially traumatic to the individual themselves and to those around them. Presumably, the old Chinese monk would have been preparing for this eventuality and still he experienced disorientation. A sudden, profound awakening will surely be overwhelming and disempowering, and will jeopardize any prospect of integrating this newly discovered awareness into everyday life. I wonder what happened to the old Chinese monk, whether he remained on the mountainside or returned to his village.

Along the enlightenment/awakening continuum, there is another way of being and living that is perhaps less dramatic, involving gradual shifts and expansions of consciousness. Pema Chödrön tells us there is no final goal to awakening, that the path *is* the goal and this is the present moment. In the metaphor of the cloak, someone who practises loosening their cloak rather than grasping it, welcoming authentic interaction with the world rather than isolating themselves from it, realizes that the cloak is a functional illusion.

At the root of Buddhism there is a deep understanding that our suffering is caused by the false construction of reality we create by our attachment and identification to the cloak, giving us a sense of separateness from others. Mark Epstein reminds us that 'Buddhism has always made the self's ability to relax its boundaries the centrepiece of its teachings'.[8] For the awakening being, this capacity to be with whatever arises does not relate only to what is inside them. In the lived experience of interconnectedness, there is no definitive inside or outside. Awakening is a word we use in an attempt to define a quality of being that is fundamentally undefinable:

> …a way of living that is an expression of reverence. It is a way of being that reveres the sacredness and dignity of all life, honours our Earth, and appreciates the implications of our fundamental interdependence and interconnectedness.[9]

As we develop our capacity for awakening, we come to see and understand just how much of our suffering is bound up in our cloaks. The patterns in our thinking, doing, values and beliefs; our rigid ideas of how things are or are not; the rights and wrongs; the views we hold of ourselves which are often judgmental. These judgments might be positive or negative; both are still judgments. The comparisons we make with others – how we measure up – measure our worth by what we do or don't do. These layers of personal and cultural conditioning are no longer left unexamined as if they are the truth and we have no choice but to adhere to them. An awakening being examines the seemingly innocuous conditioning so many of us are subjected to in so many of our cultures that leaves us feeling less than, inadequate and needy. So many of the institutions in our lives – family, education, politics, religion and the financial world – have successfully trained us to look outside ourselves for fulfilment. Buddhism describes these as the Lords of Form, Speech and Mind.[10] When we can be truly honest with ourselves, we can see that the Realm of the Hungry Ghosts, so movingly described by Gabor Maté, is a place all of us know well, not only Maté's chronically addicted patients. In essence, we are all trained to look to things outside ourselves to define who we are and to shield us from the direct experience of reality. This is the nature of the cloak. It is liberating to realize that our well-being and happiness are not entirely dependent on people and materials that are completely outside of our control. What we can control, however, is *the quality of attention we bring to them.*

Our cloaks concretize reality, making it this or that, so that we hide behind our beliefs and our dogmas and feel threatened when these are challenged by someone else (also hiding behind their beliefs), bringing about the illusion of separateness and, often, in conflict with it.

If we believe that awakening/enlightening is either a process *or* a product, we would inadvertently be falling into the dualistic trap of the conditioned cloak. Surely, it is a process and a product being 'the final goal of human existence'.[11] Awakening is a moment-by-moment experience as we open our eyes, our ears, come to our senses and be in the present moment. Just as every moment offers us an opportunity to awaken, so too can we fall asleep. This is our individual choice.

My client Natalie, whom we met in the Prologue, was inspired to enter psychotherapy having read Mary Oliver's poem 'The Summer Day'. Natalie did not want to continue living her life according to the old patterns that she knew brought her dissatisfaction. She was unfulfilled and deeply questioning of her sense of self and her place in the world. Natalie wanted to be happy. She wanted to find a new way of being. It was simple and yet profound. As the Buddha said, all living beings want to be happy and to be free from suffering. Stephen Batchelor observes: 'We too sense that there is more to life than indulging desires and warding off fears.'[12]

Natalie could be said to have 'heard the Call from the Great Below', an invitation to enquire more deeply into her life, who she is and how she wishes to live out her days. Hearing the call does not need to emerge out of acute suffering such as a major loss or trauma in one's life. It could be a steady growing awareness of unfulfilled potential, as Christina Feldman describes it, 'initiated by divine curiosity'.[13]

Fundamentally, the question of 'Why awaken?' is the response to Pema Chödrön's question: 'Do the days of our lives add up to further suffering or to increased capacity for joy?'[14] Given the opportunity, who would choose *not* to embark on this path? The main obstacle, I believe, is fear. Fear of change, how we might lose ourselves, fear of the unknown, perhaps even fear of becoming psychotic. The Emptiness (Sunyata), as the Chinese Master of Zen Buddhism Huang Po observed almost 1200 years ago, is not the abyss that we fear if we surrender our attachment to the cloak. Rather, it is our true nature, our buddha nature.

> Often we are afraid of falling apart, but the problem is that we have not learned how to give up control of ourselves.[15]

It is our cloaks that obstruct this knowing:

> The only way to find out where I was was to get out of the way and let myself happen.[16]

We are already awakened beings with buddha nature. We already have an unlimited capacity for insight, love, compassion, equanimity and joy. The problem is we just don't realize it and instead we tie ourselves up in thoughts and actions that bind us to being so small. All the realization we need is already latently present. Obscuration by the cloak hides our true nature. If we were to call upon the Fool and the Fool's way of understanding language, we would understand the true meaning of the word 'dis-cover' – that is, to uncover what is already there. So this practice of awakening is simply an affirmation.

> It's an affirmation that consciousness is one of the essential ingredients of this universe, of all existence, of all reality. All the consciousness of every sentient being bears limitless potential for compassion, insight, and power. The whole of life and explicitly the whole of spiritual practice is simply designed to bring forth this potential.[17]

The way to enlightenment, said the Buddha, is through meditation. In meditation, one practises an attitude of attentive openness to meet whatever arises – good, bad and indifferent – and to meet it with an unwavering mind. In this state, we can cultivate the wisdom of insight, and it is insight that allows us to cut through the illusion of the cloak: the illusion of our separateness.

It leads to a realization that this 'I' we have been clinging to for so long doesn't exist at all. It's not that we don't exist – that would be a silly conclusion – but that this particular 'I' that we sense as separate and autonomous is simply non-existent.[18]

In this mindful state, the cloak – all our habitual patterns of behaviours, thoughts and feelings, our past histories, our future desires, in fact, our own sense of who we believe ourselves to be – begins to unfold and reveal its real nature: that it is a necessary illusion.

[Awakening] is a process from which there is no turning back. Once we discover the joy of being awake, it is no longer possible for us to reconcile ourselves to a life of limitation or unconsciousness.[19]

When I was first introduced to the Brahma Viharas during my psychotherapy training at the Karuna Institute, I had an intense, visceral experience. I felt I already knew these qualities, although I had never consciously sought to name them. I didn't even realize they had names! And because they remained vague, nebulous and unnamed, I had never enquired more deeply into them and I certainly hadn't spoken to anyone else about them. The closest approximation I had was the term 'angel' as I had been brought up in a loosely Christian home and in a culture that defined itself along such lines. I had experienced the Brahma Viharas at times of great challenge in my professional life as a therapist and in my personal life, especially in relation to fear, rage, profound uncertainty and shame. There were notable occasions in my work with children and adults who had been subjected to years of pervasive and depraved abuse by those professing to love them when I sincerely felt utterly inadequate encountering such suffering. I prayed for guidance and support to sustain not only my client but also for myself in the face of such hopelessness. The discerning words of Paracelsus, 'nothing comes from me; everything comes from nature of which I too am a part',[20] brought me some reassurance that I was not alone. There were many moments of something bigger holding both of us in an energy. How could I speak to anyone about these experiences when I didn't even have the language? I also feared others may think me weird or 'New-Agey'. And so I kept silent. Learning the names of *metta* (loving-kindness), *karuna* (compassion), *mudita* (sympathetic joy) and *upekkha* or *upeksā* in Sanskrit (equanimity) was with a heart-warming familiarity.

The Brahma Viharas are known by different names to describe their qualities. They arise from the place of Source (Brahma meaning the Creator in Hinduism, Vihara meaning home). They originate from our buddha nature, although you don't have to be a Buddhist to cultivate them. They are transpersonal. They belong to everyone and to no one, and yet every being can access and practise them. They are omnipresent and we need only open to their presence to know them. They are known too as the Illimitable or Immeasurable Minds because they are infinite – infinitely greater than *any* suffering. They are also described as the Necessary Conditions or the Four Great Catalysts of Awakening because without their presence in our lives we will struggle with staying open to whatever arises within us. Besides the fear of losing something we may treasure, as the Recently Dead character experienced in Bax's play, we may also fear what we will discover about ourselves when we start to respond to the Call. Most likely, we will grasp and cling to the cloak more fervently. As B. Allan Wallace observes, 'some groundwork is needed to ensure that you welcome and embrace deep insight when it occurs'.[21] This loosening of the cloak is primarily an *experience* of the sensations, feelings and movements within our bodies, rather than an intellectual exercise.

Another reason to cultivate the Brahma Viharas is so that realizations gained through the insight of awakening can be both sustained and integrated; otherwise, those experiences are going to fade from memory over time. What is needed is reliability and continuity.[22] These practices are not easy. They will challenge many traditional ways of viewing humankind, for they are based on love as opposed to hatred and violence, forgiveness rather than revenge, empowerment instead of power over.

The Brahma Viharas also have 'near enemies', as stated in Act 2. These are mental states that may share some of the qualities of the Brahma Viharas but are really quite different, arising as they do from our conditioned states (the cloak) instead of Source. It is important to recognize when we have become caught up in a near enemy as it is both limiting and will take us in a different direction.

So much of what we do to ourselves is harmful. We might look at others who are addicted to drugs such as crystal methamphetamine or heroin, or view as 'self-harming' those people who make repeated incisions on their arms, or those who stay with violent partners despite being physically and emotionally abused, but what about all the times that we tell ourselves we're stupid, useless, ugly? What about the times we hold on to anger or resentment or allow ourselves to be swallowed up by revenge or malice? Or our sense of worthlessness or inadequacy, to stop us from recognizing our own needs, let alone being able to express these needs to others? Although these injuries may not be visible to others, they nevertheless prevent us from truly living and thriving in the world. Also what we know is that if we see ourselves as worthless or inadequate, others are more than likely going to see and relate to us as such and so our sense of ourselves is validated. A negative, vicious cycle ensues. Our cloaks display this even if we are deeply unconscious of it. Despite many people's tendency towards feelings of unworthiness and self-denigration, generally we *still* seek to find happiness.[23] This yearning for happiness is, according to Wallace, 'the fundamental expression of the buddha-nature'.[24]

The word for loving-kindness in Pali is *metta*, and in Sanskrit, *maitri*. Loving-kindness means essentially a friendliness and a wish for oneself and *all* other beings to be well and happy.

May you be free of hatred. May you be free of anguish.

May you be free of anxiety. May you be well and happy.

It seems that so many people struggle to practise loving-kindness towards themselves, yet maintain they can have it for others. This practice is very clear in its intention to begin cultivating unconditional friendliness towards oneself. If we ignore or deny our own pain, we are simply 'spiritually bypassing'.[25] If we only focus upon ourselves, we are in danger of self-indulgence and quite likely mistaking wants for needs. Loving-kindness has a very significant component of honesty. We can only really love ourselves unconditionally if we can be utterly open and frank with ourselves. Warts and all. This entails recognizing and accepting all aspects of who we are, including those parts of us consigned to the shadow.

It is relatively easy to practise loving-kindness towards some people in our lives. Others, less so. What about those who have caused us or someone we love harm? What about the perpetrator of sexual abuse? The bully who tormented us for years and made our lives hell? What about the serial murderer? To practise loving-kindness for a perpetrator, a murderer or a psychopath is a wish for them to face those aspects of themselves that have caused harm to others, to take responsibility for themselves, not with the intention of hating themselves but to begin to love who they are. The Buddha said, 'Whoever loves himself will never harm another.'[26] Embracing loving-kindness is by far the most powerful antidote to recidivism known to humanity. Furthermore, if we harbour hatred towards another, we are inflicting harm on ourselves.

Hatred is the far enemy of loving-kindness. The antithesis of it. They arise from the same place, but hatred is a distortion and, as Wallace notes, 'There are greater powers than hatred, those that emerge right out of buddha-nature without any distortion. That power is fathomless.'[27] It is important not to confuse hatred with anger. Practising loving-kindness is not about being passive, especially in the face of cruelty. Aristotle identified anger as *ira*, which translates as spiritedness. In Nonviolent Communication, anger is regarded as an immensely valuable feeling because it alerts us to a significant need being unmet. Most cultures (familial and societal) have a deeply ambiguous relationship with anger, seeing it as dangerous and something that must be repressed. Anger is a quality that has a passion. If we suppress passion, we also suppress compassion ('com' meaning with or together), and instead we create apathy. In other words, *we fall asleep*. Misused or misplaced anger can become twisted into aggression and hatred, which serve no purpose other than creating further suffering. I accept that this is a challenging practice. In later scenes, we will meet individuals who would have been unarguably justified in hating those who tortured, raped, imprisoned and murdered, yet they found another way.

The near enemy of loving-kindness, which masquerades as loving-kindness, is attachment. Human beings (and most other sentient beings) rely upon a secure attachment to their parent/s for survival and well-being. Clearly, we *need* this quality of attachment, and those who lack a secure enough bond will likely suffer throughout their lives. Attachment as the near enemy of loving-kindness is subtly yet markedly different to parent–child secure attachment. The near enemy of attachment has little to do with the well-being of the other and a lot to do with meeting your own wants and needs. The easiest way perhaps of understanding the near enemy of loving-kindness is in the context of a romantic attraction where one person might say 'I love you' but really mean 'You are beautiful and I want you to satisfy my sexual needs.' The near enemy is not exclusive to sexual relationships, however. It can equally exist in professional relationships. It can prevail too in a parent's relationship to their child. Sadly, I have encountered many young women, unloved themselves, who have unconsciously had babies to fill the void they felt within.

What is vital to remember is this. The Brahma Viharas, and their near and far enemies, *all exist on the same continuum.* They are connected to one another, they are not separate. The near and far enemies, therefore, with acknowledgement, insight and perseverance, *can* be transformed into the authentic quality.

The Sanskrit word *karuna* translates as compassion. If we feel compassion towards another, we empathize with their suffering and we have a strong wish to alleviate that suffering because we also know suffering. Compassion is a mutual experience.

May you be free from suffering and the root of suffering.

The far enemy of compassion is cruelty. The near enemy is pity. Although it looks like compassion, pity is primarily self-referencing. It has a 'thank God that wasn't me' feel about it, setting up a separation between the sufferer and the observer of the suffering, rather than having true compassion for the suffering of another. Often, there is a sense of superiority attached to this pity. Conversely, compassion is an active state, a questioning of 'What can I do to lessen this suffering?' We may not always know what can be done, and so we sometimes need to wait, to contemplate and to bring our wisdom to the situation. We also need to bring awareness and sensitivity to the one who is suffering and not impose our will (believing we know what they need). I have witnessed many occasions (personally and professionally) when someone has ridden roughshod over another person's feelings and needs, with little or no regard for that individual's right for respect and autonomy, simply because they believed they knew best. I've done it myself. It's important to ask ourselves the question 'Why am I making this intervention?' and to answer honestly. Perhaps I am acting from a defensive position ('covering my own back') or perhaps *I* can't bear to see such pain?

Sympathetic joy, *mudita*, is that quality of being able to celebrate or rejoice in the happiness of others. Although this practice is usually seen as being straightforward in Buddhist traditions, for many Westerners brought up in cultures of rivalry, seemingly limited resources and habitual comparison, I think the practice of *mudita* is far from simple. The far enemies of sympathetic joy are envy, jealousy, cynicism. The quality of envy can be experienced in the body, quite literally like a constriction in the chest, in the heart. We may feel a person does not deserve to be happy or to receive something that brings them joy, especially if we believe we deserve it. This distorted thinking is based on the premise of there being a finite amount of happiness, love, contentment and opportunity, and that by this person receiving, we will be denied.

The near enemies of *mudita* are understood to be frivolity and also an egocentric wish for gain or reward for oneself. For example, if your friend wins a sum of money in a competition or is successful in getting the job they applied for, you might think how much will I be given or would this open up employment opportunities for me with that company?

Although equanimity, *upeksā*, is usually introduced as the last of the Brahma Viharas, it is also recognized as the crown in which the others are jewels; the foundation of the Spirit of Awakening.[28] As the crown, equanimity provides the setting for loving-kindness, compassion and sympathetic joy. Equanimity is that quality of even-temperedness and composure, especially in challenging and difficult situations, because it is based in a deep awareness of the transient nature of reality. The far enemies of equanimity are understood to be attachment and revulsion and also overwhelm, all of which will unbalance the mind. The near enemy of equanimity is indifference or aloofness. It looks like equanimity, but is instead based upon a disconnection and a lack of care. Equanimity is fundamentally based on connection and interdependence, generating a warmth and luminosity of being. The Buddha described a mind filled with equanimity as 'abundant, exalted, immeasurable, without hostility and without ill-will'.[29]

The Brahma Viharas, although introduced as apparently separate and distinct qualities, are holographic in nature. If we practise loving-kindness for another, for instance, it follows that we will rejoice in their good fortune and wish for them not to suffer. As the practice relates not only to those we find easy to have loving-kindness for, but also those who challenge our practice, then we will be presented with many opportunities to practise equanimity. When we are struggling to feel compassion towards someone else (maybe they have caused harm to us or a loved one), bringing loving-kindness to ourselves at such a time will support this endeavour. When we feel hatred, want to inflict harm, and feel resentful or indifferent towards either ourselves or another, it is valuable to know these qualities are fully acknowledged in this practice and are, in effect, invitations to cultivate loving-kindness, compassion, empathetic joy and equanimity.

> We do not suspend our judgments easily, nor do we generally have access to our childhood capacity for curiosity and exploration.[30]

Play provides the means of being able to access our childhood capacity for curiosity and exploration as adults. In play, we are able to suspend our judgments and to enquire into the 'what if?' In addition, in its many forms – ritual, art, theatre, music and song, poetry, myth and dance – play has been a vehicle for the expression and exploration of humankind's relationship to the divine. Through play we are able to use imagery and metaphor that bring us closer to experiences which are by their very nature illogical, irrational and beyond everyday language. Play takes us out of our concrete existence where this is this and that is that, and opens up a whole other reality far more expansive and mysterious than our intellectual minds can accommodate. The great mysteries in life and death are not understood by cognitive analysis or literal language. How do you describe, for instance, the experience of falling in love? Or seeing your baby's face for the first time? Or being present at the death of a loved one?

Due to its paradoxical nature, play challenges us to reify anything that we may create as we experience first the empty yet potential space, the making of a creation and the deconstruction/deroling/destruction of that creation. It doesn't exist, it exists, now it doesn't exist, and yet we are changed by it having existed. It takes only the smallest amount of imagination to apply these principles to our own emotional states, our thoughts, our own lives, the life of this planet and so on. The realm of play brings us into direct and unequivocal relationship with impermanence. Everything changes. *Everything*.

In play, as Winnicott realized well enough, we are truly ourselves. In the space of play, we can soften, relax and slow down the analysing, intellectual mind that jumps in to label and to categorize, that closes down the enquiry. Play, when we are fully engaged, opens up the channel of creativity. Play is a physical, bodily experience that happens in the present moment, reconnecting us with that childhood capacity for curiosity and exploration.

A myth is a sacred tale that may or may not have its roots in factual origins. The word 'myth' derives from the Greek *mythos*, which simply means story. Humankind has engaged in mythology from time immemorial whether simple or complex, passed down orally through generations, written or drawn on the walls of caves. Story is a form of projective play that gives the listener opportunity to create their own meaning. Perhaps one of the most significant contributors to the study of mythology is the American writer Joseph Campbell, himself deeply influenced by Picasso, James Joyce and Nietzsche among others. His understanding of mythology in relation to the human psyche was also greatly affected by Carl Jung and Jung's use of the archetypal collective unconscious.[31] Campbell, through his comprehensive study of many different cultural myths, was able to realize the universal significance of these archetypal themes and images.

Campbell saw myths as portals to the psyche's inner world. Not only portals – landscapes, inhabitants and guides too. As he says, 'Myths are clues to the spiritual potentialities of the human life.'[32] They do not, however, provide us with literal meanings. They allow us to engage in the enquiry of understanding what they mean to us now both personally and culturally, and that can and will change over time.

> We're so engaged in doing things to achieve purposes of outer value that we forget that the inner value, the rapture that is associated with being alive, is what it's about.[33]

Myths remind us of our shared humanity. Our deep, long-standing interconnection as opposed to capricious, divisive tabloid messages that sensationalize individuals' lives, idealizing them one day and demonizing them the next. It is the myths that survive, not the headlines. All are stories, yet it is the myths originating from cultures lost thousands of years ago that still resonate for us today and have much to reveal if we take the time to listen. Jung believed that we are in search of our soul and in search for meaning. He sensed we could not live a meaningless life. For Jung, this meaning comes from an inner experience and a connection to the timeless aspect of ourselves, that which is beyond the cloak. Jung calls this 'the Self', and for him the relationship with the unconscious Self meant allowing symbols and images to resonate and release us from the narrow confines of the cloak. Jung held the belief that it was our individual responsibility '*to create a dialogue* with the unconscious Self...to acknowledge numinous experience and to discover our personal myth'.[34]

As myths contain within them archetypal themes and characters, they are as relevant to today's generations as they have been to countless others who have gone before. As with all archetypal forms, myths are reinterpreted and invested with new and relevant meaning by every generation, yet the themes are universal, existing beyond the bounds of time and space. They speak of creation, birth, death, the light and the shadow sides of humanity, suffering and celebration. They tell of our relationship to the divine and the dance of power that exists between. Universal symbols, such as the Trickster, the Shadow and the Wise One, can be found in every culture across the world. The resonances are often uncanny and quite remarkable.

If myths no longer fed our imaginations and gave us meaning in our modern lives, we would cease to feast at their table. The key element here is how we bring these archetypal energies into form and allow them to illuminate our own darkness, giving us opportunity to open up the mysteries in our own lives. Originally oral in transmission, when the tales came to be written down, the people best equipped to carry out the task were men, as most women, even if they could write, were not considered capable of undertaking such an important task. So we have stories written by men who could not avoid conveying the patriarchal conditioning of societies and cultures of their times.[35] There have since been many female writers, often Jungian analysts, who have gladly taken up the challenge of reclaiming archetypal themes and making them relevant to the other half of the world's population.[36] There is a particular series of myths, though, that predate the patriarchy, and it is one of these myths that I would like to share with you now.

The Call from the Great Below – Goddess Inanna's Descent into the Underworld

...in this time of descent – one, three, seven years, more or less genuine courage and strength are required...with no certainty of emergence.[37]

The subtitle for this scene is taken from the 7000-year-old Sumerian myth derived from an epic poem of Inanna, Goddess of Heaven and the Earth, and with thanks too to Starhawk.[38]

Although the myths of Inanna have most often been associated, understandably, with the initiation of women, the Call from the Great Below does not exclude men. These myths, like those of many pagan traditions, predate all the patriarchal religions we know today including Christianity, Islam and Buddhism, and so offer us a very different perspective. The myth of Inanna's initiation addresses the archetypal theme of awakening.

Inanna hears the Call from the Great Below. She is drawn to death, to understand the nature of death and she knows this is what she will encounter in the Netherworld where her sister Ereshkigal reigns. Inanna is impelled to witness the funeral of Ereshkigal's husband. She prepares herself to go to the place from which no one returns. The Goddess takes her seven attributes that have served her so well in the Land Above and advises her faithful servant Ninshubur to seek help should she fail to return after three days. Inanna arrives at the first gate to the Underworld and is met by Ereshkigal's gatekeeper. She is stopped and asked to declare herself and her business. Upon learning of Inanna's arrival, Ereshkigal is enraged. She instructs the gatekeeper to allow Inanna to enter only when she removes one of her attributes. As there are seven gates that protect the Underworld, Inanna will enter Ereshkigal's kingdom 'naked and bowed low'. In the Underworld, Inanna's need to know death intimately is fulfilled by Ereshkigal. Inanna is inviting death and Ereshkigal gives it to her, but she does not give it easily. Ereshkigal demands that Inanna undertakes this sevenfold process of letting go of her earthly qualities as she enters the gates to the Underworld. Here, Inanna dies to her old self and her corpse is hung on a hook to rot like a piece of meat. Three days pass, and the faithful Ninshubur begins her lament and goes to seek help for her mistress as commanded. She is turned away first by Inanna's paternal grandfather, then her father, both refusing to interfere with the ways of the Underworld. Then Enki, Inanna's maternal grandfather, the god of water, wisdom and creativity, hears Ninshubur's plea and has compassion for his granddaughter. Enki removes two pieces of dirt from beneath his fingernails. These he gives the gifts of the food and water of life and instructs the two to fly through the seven gates into the Underworld. There they will hear the cries of Ereshkigal as a woman cries in childbirth. Enki tells the two creatures to echo her moans. With this, the Queen of the Underworld will show her gratitude by offering the tiny mourners many gifts. They are to refuse all but to ask only for the rotting corpse hanging from the hook. Ereshkigal will grant them their wish and they are to bestow the gifts of the food and water of life upon the corpse and Inanna will rise again. Although Inanna is permitted to return to the Land Above, she must, according to the laws of the Underworld, provide a substitute. She refuses all those who have mourned for her – Ninshubur, her two sons – and then she encounters her consort, Dumuzi, dressed in his splendid regalia, sitting upon his throne and far from mourning in denial of Inanna's death. She identifies him as her substitute, but Dumuzi flees. He cannot escape for ever, though, and the demons of the Underworld eventually catch up with him. Struck by grief, Dumuzi's sister, Geshtinanna, offers to go in his place. Inanna decrees that the two will share the fate, and so it was that for half a year Dumuzi inhabited the Netherworld, and for the following half, Geshtinanna took his place.

Jungian analyst Sylvia Brinton Perera recognizes the myth's resonance with the narrative of Christ's death and resurrection 4000 years later:

> Inanna's suffering, disrobing, humiliation, flagellation and death, the stations of her descent, her 'crucifixion' on the underworld peg, and her resurrection, all prefigure Christ's passion…[39]

In the Jungian approach to working with myths (fairy tales or dreams), it is acknowledged that the characters are archetypal motifs and therefore collectively belonging to each of us. They are not necessarily considered separate and distinct beings.

In the myth, we see the archetypal theme of inner spiritual work, the union of light and dark, the cultivation of resources that were in potential and the discarding of external 'attributes' that had previously served Inanna to some degree. Like my client Natalie, Inanna heard the Call from the Great Below. An invitation to open to the depths of her psyche, initiated by a 'divine curiosity'. This is the response to the realization of inner disconnection, the alienation from oneself or deeply felt dis-ease. Inanna is intent on encountering her sister, Ereshkigal, also known as the Dark Sister for she inhabits and reigns over the Underworld. It is valuable to see that this awakening process is not a transcendence from the Shadow; rather, it is an encounter and ultimately an integration with the Shadow.

Ereshkigal responds to the presence of Inanna with rage. Perera suggests rage and fury are inevitable expressions of the archetypal underworld, having been banished and imprisoned for so long – neglected and forgotten about: '[They] are the ways the unconscious reacts to unwelcome visitation. We see them when a complex is probed, for the unconscious has its own powerful defences.'[40] It is necessary that Inanna enters the Underworld stripped of her worldly attributes. Those precious items that have served her in the world above. Ereshkigal demands that she unveil, disrobe, uncloak herself to reveal her true nature, her vulnerability, and to have a direct experience of reality. Inanna learns first-hand that her body, once adorned, beautiful, coveted, pampered and revered, is ultimately a piece of flesh that will rot like any lump of meat. What Inanna does takes enormous courage. First, she enters a place reputedly from which no one returns. Second, she seems to go against the advice of others (her own father and paternal grandfather refuse to help when she fails to return, both angry with her for daring to make the journey). Third, she is willing to surrender and die to her old self.

The seven attributes which Inanna equips herself with – her crown, her lapis lazuli earrings, her lapis lazuli beads, her breast plate, her golden hip girdle, her measuring rod and her breechcloth – each corresponds to chakra. Chakra, a Sanskrit word meaning wheel, signifies the seven energy centres in the body which are the openings for the life energy to flow. Each chakra corresponds to major ganglia branching from the spinal column and correlates to levels of consciousness, archetypal elements, developmental stages in life, colours, sounds and bodily functions.[41] By relinquishing each of her prized garments, Inanna opened her energy centres to allow the life force to pass through her.

A very significant character in the myth is Ninshubur, Inanna's faithful maidservant who keeps watch at the entrance of the Underworld, paying close attention to events, and when Inanna fails to return after three days and three nights, Ninshubur raises the alarm by beating her drum and lamenting Inanna's disappearance. The faithful servant symbolizes our witness part: that aspect of us that stays above the ground while the soul descends into the Underworld.[42] Ninshubur goes off to seek help from her mistress's 'fathers' (it is interesting that the womenfolk are not summoned…). She is undaunted by the first refusals to help and eventually finds Enki, Inanna's maternal grandfather and god of wisdom. Enki is the archetypal Wise One. He listens intently and does not turn Ninshubur away. Instead, his heart is touched as he already knows her fate (Ereshkigal is also his granddaughter) and he implements a plan to bring Inanna back to the land of the living. According to Perera, Enki 'improvises to create what the moment needs'[43] and what he creates are witnesses that can manoeuvre seamlessly into the darkest places. There, these witnesses hear and resonate with the cries of the Dark Sister so that she is stopped in her tracks:

> Their echoing makes a litany, transforms the pain into poetry and prayer. It makes out of life's dark misery a song of the goddess. It establishes art as a reverent and creative and sympathetic response to the passions and pains of life.[44]

Perera describes Enki as the patron of therapists.[45] As the god of play, he can use anything (even pieces of apparently useless dirt from under the fingernails) and bring about a transformation by creating an empathic connection. The archetype of Enki is present and ever ready to intervene in any therapeutic endeavour. This archetype does not only 'belong' to the therapist. It is in potential too within the client.

Inanna is returned to life and to the Land Above, ever changed by the experience she has had, but this is not the end of the story. Dumuzi and Geshtinanna's fate, to each spend time in the Underworld and yet to return to the Land Above, implies an ongoing, continuous relationship with the Shadow rather than a once-only encounter.

This 7000-year-old myth shows us the journey of awakening. Of healing. It is a container, providing images in the form of a story with a narrative and characters, that gives us a means of exploration into our own lives. Besides offering many symbols for the individual, the Descent of Inanna can also be understood on a more collective level…

Inanna senses the world changing – and not for the better. She feels she no longer recognizes this peaceful Gaia; she senses herself separating from her beloved Earth, so when she hears the call from the Great Below, she cannot be sure if it is her Dark Sister, Ereshkigal, mourning the death of her husband, or the Earth itself that is weeping. What is the purpose of Inanna being the Goddess of Heaven if she is disconnected from the Earth she loves? The planet is decimated by warring nations, each one building up its arsenal of increasingly vile weapons. All the while, her populations are starving despite the multitude of grain, maize, citrus fruits; in spite of the plenitude of fish and shelled creatures the oceans so generously offered up to the fisherman's net. Great swathes of her people are moving on foot, carrying their elderly and infants away from their homes that have been razed to the ground. Her position as Goddess of War, always a contentious one, had been strictly reserved for the protection and defence of her people; now wars start, it seems, for the sport of it, to fight for beliefs that contravened the higher powers. Inanna has lost her matriarchal status and, for now, the patriarchy rules. And yet, Inanna knows, everything is in flux.

What feels important is to find ways of bearing witness to the changes that are happening within and outside ourselves. To find ways of expressing, means of telling, channels for showing, to make life more bearable. Perhaps, too, in the hope that another will see, understand and validate our experience. In the next scene we will explore some of these manifestations of play.

Act 3

Scene 2

MANIFESTATIONS OF PLAY

The poem, the song, the picture
Is only water
Drawn from the well of the people
And it should be given back to them in a cup of beauty
So that they may drink
And in drinking it
Understand themselves[1]

If truth is that which lasts, then art has proved truer than any other
human endeavour. What is certain is that pictures and poetry and
music are not only marks in time but marks through time, of their own
time and ours, not antique or historical, but living as they ever did,
exuberantly, untired.[2]

Children learn who they are in the world and their relationship to it through the medium of play. Our engagement in play (with luck) does not end when we become adults because who we are and our relationships are dynamic, not fixed. We change and are changed by life. Instead, it transforms into, perhaps, more sophisticated, skilled forms. In this scene, we look at specific 'players', their 'plays' and some of the processes involved in their creation. 'Players' are those people whom I regard as skilled artists in their particular field, courageous in their commitment to integrity and self-discovery. In Act 1, Scene 2, we learned that a play is Jonathan Kay's generic term to define the residues of play and The Play, 'combusting' as they do in the imagination of the artist, sculptor, actor, musician, fool, dancer or writer to create *something*. Our player artists who have devoted their time, skill, energy and often their lives to their art form act as witnesses to us, to events, to the times we are living in. They are the narrators of our personal stories as well as the archetypal, primordial stories. Sometimes theirs is the *only* voice or vision that can be heard and seen, encapsulating the horrors of suffering and making this suffering accessible to all of us without the danger of overwhelm. These player artists have taken on the task of inviting us to see, feel, sense with an aesthetic distance that saves our own hearts from being crushed, allowing us to engage in ways that are helpful rather than hopeless. The player artist creates form from emptiness; order from chaos.

These are the artist players I am particularly drawn to for a variety of reasons – some I know personally and I have been able to explore their work and their process of playing with them directly; others I am inspired by from afar. Each one, besides their work being (in my view) beautiful and compelling, also sheds some light on this mystical process of playing.[3] They are all what I consider to be 'true artists' as defined by Jeanette Winterson:

> The true artist is connected... The true artist is interested in the art object as an art process, the thing in being, the being of the thing, the struggle, the excitement, the energy, that have found expression in a particular way.[4]

The main criterion, though, for including these player artists and their plays is because they have opened my heart and my mind, bringing me into connection with myself and others. I hope they might do the same for you too.

> Where there was nothing, there will be something that has come from within...[5]

Some players are driven to create something tangible beyond their own bodies which then exists independently of the maker and is available for others to project their own meaning and understanding on to. Whatever the material used – words and language, clay or stone, oil or acrylic paints, watercolours, textiles, paper – the creator will have a sensory and intimate experience of their material. They experiment with colour, texture, shape and pattern, 'pushing the materials beyond the probable',[6] finding the material which best serves them to embody whatever it is that needs to find form. The choices of material may be born out of necessity or a challenge to use only what is freely available.

Some creators use only recycled materials. Some work on vast scales, others in miniature. Some create literal objects, others abstract or fantastical. Whatever the form, the creator projects something of themselves into whatever they create, which is a coalescence of their own personal experiences – their inspirations and observations, skills, techniques, feelings and thoughts. Some call themselves artists; others eschew the word. Some, like tradigital painter[7] David Cowell, do not even consider what they make as art, preferring instead to see it as a process, an artefact of the creative process. Whatever is made, however it is made and by whom, the single consistent truth I can find is that the process of making *something* is a profoundly satiating and pleasing one. In adulthood, the play of childhood evolves into the act of making and creating that allows us to bring to bear the whole of ourselves. BBC Arts Editor Will Gompertz describes the creative process as a dynamic 'call and response'[8] happening in the maker's head, which, without distractions and self-sabotage, is a highly playful and productive unfolding. This call and response broadens to incorporate whatever is being made and the senses, the body, thoughts and feelings of the maker. The maker's style ripens as new boundaries, both internal and external, are pushed to their limits.

Art forms are a means of expressing our truths, mirroring back the patterns in our cloaks, but also, and crucially, they are a means of uncovering, dis-covering, revealing the truths we have forgotten. Art allows us to re-member who we are. To remember not only the Cain aspects of ourselves, but also the Abel parts, for, as Jonathan Kay reminds us, we are both of these. Art offers us a medium to bring the twins into relationship. Twyla Tharp recognizes the twin experience as *zoë* and *bios*, terms used by Greek philosopher Plotinus to represent universal life and an individual life – that is, a cloak. Another way of understanding *zoë* and *bios* would be emptiness and form. In artistic expression Tharp understands *zoë* and *bios* to be 'competing natures', where 'sacred art is zoë-driven; profane art stems from bios'.[9]

She goes on to talk about the ideas that originate from Source – their enigmatic, spontaneous nature that is not always comfortable nor welcomed – yet concedes that her finest work evolves from a union of the two. I do not believe it is a given that the two will *always* be in competition with each other. For me, it is a dance, sometimes jarring, other times flowing. At times of fluidity, perhaps we can relate to the Dead Woman in Bax's play when, having cast off her cloak, she exclaims, 'I am free! Now I know *what* joy is...' I don't believe we need to wait until we die either.

Jeanette Winterson in her book *Art Objects* (note the ambiguity of 'objects' as a noun and a verb) speaks of 'art, all art, as insightful, as rapture, as transformation, as joy' and that this experience is not limited to the select few but to *everyone* 'if we let it. Letting art is the paradox of *active surrender*'[10] (italics added). According to Winterson, art objects to humanity's self-imposed limitations, our ignorance in realizing that we are not only the bead but also the thread upon which the bead is strung.

The artist's mission is to bring something new, to shake up the ordinary and mundane, to waken us from our stupor. Like a modern-day shaman, the artist offers herself as a conduit, in the service of creation, that allows us to connect to those aspects of ourselves we have forgotten.

In the West, the conventional way to look at art is to understand and critique it through the narrow lens of the intellect, or, even worse, through the eyes of the financier or investor, viewing art no differently to the way we view most other commodities, looking for affirmation, approval and validation of the 'I'. For art to work on us, though, we have to drink it in like Lorca's water. The artist may give it back to us in a beautiful cup, but if we only marvel at the cup without drinking, we have completely missed the point. We see art through what Winterson terms the 'protection of assumption',[11] which is the antithesis of 'beginner's mind'. When we assume, as my brother David would delight in reminding me in our childhood, we make an ASS out of U and ME. This is the realm of the cloak. This is the mirror of everyday reality. The 'true painting', as Winterson notes, however, 'in its stubborn independence', can only do this by coincidence. The true painting's reality is playful; it beckons us to go beyond the cloak, beyond the earthly and prosaic, and to discover a new freedom without the constraints of the cloak. In this place, liberated from our *bios* with its biases, power struggles and the distractions of everyday life, we can waken up. And it is this that the painting (or the dance, the poem or the sculpture) demands of us – 'Waken up!' 'Come to your senses!' In the theatre, Peter Brook describes this as 'A Happening'.[12] Yes, I want art to open my mind, but most especially I want art to open my heart.

I met artist, sculptor and therapist Sara Fairfax at a talk I was giving on play. Sara had arrived with a clay bust of herself with a view to promoting her forthcoming workshops. I asked Sara if I might have the sculpture next to me while I gave my talk and, courageously, she agreed. Later, she wrote these reflections:

When I came home I realized I was still blushing from having been so open with you about my experience of my head being up front during your talk and so clearly illustrating the power of the transitional object. Making stuff has always been the process whereby I externalize something felt deeply internal but not entirely known to me. Play/making art allows that something to emerge. It is also 'a place or space' where I can hold things at arms length and look at them, talk to them and engage with it – I hold a conversation with myself through the object, especially while I'm making it or playing with who I might be, what I could be – experimenting with roles and meanings and even feelings – what does this feel like or that, what if this, what if that. The making not only provides a space, it also provides 'time' for which to muse on a multitude of feelings and thoughts – and because it is often in silence I experience things at a deep level – deep awareness and clarity of what I am or have experienced and it is indescribably satisfying – even when it is painful. It is also about, as you said, a way of bringing the past into the now and being fully present with it, and the longer I stay with the creative process the more this is clearly experienced. There is a real sense of being so deeply engaged and connected that the energy feels healing.

At the beginning of the evening I felt the head had its own existence separate from me and my stuff – it had become itself – though by shifting the head into discussing it in a therapeutic context I was aware almost as soon as you began your talk that the original connection I had to the head was going to emerge and it did. I think when an object has been imbued with strong meaning, relationship, or significance it is like a living breathing organism – it is alive. The head felt alive, it felt a part of me was really up at the front with you too – and that was OK.

One aspect of the clay head for me was to connect with the idea of being able to listen very deeply to oneself as well as about listening intently to others – particularly at times when one is finding that really hard to do. I had a feeling of having listened to you twice, that was really quite a strange feeling. And so my clay head now contains your talk, adding something quite profound to the experience.

I know you were concerned about how safe it felt for me – you emphasized safety so much and I felt that you had not wanted me to have felt too onerously exposed – I also take responsibility for that because I made a conscious choice to bring the head that evening. I committed myself to the head having an existence beyond the one imbued by me. One of the challenges of being an artist is that you reach a point where the work will be out there and be exposed to the eyes and questions of others.

I am indebted to Sara for her generosity and the depth of her awareness. I experienced the power of Sara's clay head and sensed the life it imbued, so much so that I asked if I might be able to include the image on the cover of this book. Sara generously agreed.

At the root of this discovery process, as Alan Yentob notes, is play.[13] Play that evolves from our *bios*, our cloaks, *and* it emerges from Source, from *zoë*. Whatever our medium of play, what lies at the heart is the motivation, as Sara notes, to express, externalize and realize what is within. To make the unconscious conscious. Human beings are relational beings and so we may express ourselves in the anticipation that others will validate the external and thus, by default, validate what is internal. We all want to be seen as Winnicott said of the infant: 'When I look I am seen…therefore, I exist.'[14] In our earliest days, we are mirrored by those closest to us, and in this reflecting we become who we are. Yet this is no one-way mirror. The tiniest of infants are also mirrors to others, casting back images as parents, carers, relational beings.[15] This process is continual throughout the life cycle, and consciously or unconsciously we are each engaged in this mirroring with all those we encounter. Our need to be known and understood by another co-arises with a need to understand ourselves. Player artists and the artefacts they create serve to, as dancer and choreographer

Akram Khan notes, 'put a mirror to the audience'.[16] Our play forms connect us to others long since passed, reminding us that the human condition – to seek deeper understanding of our purpose, of our suffering, of our joys – transcends time and space. Tharp says of 'our' artists that we want them 'to take the mundane materials of our lives, run it through their imaginations, and surprise us'.[17] For the artist to surprise others, they need first to be surprised. One of the challenges any artist must face is to reconcile their skill in their artistic field with the spontaneity of Source. They have to marry the belief in their ability with a deep-seated trust in what is emerging. The artist is the shaper of the energy flowing through them, creating form from the emptiness. If they stay attached to their previous success, they fail to play. They will then only repeat, rather than create. Grayson Perry speaks of trying to keep the freshness of the play he knew as a child playing in the freedom of his bedroom despite the fact that a camera crew is watching his every move.[18] Ernest Hemingway described it as becoming the master of one's art form, yet maintaining the courage to do what the child does when he knows nothing.[19]

The theme of remembering, reawakening something forgotten, recurs throughout this scene. Actor and dramatherapist Roger Grainger, in his enlightening research into why actors act, describes the *raison d'être* of the dramatic impulse to 'remind us of the things we know, whose significance we have managed to forget'.[20] All art, not only acting, beckons us to reconnect to our deeper nature.

Andrew Motion is a British poet and was Poet Laureate between 1999 and 2009. When asked to partake in a discussion regarding the purpose of poetry, he reflected on the value of poetry in the most natural way a poet would – poetically. He said:

> Why does poetry have to be for anything?
> ...
> But for the most part it's a unique and liberating blessing
> A fabulous difference
> By virtue of being 'for nothing'
> Poetry is for the Self
> ...we read poetry to be reminded of things that have faded from our memories
> Or to be reacquainted with things in this world and beyond that we have stopped noticing

... Poetry is in fact as natural to the human race as breathing
I'm tempted to say – it is a kind of breathing
It's the imagination breathing
It's the sound of the Self saying,
'I am here and I matter.'[21]

Jackie Juno is a witch, a performance and page poet, comedian and musician. Jackie writes on subjects highlighting social injustice and environmental issues, serious matters which could evoke overwhelm and dissociation in her audience; however, she skilfully uses comedy to make bearable what is often unbearable. Jackie, like Jonathan Kay, knows the territory of the Fool intimately. One of her most poignant poems is 'The Word', which is a particularly beautiful version of a creation myth. It begins:

In the beginning was the word
And it slipped from her lips like a fully-fledged bird.
Something stirred in her womb and it swelled like the moon
Til there was no more room in her skin.[22]

Poetry allows us to glimpse the essence of something. There is an emptiness around the words, creating space that invites the reader to fill it with their own meaning, images, textures and feelings.

Play offers us a unique gift because it exists in that space in between – the potential space – between you and me *and* between who I think I am and am not. It challenges the *bios*, the 'I', mirroring this back to us and enquiring, 'Really?' When we allow ourselves to be touched by the plays of others, we enter the space of non-separateness, reminding us of what Hillman says is '[n]o longer polarity, but plurality'.[23]

The remembering made possible through the spectrum of plays relates to both our *bios* and *zoë* natures. The self and the Self. Cloak and our Being nature.

In her book *The Little Red Chairs*, Edna O'Brien, has sought to fictionalize 20th-century war criminal Radovan Karadzic, the 'Butcher of Bosnia'.[24] The novel is a study into the nature of evil and enquires into the question: How can a man reconcile such barbaric actions with any semblance of sanity? When asked why she created a piece of fiction rather than just presenting the facts, O'Brien replied that first the writer, then the reader, lives that experience, 'making the journey on foot'.[25] When we are confronted with a figure of many thousands massacred in conflict, we simply cannot comprehend it. We can objectify these humans, seeing just the number and safely distancing ourselves from them by not knowing their names, faces, families, hopes and dreams. We protect ourselves from overwhelm, from what is unbearable. An adept writer like O'Brien makes the unbearable bearable and makes it possible for us to step into the shoes of these characters, awakening our feelings. The skilled and insightful writer 'makes that world live again so it has not died'.[26]

When we read or hear a story, we cannot help but place ourselves into the role of the subject. Harris cites several experiments that verify the degree to which we (as young as three and four years old) mentally follow the protagonist as they move through their experiences; moreover, we are able to work out the emotional implications these experiences have for the protagonist.[27] Through our imaginations, we develop the capacity to empathize.

The novelist, like any other artist, draws upon their own life experience, fictionalizing it, anonymizing it, at times ameliorating it for the reader to make it more bearable yet without losing its potency. In her novel *This Must Be the Place*, Maggie O'Farrell's young character Niall suffers from aggressive eczema. In one scene, while they are waiting for Niall's regular appointment at the clinic, his father Daniel can no longer contain his outrage with the many posters displayed around the walls advertising underwear for eczema-suffering children: every single one of the child models has perfect, flawless, eczema-free skin. Daniel defaces the images, adding stretches of sores on faces, torsos, arms and legs.[28] As a reader, I was deeply affected by this passage. Its energy bounced off the page. Later, I read that Maggie O'Farrell herself has a daughter with extreme eczema. During the writing, she commented that her husband had scrawled in the margin 'still too angry'.[29] Creating from a direct experience can be powerfully cathartic for the artist, yet the artist always somehow needs to hold the reader or audience in mind – to take them with her and not alienate or overwhelm them. O'Farrell certainly managed to convey proficiently the desperate helplessness of a parent watching their child suffer such intolerable anguish.

Grayson Perry has been frequently referred to in this book as he has inspired me in many ways. As a ceramicist, he is known notably for his large pots depicting collages of images, phrases and photographs of people's individual stories, often brightly coloured, the mundane juxtaposed with the profound. Much of his work is autobiographical, and Perry has spoken candidly about his upbringing and what it is to be a man in Western society. One character appears repeatedly in his images, and that is his childhood teddy bear, Alan Measles. The presence of the bear offered the artist a way of meeting the world that he would not have been aware of/able to articulate at the time, until, in his forties, he realized that Alan Measles had been the repository of his shadow material. He explains how, in an unconscious process, he transferred significant aspects of his masculinity to the teddy, while rejecting/retreating from/disowning/surrendering other aspects of himself that might be called feminine.[30] Alan Measles was subjected to innumerable life-threatening situations, such as accidents and attacks, yet he always survived. In recent times, Perry has become what might be described as an anthropological artist, meeting ordinary individuals in particular circumstances and depicting aspects of their lives through his vases, tapestries and drawings. The artist literally mirroring back to others the stories of their own lives. For some, Perry has become almost the Artist Laureate, an artist who is not afraid to comment on the process and business of being an artist. His recent contribution through his television programme and subsequent book explores how contemporary masculinity affects the lives of men.[31] Critic Matt Haig in his recent review comments how '[m]en reap many economic and social benefits from adopting *the cloak of masculinity*'[32] (italics added). Not everyone, however, is in praise of Perry. Another *Guardian* critic, Jonathan Jones, describes Perry as having a 'rational dryness to his art that makes it dead on arrival'.[33] For me, this highlights how subjective are the eyes that view art, how for some the work is alive and others it is deadly. We must, of course, each make up our own minds.

For the painter, sculptor or even the novelist, their expression (even though they themselves have lived it in their imagination if not in life) is projected outwards, beyond their physical body. For the actor, dancer and, in some ways, the musician, it is their own psyches, bodies and breath that become the material for expression. For these players, there is a fluid interplay between the three stages in the developmental play paradigm – embodiment, projection and role play. For the highly trained dancer, her practice allows her to attune to the subtle stream of energies that emanate through her body even though she has performed the movement a thousand times. She knows she has never performed *this* movement ever before, nor will again. In her well-known letter to her biographer, Agnes De Mille, dancer and choreographer Martha Graham speaks about a vitality that is executed through the dancer's body into a unique form. She goes on to advise how it is not for the dancer to judge her work's merit, believe in herself or to compare the work to other expressions, but, instead, simply *to keep the channel open*. Graham understood the necessity for the artist to allow herself to be used by the life force despite the strange and sacred discomfort this generates within.[34]

For the actor, the words of the playwright and guidance from the director coalesce in the actor's body and mind, merging with his own experiences to create someone new. The actor's whole being is needed to birth a previously unborn Hamlet or Willy Loman. Each new human being has their own way, their own motivation, their own presence which every actor must discover for himself in every performance. Without this active surrender, or as Polish theatre director Jerzy Grotowski defines it, an act of sacrifice,[35] we are likely to experience the Deadly. When the actor brings the whole of his being into the present moment and makes himself available, he might then, if he is fortunate, become a conduit. Making the invisible visible. Bringing form from emptiness. The skill and technique required are essential aspects in this process, for it is through these that the character will be seen and heard; however, something else has to happen *in the moment* to bring it alive for the audience.

Theatre director Peter Brook had his own definition for the cloak. He called it 'a crust', akin to the Earth's surface, and, pursuing the metaphor, enquires, '[H]ow can we access the energy, that boiling volcanic matter, that lies under its surface?'[36] In his Holy Theatre, this is precisely what the actor aspires to do. The Holy Theatre transcends the *bios*, bringing the actor and audience into direct contact with *zoë*. Roger Grainger interviewed one actor who articulated this rare and precious moment of balance between the two: where Cain and Abel were no longer in conflict and the sacred and the profane could co-exist. Grainger reminds us that theatre emerged from religious and spiritual practices, a reference made by one of his interviewees.[37] Actors in the ancient world would surrender themselves to the spirits of the dead, thereby allowing their own bodies to become a home for the duration of the play. Perhaps, in this respect, it is the actor who comes closest to shamanic practice?

Shakespeare believed that humanity could only glimpse the sacred intermittently and so he ensured the actors and audience were frequently reminded of the profane. Perhaps it is for this reason that Clifford Bax's play *The Cloak* is a single act in which the playwright directly invites the audience into the realm of the absolute with an unambiguous enquiry – into the nature of suffering:

> We do not purpose now to bring you mirth
>> But rather, if we can,
>> To show how strange is Man
> And what it is that cankers life on earth

The Angel is not referring here to the suffering of birth, although she does also speak of this to the Unborn Spirit; rather, she is alluding to the irrelevant and extraneous suffering we cause ourselves through our attachment to our cloaks and our ignorance of our true nature. To aid our understanding, he also gives the Angel the dialogue:

> Let us be
> Imagined out of our mortality

She is entreating us to experience the play, the words, the images beyond our own individual *bios* and instead to soften and open into *zoë*. The Dead character is adorned with her richly patterned *bios*, her cloak, to which she is most insistently attached. It has given her identity, status, power over others and, crucially, because she is tormented by fear, protection from the control and abuse of others. Without the cloak, she fears she will be a nobody and unbearably vulnerable. Faced with the situation of remaining in this state of limbo, she is forced to confront both her fear and her desire. She has a choice. She takes the risk and, discarding the garment, is instantly liberated.

> The universe and I
> Flow to one rhythm, – as the sea bears the foam.

Here, Bax is drawing on a familiar metaphor used in many spiritual traditions, including Buddhism, to convey the meaning of *zoë* and *bios* – the sea bears the foam just as the thread bears the bead. He is defining absolute and relative realities, and it is when the character surrenders her attachment to the self that she realizes (real-eyes) her true nature – the nature of Self. In that moment, ironically, the Dead Woman has woken up! Frightened, though, by the Dead Woman's portrayal of life on Earth, her warning to:

Be wise, –
Weave yourself a protection and disguise

the terrified Unborn Spirit succumbs to the fear and, taking the abandoned cloak, enrobes herself before continuing on her journey to birth. Is Bax suggesting reincarnation or rebirth? This view is also supported by the Unborn Spirit's earlier recollections of previous earthly existences. The playwright leaves the audience with many unanswered questions, inviting them to continue the enquiry for themselves.

Bax, initially a painter, found writing a more fruitful medium through which to explore his ideas. He was a prolific playwright and biographer. Living in London, Bax, together with many creatives and intellectuals deeply affected by the unprecedented loss of life and the terrible destruction of the First World War, sought to enquire into the profundity of life. His circle of friends included the occultist Aleister Crowley and Allan Bennett. Bennett, who widely travelled in India, is credited with the introduction of Buddhism to England and was only the second Englishman to be ordained as a Buddhist monk.[38] Bax was clearly influenced by him. *The Cloak*, written in 1937, was followed in 1947 by a full-length radio play, *The Buddha*. I was 'caught' by *The Cloak*, as I outlined in the Prologue, over three decades ago, and its influence, largely unconscious, is woven deeply into my own *bios*. I wonder what plays or players, in the widest sense, have provided a footnote to your life?

The Dead Woman learns something about life, only, for her, it is too late. She cannot, having removed the cloak, then turn to the Angel and say, 'This is astonishing, thank you! I've got it! Let me travel back down there and try that again...differently this time.'

Every letting go, every surrender, every decision not to get caught up in the push and pull of our fears and our desires is a death of sorts. A death of the neurotic self that allows for further awakening of the Self. We all have choices, many choices every day, and to ask ourselves the question 'What do I plan to do with my one wild and precious life?' is an invitation to awaken. The true actor can, as Grainger observes, 'defeat narcissism', and in so doing support the audience in finding 'the confidence to abandon, at least temporarily, the entrenched positions they are so used to occupying'.[39] In other words, casting aside their own cloaks and experiencing non-separateness.

Jessica Williams Ciemnyjewski is very familiar with the territory between *bios* and *zoë*. As an actress, theatre director and visual artist, her work has been to enquire into the profound process of play. Latterly, much of her work as an actress has been in solo performance, and she has brought particular enquiry to that act of sacrifice, the de-cloaking and revelation of something beyond, without the security of another actor on stage with her. Jessica is also a dramatherapist and so recognizes in herself when resistance and defence emerge, whether in the process of acting or creating an image on canvas, and she has cultivated the discipline to 'hold and not destroy' and to stay with the unbearableness of her own revelations. Although her performances are solo, she values the contribution and dialogue with others, most especially her director, technicians and musicians. During an original performance of the play *Thursday's Child*,[40] Jessica had a profound and disturbing experience. The play depicts an apparently successful young woman, Carol, whose façade masks a fractured and deeply troubled life of devotion to a domineering and once-glamorous mother, now speechless and bedridden. The play is an exploration of an extremely ambivalent and sadistic mother–daughter relationship. Since her mother's stroke, Carol has not only taken care of her sick mother but also managed the family's dress boutique. It is a dramatic study into the fragmentation of a fragile ego, leading ultimately to the character's psychotic breakdown. Marina Jenkyns observes:

> The wars raging inside her make her ultimately vulnerable to the breakdown of her personality.[41]

During a performance, the actress, while engaged in a highly charged encounter with a life-size mannequin, perceived the dummy's head turning to meet her gaze. She heard the inner voice of her own witness pulling her back to herself with the words 'Watch it'. Jessica knew she was at the threshold between her own sanity and madness. Her presence of mind and skill as an actor served as witness and anchor to the disturbing experience. Furthermore, she succeeded in giving the audience an experience of standing at the edge of an abyss and looking down into the madness below.

Dijana Milosevic is a Serbian theatre director and co-founder of DAH (meaning breath), a laboratory theatre company based in Belgrade, Serbia. When the war started in 1991, the company of actors asked themselves what their responsibilities and obligations were during such times of violence and suffering. What was the purpose and meaning of theatre? Dijana said, 'When the map is torn – your world is torn.'[42] The DAH theatre, like the theatres in Britain and Germany after war, was responding to a 'hunger'.[43] Peter Brook asks:

> What, however, was this hunger? Was it a hunger for the invisible, a hunger for reality deeper than the fullest form of human life – or was it a hunger for the missing things of life, a hunger in fact, for buffers against reality?[44]

Unlike the theatres Brook witnessed, the DAH theatre was active *during* the war. The DAH actors responded to its people by going out into the war-torn streets, improvising and evolving their performances in the true tradition of laboratory theatre in response to their collective despair. Theatre, at times of war, 'comes like water to the thirst of dry lives'.[45] Milosevic continues, 'We start from the personal, that reaches the universal', referring here both to the individual *bios* – acknowledging differences in their nationalities, their political, religious or spiritual orientations, and the personal feelings connected to the actors' performance – and to the recognition that beneath the *bios* is the infinite life force, *zoë*, that does not distinguish such separateness. This reminds me of a quotation by Jung that reflected on the need to hold the universe in one hand and the particular in the other. Jung was referring to the therapist, yet it can equally apply to a therapeutically orientated theatre company such as DAH. The company understood the need to speak directly from the wound, both their own and their audience's. Dijana acknowledged the need for the skills and precision of the actors that created an invisible shield around them. My understanding is that their discipline enabled them to contain and shape the potentially overwhelming material (both their own and others') and to re-present it in ways that offered hope, without becoming overwhelmed themselves. I am reminded again of Nietzsche's words: 'We have art so that we can tolerate the truth.' Such artistic work in times of humanitarian darkness is especially significant as it provides a channel through which voices can be heard and feelings can be expressed, creating connection and some sense of empowerment and meaning. The necessary conditions that serve to reduce the impact of trauma.[46]

Any authentic play brings about healing because it reminds us that we are more, much more, than our own individual cloaks, however elaborate, intricate and beautifully woven they may be, but is it art or is it therapy? I ask this question not because I have the answer, but to open up and continue an ongoing enquiry. Many plays, artworks, artefacts may have been therapeutic for the player in that there is a catharsis and a validation.

In the 1890s, seamstress Agnes Richter became an inmate in a German psychiatric institution. The jacket she painstakingly unpicked, embroidered and resewed now sits in a museum in Heidelberg. The cryptic language appears to be an archaic form of German, rich with fluidity and artistry. It seems to have no beginning, middle or end, yet the word that stands out most clearly is 'Ich'. Much of the text is on the inside, worn away by Agnes' body and sweat. The sweat stains are still visible. Gail Hornstein writes, 'Encountering her jacket feels more like seeing a ghost than inspecting a work of art.'[47] The jacket, together with more than 5000 other items created by asylum patients, came into the possession of Hans Prinzhorn, who as well as being a trained psychiatrist was also an art historian, with a particular interest in madness and creativity. Prinzhorn launched what came to be known as psychiatric art.[48] No one knows why the jacket or any of these other objects were created, nor what purpose they served. What is evident is the sheer determination on the part of the makers to make them and to use whatever material was available, including water-soaked bread, faeces and blood. Each piece is a tribute to the human spirit, to create, to bear witness, to shape *something* from their life experiences. To tell their stories. Perhaps Agnes Richter inspired 'transewing' artist Rosalind Wyatt to sew the most intricate text on to items of clothing that once belonged to others. What is quite remarkable about Wyatt's work is that, after studying the flow and shape of the owner's handwriting, she recreates it freely on the garments. Wyatt is currently curating an extensive art project, *The Stitch Lives of London*. One of the garments is a running vest that had belonged to black teenager Stephen Lawrence, murdered in a racially motivated attack in South East London in 1993. The vest, donated by Stephen's mother Doreen Lawrence, has been stitched by Wyatt with remnants of Stephen's last piece of writing, an unfinished essay.

Bobby Baker is a nationally acclaimed performance, drawing and multimedia artist. In 1996, BB, as she is known, was diagnosed with borderline personality disorder and spent the next 11 years managing to overcome this severe mental illness. She attended a day centre while still living at home and, astonishingly, still maintaining an international programme of performance work. During this time, BB made a commitment to herself that she would create an image every day, however she was feeling. The 700 diary drawings are a unique documented history of her inner world – disturbing, harrowing, playful, tender and truly authentic. The exhibition *Diary Drawings: Mental Illness and Me 1997–2008* premiered at the Wellcome Collection in London in 2009, and the accompanying book by the same name won the Mind Book of the Year in 2011. Mythographer and writer Marina Warner observes that 'the act of making art helped in itself: sometimes…making the image, following her feelings with paint and brush or pencil and, later, pen and ink, simply made her feel better'.[49] I am particularly drawn to Day 403 entitled *Mindfulness??* BB explains:

> One of the DBT[50] skills, taught endlessly, was something called mindfulness – a simple version of meditation. They started the practice sessions with a gong. I seemed to be the only one with steam coming out of their ears with irritation. This drawing was my riposte.[51]

The image shows BB with a look of sad resignation, her skull opened like the top of a hard-boiled egg and a hand holding a watering can pouring water into her bisected head. As a Buddhist psychotherapist and a trainer of a mindfulness programme often engaged in supporting others to 'come into the moment', this image offers me valuable feedback that this experience is not always beneficial. Sometimes we need a more active form of meditation.

> [V]ery occasionally in a drawing or painting one can hit the jackpot and create an image, using the power of the line, form and the delights of colour, that expresses far more than complex packages of words, images and actions.[52]

Although the drawings met particular needs at different times throughout the process, BB recognizes that the commitment to making, however she might be feeling at that time, was pivotal in her survival. The sensory experience of 'sploshy, succulent wet blobs of paint',[53] the heightened absorption, the opportunity to self-reflect, her words echo Lorca's, 'which has led to a greater awareness, acceptance and understanding of the world and its ways – and ultimately helped me to recover'.[54] BB's capacity to play is evident in her work, not only her drawings and paintings, but her extensive and diverse performance art. She describes herself as having a 'magpie mind' – gathering material wherever she finds it, putting together seemingly unconnected objects, images and ideas to create something new. This resonates with Picasso's description of the artist being a receptacle for emotions that come from the sky, the earth, a scrap of paper, a spider's web. Bobby Baker concludes this scene with these words of unmistakable joy:

> I find that trying to create a picture composed of subtle elements and visual references that successfully communicate new ideas is probably the most enjoyable occupation in the world.[55]

FROM SURVIVING TO THRIVING

The Space Between

The liminal space,
Between land and sea,
Between day and night,
Night and day,
Light and dark,
Dark and light,
Between breathing out and breathing in,
The razor's edge,
Expanded.
Winnicott's potential space,
Magnified.
The space where anything is possible.
Where there becomes here,
And then becomes now.
The space of change,
Transformation,
Healing.
The sacred place of play.[1]

[Play] is a naturally arising, spontaneous expression of the [S]elf's need to negotiate all kinds of threatening situations, situations that throw a person into confrontation with his own aloneness…the truth and the falseness of these threats…become trauma only when there is no way out.[2]

In the previous scene, the reasons for play at times of great personal challenge, such as incarceration and mental health difficulties, were introduced. What are we needing at these times? To hide our vulnerability and become invisible in an attempt to protect ourselves from increased suffering? A desire for transcendence? A hunger for meaning? A longing to bear witness to ourselves, to tell our own story? To fill the emptiness? For escape? Play possesses the qualities able to serve each of these needs and more. In this scene, I would like to pay homage to those people who have called upon the genius of play to support themselves during the darkest times of their lives, enabling them to survive, using play's capacity to keep in relationship to themselves, offering a sense of empowerment and helping to find meaning to mitigate the full effects of trauma. David Elkind, cited in Act 1, proposed that play was the child's only defence against the world. Here I am supporting that claim and expanding it to include adults as well – whether we use play as a refuge, respite, meaning-maker or agent for transformation and healing. These gifts that play offers, though, are not separate and distinct from one another.

Nietzsche's statement about having art so that we may not perish by the truth is acutely poignant when our own truth, our own reality, is precariously overwhelming. Despite the dangers of the outside world, some have been able to create an internal world that supports conditions for play to emerge – the spirit of play then becoming a vital factor in saving life.

One such person is Alice Herz-Sommer. The pianist, who lived to the remarkable age of 110, survived imprisonment in Theresienstadt concentration camp during the Holocaust. She attributed not only her survival but also 'her continued capacity for hope in the face of unimaginable suffering' to music.[3] Music sustained her spirit. In the camp, she gave over 100 concerts (some to her fellow inmates as well as camp guards). Her extraordinary life has been documented in the films *We Want the Light* and *Everything is a Present*,[4] and in the book *A Garden of Eden in Hell*.[5] In an interview with Michael Thallium at the age of 108, she attributed her longevity and vitality to her optimistic outlook on life. Refusing to hate anyone, she repeated throughout the interview, 'Life is beautiful!'

Alice Herz-Sommer's words echo the 1997 Roberto Benigni film of the same name. The film, in which Benigni also plays the main character, Guido, depicts the life of a young Jewish Italian waiter during the Second World War. He is shown as a playful, exuberant man, passionately in love with his beautiful wife, Dora, and young son, Giosue. The small family's happiness is brought to an abrupt end when they are taken to a concentration camp. Dora is immediately separated from her husband and son. Guido turns his shrewd imagination to the service of protecting Giosue from the horrors they and everyone around them are facing. He devises elaborate games with complex rules to help his son make some sense of the brutal acts of cruelty they are witnessing. In effect, the father mediates the outer world and in so doing makes it more bearable for the young boy. What makes the film even more moving is that Benigni's inspiration comes from his own father's incarceration in a concentration camp. Interestingly, the film was criticized by some for its lack of regard for the suffering of so many. Others saw it as a shining example of the tenacity and resourcefulness of the human spirit.

In 1995, David Pelzer's autobiographical book *A Child called 'It'* became an international best seller. The book documents Pelzer's childhood abuse at the hands of his alcoholic mother. The account is harrowing, but the part that particularly drew my attention was his description of an event when, locked in the garage, he knew he had to make a choice. The only food available was discarded, mouldy pie crust. If he did not eat, he knew he would be that much closer to starvation. Pelzer consciously went into role as a king because a king eats only the best food. In role, he was able to eat the rotten pastry and survive another day.[6]

In 1997, two volunteer psychologists, Camilla Carr and Jonathan James, travelled to war-torn Chechnya with the intention of helping to set up a centre for children traumatized by war. They had been there only two months when they were kidnapped themselves at gunpoint. Kept prisoner for 14 months, the couple suffered the most appalling acts of barbarism. Following their release, they wrote a book together, *The Sky is Always There*. It is an extraordinary and often excruciating account of their experiences and, most significantly, how they coped with these experiences. There are two passages from the book which I want to offer as astonishing examples of this couple's capacity to play in such dire circumstances:

[W]e withdraw to our bedchamber and sit crosslegged opposite each other on the boxes. Lighting a candle we invite three special people to join us in our circle. I bring out an imaginary peace pipe from an imaginary pocket and we hail the four directions, the heavens and the earth calling in all the powers of love and healing. Then we pass the peace pipe around, making our own prayers, thanking our families and friends, known and unknown, for all their thoughts and love and efforts towards our release. We ask them to send compassion and love to our captors and feel a wave of loving peaceful energy flow through us and know our prayers are heard.[7]

I artistically fold and cut some of the newspaper into snowflake patterns and stick them to the wall with melted candle wax... The snowflakes are followed by trees and flowers and a moon cut out of the foil inside the Nescafé tin. Camilla joins in by smoothing out gold paper sweet wrappers that she has saved from our time in the sauna and cuts out a sun to go above the paper trees. I even manage to create a symbol of unity with five intersecting circles. These decorations break up the monotony of the bare, rough concrete walls. **We are creating our own world within a world.**[8]

This sense of 'creating a world within a world' is extremely important in reducing the impact and far-reaching effects of trauma. Psychiatrist and trauma specialist Judith Herman identified two conditions that significantly contribute towards a situation becoming traumatic for the person/s involved. These conditions are disempowerment and disconnection. Camilla Carr and Jon James, thankfully, were together during most of their horrific ordeal. What is apparent in the book and during my conversations with them, without a doubt, is the strength and resilience of their bond. Both at the time of the ordeal and afterwards. They were able to stay connected to one another during the experience, each bearing witness to the other's experience. Furthermore, they were able to call upon their own playful faculties to draw on the meagre materials they had available to them in order to create such vast and beautiful landscapes of nature – snowflakes, the moon, trees and a sun. In that dark, hostile and unpredictable environment, Jon and Camilla made their own domain that no one else could enter without their permission. Although they were powerless as hostages, nevertheless, they managed to generate a sense of empowerment in their co-created world of sweet-wrapper suns, foil flowers and a symbol of connected humanity. This was *their* world.

What is remarkable and inspiring about this couple is their capacity for loving-kindness, compassion and forgiveness. Even at the time of their incarceration, they were able to hold love and compassion for their assailants. This is not to say that there has not been rage and anger. They are human beings, after all. As I understand it, their capacity for forgiveness developed latterly. Both are very actively involved in the Forgiveness Project.[9] It was during her training as a dramatherapist that I had the privilege of meeting Camilla for the first time. Later, we wept together at the opening of the ARROW project in Plymouth, UK.[10] ARROW – Art: a Resource for Reconciliation Over the World – was an organization set up by inspirational drama and theatre facilitator David Oddie at University College Plymouth St Mark and St John.

There are many accounts of the indomitable will to play and create. Bobby Baker, whom we met in the previous scene, has since gone on to become Artistic Director of Daily Life Ltd, an arts and mental health charity based in East London, with a mission to create powerful art and platforms that change the way people view mental health.[11] The artists, referred to as 'experts by experience',[12] are supported in finding creative expression for their own experiences of mental illness as well as leading arts activities for others.

Rachel Kelly had been an accomplished journalist before she became cripplingly ill with depression. Her book *Black Rainbow*[13] records her terrifying journey into the depths of the illness and how she found her way through it by discovering the healing power of poetry. Rachel is now co-founder of the iFPoems poetry app and co-editor of *iF: A Treasury of Poems for Almost Every Possibility*.[14]

Lemn Sissay's mother arrived from Ethiopia in 1966 unaware that she was pregnant and was forced, as were many young, single women in Britain at that time, to hand her baby over to the authorities to be cared for by others. She thought she was asking for her son to be looked after temporarily. Lemn Sissay (who knew himself as Norman until he was 18) did not see his mother again until he was 21, the same age she had been when she gave birth to him.[15] At the age of 12, he was rejected by his long-term foster carers and put into the care system. He is a poet and playwright, describing poetry as his refuge:

'I did it because I was trying to translate the world, because I didn't believe what I was being told. I investigated the world through my imagination.'[16] He is also a passionate advocate for care-leavers' access to further education and is the current Chancellor of the University of Manchester. Lemn Sissay is also a strong campaigner for the rights of children in the care system, a matter very close to my own heart.

Dramatherapist and psychologist Mooli Lahad is a specialist in psychotrauma work. He devised the Six Piece Story Structure and the accompanying coping resources assessment tool, the BASIC PH.[17, 18] He has practised his creative therapy methods in the immediate aftermath of natural disasters such as the 1999 Turkish earthquake and the 2004 Sri Lankan and 2011 Japanese tsunamis. He also worked in New York following the 9/11 attacks on the Twin Towers. For the past three decades, Lahad's work has focused on developing treatment methods aimed at lessening the suffering of anxiety disorders and trauma, either by reducing symptoms entirely or reducing them to a manageable level so that the individual might reclaim a life worth living. In the course of his work, he has become increasingly aware of how some of his clients used a particular resource both during and following a traumatic event. This creative tool, which he refers to as the 'as if' reality, is an ability to take themselves consciously out of the traumatic situation. Mooli Lahad termed the phrase 'fantastic reality'.[19]

> In fantastic reality everything is possible, all the limits and controls of reality are lessened, and one can explore ideas, actions, and emotions in a flexible way. This fantastic space allows and enables options and alternatives, to make suggestions without imposing them. **In short, it is an invitation to play.**[20]

Lahad is very clear that fantastic reality is not a form of dissociation or denial; rather, it is a conscious, deliberate choice made by the individual to protect their and/or other people's well-being.

Mark Epstein describes a dialogue that happened between his 11-year-old son and Hoss, his son's stuffed toy dog, two days after the 9/11 attack. When the toy, voiced by Epstein, claims that 'people don't fly airplanes into skyscrapers',[21] both son and father could begin the factual (yes, people do) and the accompanying emotional processing of this horrific event. Epstein comments, 'We needed each other [to begin digesting our feelings], and it helped to have an inanimate, yet animated, object to serve as an intermediary between us.'

In each of these cases, the individuals concerned were able to bear witness to themselves, and sometimes to others, neither abandoning nor dissociating. Each one finding a playful means of making the suffering *less unbearable…*

Dan Hughes, in his work with emotionally wounded children, uses the metaphor of a song to describe the child's Being nature, saying, 'To love a child is to learn the song that is in their heart and to sing it to them when they have forgotten it.'[22] If the process of falling asleep is one of forgetting our true nature, then awakening is the process of remembering what we have forgotten. The image of a child reconnecting to the song in their heart is a potent one. It is the realization that we are all connected at a heart level. Perhaps the song has a universal quality? This would explain how the attuned therapist would know it. This territory also reminds me of Winnicott's concept of object presentation – the presence and intervention of another bringing forth something thus far unformed or something long buried and seemingly forgotten from the depths of the unconscious. Whether the object is a nipple to the hungry infant or the heart song of a forlorn child, in that moment the life force is rekindled. This moment of connection has the power to penetrate even the most defensive cloak.

In childhood, we learn that certain aspects of ourselves are not acceptable if we are to maintain relationships with others. For the vulnerable, relational child, there is no choice here. Artist Grayson Perry projected parts of himself away for safekeeping into his stalwart teddy bear, Alan Measles. The bear was subjected to all manner of adversity, yet crucially he survived. Later, Perry was able to reclaim those banished qualities, bringing them back into relationship to himself. For the most part, it seems that this process was unconscious. In later life, Perry was able to reflect upon the journey of enquiry he had made. Healing is a process of reclaiming those parts of ourselves that were cast out and hidden in the darkest recesses of our psyche.

Both the Buddha and Carl Jung give a very clear message in recognition of our destructive capacity, and that is to know ourselves. It is in knowing and understanding ourselves that we are able to alleviate our suffering. In Buddhist practice, this knowing primarily arises through the practice of meditation. There are many forms of meditation and we each need to find the method of instruction that works for us. In Jungian psychology, this knowing emerges through the process of active imagination: in a dialogue with image, symbol and metaphor. Both men dedicated their lives to the relief of suffering. Both knew that suffering was a natural accompaniment to being alive: birth, ageing, loss of loved ones, illness and death – these forms of suffering we cannot avoid. There is a secondary form of suffering, however – what Mary Booker terms 'on top suffering'[23] – that is unnecessary and created by the mind's tendency to cling on to that which is pleasurable or comfortable and to avoid that which is uncomfortable or unpleasant. The territory between Buddhism and Jungian psychology has been much explored, should you wish to read further beyond the scope of this book.[24]

The journey of awakening is one of observing ourselves, listening to ourselves and, in the Jungian practice of active imagination, becoming conversant with the *daimons* that reside within ourselves. This way, we can develop an awareness of the grasping and aversion that add to our suffering. We need to resist the temptation and inclination to grasp or avoid the images themselves and to reduce them to a literal understanding, and, instead, if possible, to adopt a soft focus, develop another way to listen and to stay as true as we are able to 'beginner's mind'. This journey takes immense courage because we cannot know what we will discover, or how we will be altered by those discoveries. As Hillman cautions:

> It is a rare courage that submits to the middle region of psychic reality where supposed surety of fact and illusion of fiction exchange their clothes.[25]

It could be argued that the creative process is the antithesis to meditation. In meditation, thoughts arising are named as such with the intention of letting them go. In the creative process, the player invites thoughts (and ideas, images and sensations) from the unconscious out into the light and engages with them – dances, moves, peers into, untangles them and moulds them to create form in the outside world. Sometimes the player drops an idea back into the unconscious and waits for a while to see what might happen. Upon closer enquiry, though, the two are actually not that dissimilar. There is a lightness of touch, a spontaneity, an endeavouring not to grasp hold, allowing an unfolding, witnessing and, ultimately, the sense of knowing oneself better through the experience. Buddhist teacher Rob Burbea, whom we met in Act 1, has brought a rich enquiry to the sacred teachings of the imaginal path.[26]

When traumatic memories are emerging, there is a compelling need to process these with the aim of releasing blocked emotional energy and integrating the experiences into the personal narrative – that is, the cloak. As Winnicott describes:

> Psychotherapy takes place in the overlap of two areas of playing, that of the patient and that of the therapist. Psychotherapy has to do with two people playing together.[27]

Mark Epstein supports Winnicott's view, saying:

> Good therapists are, by nature, playful – and good play is, by nature, therapeutic.[28]

Therapy which intentionally uses the vehicle of play can support people in bringing awareness to the layers of defences that make up the cloak and, because play is entered into voluntarily, there is a tendency for the cloak to naturally relax its defensive qualities. Play offers an opportunity to dissolve what we think we know and to make space for something new to appear. We can always revert to our former selves, for there is no demand to change. Core Process psychotherapist Francis Deas notes:

> Play offers a liberation from the crystallization of ego.[29]

Play is inherently precarious owing to its liminal nature, sitting as it does in the place of *sambhogakaya* – the place of magic and mystery.

As a therapist using play, I must always keep in mind, however, that for some clients play may not be a blessed relief but another way of being manipulated and possibly abused. In such cases, it is imperative that the therapist does not attempt to introduce play into the relationship until the client feels safe enough. One of the aims of therapy is to help explore, re-evaluate and rework the cloak to better suit the individual and to create a more adaptive and resilient engagement with life. This is particularly true for the abused child, removed from their abusive home and placed with foster carers. The strategies once necessary to simply survive need to be re-evaluated. This process is an integral aspect of the healing process.

The Role of the Witness

Ten-year-old Caleb had suffered extensive early childhood neglect by his mother and sexual abuse by his stepfather. He was received into care at the age of seven, remaining with the same foster carers. His behaviour was very controlling towards other children and became aggressive when they would not do what he wanted. His school and the carers were acutely aware of the possibility of Caleb becoming sexually aggressive towards other children. He isolated himself from his peers, which exacerbated his rage as he felt the other children were leaving him out. He began play therapy after the court case that found his stepfather guilty of sexual abuse and his mother guilty of neglect. Caleb's play, which started immediately he entered the play room, was repetitive and controlling. At times it became cruel. In the play he was showing the therapist a map of his inner world which was inhabited by terrifying monsters that frequently punished, silenced, starved and killed the small child. The scene, with slight variations, was played out again and again. The play therapist Miriam was always directed to play the victim. The therapist spoke of Caleb as 'waking dead', lacking spontaneity and joy, yet she understood that this rigidity and control had been the only things that had helped him survive in his life. In supervision, she explored whether this was reinforcing the trauma Caleb had experienced. Furthermore, she was concerned that Caleb was enjoying the sadistic power he was exercising over her and would then inflict it on children outside the sessions. Holding this in mind, Miriam complied with Caleb's directions but showed him how he could demonstrate what happened to the child by substituting a large teddy bear for herself at these times. From her witness position, she could speak as the child victim: 'I am so scared/I am alone/please help someone/I don't know why this is happening to me/I must be so bad/please stop.' She could also model empathy for the child: 'No child should have to bear such cruelty/This needs to stop/Helpful adults can make this stop.' Caleb found her commentary infuriating and tried to silence her. The therapist knew though that he was listening, despite his resistance to hearing her. She felt it was vitally important that the victim's voice be present in the room. Miriam was also aware that the abuse and neglect began when Caleb was preverbal and so he would have no language for these experiences. Crucially, the victim returned week after week, despite being hurt and sometimes killed. For many sessions, Miriam felt herself to be an object that Caleb directed. Miriam knew her interventions must be attuned in order for the child to make use of them, and they must emerge from a genuine place of loving-kindness and compassion. As the play evolved, the powerless child would be punished for misdemeanours by the other, now no longer a nebulous monster but a heartless and cold witch. The fact that the rules were often changed by the witch made no difference. It was clear that punishment rather than education was the priority. In one session, the child victim had again been imprisoned, surrounded by an electrified wall. The therapist-as-child was threatened with having her tongue cut out if they spoke at all. Miriam stepped outside the role of the child, narrating as she did so, explaining to Caleb that they were going to leave that Miriam in prison (represented by the teddy bear) and that now she was going to speak from the place of Miriam-as-therapist. From this meta-witness position, the therapist could commentate on the play – dialoguing directly with the witch and being outside the punitive treatment. Very quickly, the witch released the child from prison and allocated a new role to the therapist – that of the child prince. The therapist then switched between this frightened, small and vulnerable role and Miriam-as-therapist, narrating and co-directing the drama. Caleb, unsurprisingly, attempted to take on the role of therapist himself. Gently but firmly, she responded, 'Ah, no, Caleb, this is a role that only I can play.' He accepted this with what the therapist felt to be the quality of relief. The child seemed to be accepting that he did not need to control everything in his life and could be safe.

This extract from the play therapy spans a period of two years. Caleb had been with his foster carers for a year before the therapy began to allow him to settle and for the court case to be completed. Caleb, at the time of writing, is still in therapy with Miriam. This excerpt was chosen because it illustrates several of the qualities of play that facilitate significant shifts in the healing process. The therapeutic relationship is key. *All* the play therapist has to do is to create a safe space for the child. For a child like Caleb, this can take a long time and requires patience and trust on the part of the therapist. She also needs assurance that he is now living in a safe environment.[30] When the therapy space is safe — free from judgment, harm, intimidation, hidden agenda — an abused and neglected child will still have, as a significant part of his internal working model, an abuser and neglecter. A child will act out his inner world, in or outside the therapy room, as Margaret Lowenfeld notes:

> This necessity of the human mind to dramatize the elements of its environment that it perceives, in order to emotionally assimilate them, is a characteristic that runs throughout the whole fabric of human life.[31]

What the play therapist does is create a safe space in which the child can be held, witnessed and trusted to rework the traumatic material. Play is the vehicle for externalizing what is internal, whether that is through role play, story or sculpting. This externalizing gives the player an opportunity, especially in relation to another, to step back, out or away from the action to gain more detachment.[32] When the therapist initially used the witness position, Caleb was not ready to engage with it, although he did hear it, and it was valuable in the sense of being able to promote empathy for the child victim. The witness role cannot be underestimated. Noticing is a prerequisite before we can fully exercise our freedom to make choices. This awareness is the greatest agent for change and is traditionally cultivated through the practice of meditation. In Core Process psychotherapy, this awareness expands to 'witness consciousness'.[33] Eckart Tolle refers to the power of witnessing:

> [the] longing in each person, child or adult, to be recognized on the level of Being…that recognition brings forth the dimension of Being more fully into the world. This is the love that redeems the World.[34]

When Caleb began in play therapy, his play was Stagnant Posttraumatic Play[35] in terms of his interactions with his therapist: the rigidity of the theme and how it was acted out and most especially in the unresolved ending. This shifted over time as Miriam stayed present, witnessing and empathizing with the abused and neglected parts of Caleb. Miriam was also articulate in her judgment of the adults' behaviour, without attacking the adults themselves. It is very important not to denigrate the attachment figure, even an abusive or neglectful one. To do so would create a 'moral defence'[36] in the client, where they would feel a need to protect the parent against the therapist's perceived attack. Rather, the therapist needs to give time for the client to arrive at their own judgment of their parent.

The metaphor of the cloak has afforded me the opportunity to have a clearer visual image of the layers of wounding we all carry. How often it is that wounding and the protection we unconsciously weave around it impinges on practically every, if not every, aspect of our lives – our self-image (of mind, body, heart, intellect), how we come into relationship, how we love, how we hate, what dreams and aspirations we have (or not), how we learn and remember, our general trust in life (and maybe death too). Like any sensory organism, we contract and move away from pain – whether physical or emotional. The earlier in our lives and more prolonged that pain, the deeper the wounding. These early traumatic experiences become, as Peter Levine describes, 'riveted'[37] into the very foundations of our identity, the inner layers of the cloak.

For well-being, I believe we are aiming for the creation of a coherent narrative. A cloak with coherent patterns, not one that denies or excludes the wounding, but one that incorporates it into the meaningful whole. A cloak available for adjustment, open to new experiences, alert without being afraid, and able to be enriched by life's experiences, even the hardest ones. I also believe we need cloaks that have a permeability that allows our Being nature, our Brilliant Sanity, to shine through. Where there is trauma, especially early trauma in the deepest layers of the cloak, the enquiry *has* to be gentle, respectful and, above all, safe.

Behind the Barricade

Maria turned up for her session on the wrong day, forgot the next session and then arrives an hour early for today's session (realizing this, she went for a walk before coming). A well of emotion rises as she sits down. Bringing enquiry to this, she names the feeling of shame. As we peel back the layers of judgment, she arrives at a new awareness: that week after week she feels she brings her 'clutter' and does not get to what is really happening. By enquiring into her process, she opens to the possibility of how valuable the clutter might be as a protection. I invite her to create this in the space and she builds a wall of cushions around herself, squeezing into a tiny space in the middle that constricts her breathing but crucially where she feels safe. She looks like a soldier hidden behind sandbags and under attack from the enemy. The memory of being a child comes up where she had to create a safe space under her desk, the battle raging outside in the rest of her bedroom. The battle was between her and her mother, ostensibly about the mess in her bedroom. For Maria, it was about her right to exist and to have her own needs met.

Anger, sadness and longing rise from the child within Maria. Her vow never to have her own children lest she treat them the way her own mother had treated her, and her fear that her children would almost certainly detest her as she hated her own mother. Other memories arise of her mother scorning or laughing at her as a child when she came to her in need. Maria is quick to find reasons for her mother's cruelty. I gently guide her back to being with her child-self, what she did not have then and what she may be able to give to herself now.

From behind her barricade, arms now resting upon the cushions, she recounts a recent meeting with her niece. Maria experiences a warm sensation in her chest. I notice her face softening, still wet with her earlier tears. I comment that perhaps the next generation do not need to carry the wounds of their ancestors. She nods.

Maria remembers a poem about leaving petals around as an invitation to the other. If the other picks up a petal, then they can be invited into the garden. Metaphorically, she feels her niece has picked up her petals, responding to her invitation, and she picked up her niece's. I ask her if she feels the need for the barricade when she is with her niece. No, she replies.

Healing happens in the present, in the here-and-now. Maria used play to externalize the internal barriers (in effect, her cloak) that she had erected to protect herself as a child. Her realization that the barriers were still there and were blocking her from living her life as fully as she knew was possible brought her to crisis point. Something *had* to change. Although she had been in therapy for some time, I do not believe this process of revealing herself could, or should, have been hurried. The impetus to change had to emerge from the individual. Maria felt safe enough with the therapist to name the clutter. Even then, it was necessary to create the defences. Then she could give herself the permission and awareness to truly inhabit her sanctuary. Note how quickly she abandoned her own child-self to empathize with her mother. It is vital that the therapist at such a time stays present to the child and firmly but gently brings the client back into relationship with that wounded part. If this does not happen, the client will be re-traumatized as the old patterning is simply replayed. Healing is a reworking of that old material, not a reiteration of it.

Although the overlap of two people playing can involve the use of imagery and metaphor while sitting in chairs or on cushions, introducing other creative methods opens up a wealth of other possibilities. Psychotherapist Fiona Lothian reflects on her own practice:

> Just talking limits how my clients and I experience the world... introducing a photograph or an object engages the unconscious mind because it uses the senses, bringing us into the present moment... the only time healing is possible. You never know what is going to come out so it can be scary and needs to be used wisely. Often with a client I will introduce them to the sand tray and invite them just to choose objects they are drawn to and suddenly they are revealing aspects of themselves I don't believe can be discovered through cognitive means.[38]

Fiona's words remind me of Jung's wise advice:

> An emotional disturbance can also be dealt with another way, not by clarifying it intellectually but by giving it visible shape.[39]

In my experience, when we open to the genius of play, we are frequently surprised by the discoveries we make. There is, however, an inbuilt safety mechanism in play. Because of its paradoxical nature, that real/not real aspect of play, we can always dismiss the discovery if it is too much to bear at that time. Sometimes it is better to let go of the realization in the same way an artist may allow an idea to drop back down into the unconscious so that it might percolate a little while longer. My young adolescent client Izzy saw herself as ugly. She arrived for her session one day wearing make-up, out of her usual jogging pants, and smartly dressed with her hair brushed and tied up. I was astonished how different she looked; I barely recognized her. She beamed a wide smile. I had noted previously that she could not accept any compliments and so I said to her, 'Hey Izzy, if I was to tell you how wonderful you're looking today, what would you say?' She contemplated for a moment with a serious expression, then, looking me straight in the eye and smiling again, she said, 'Hmm, I'd still tell you to fuck off!' We laughed together. So I did not tell her she looked great and she did not respond with an expletive, but we both knew where we were. As we held this exchange through the medium of play, it was simply an experiment without consequences.

Scene 4

STAYING AWAKE

Some have I seen in whom love was a flame
So bright that men remembered whence they came.[1]

My wish, indeed my continuing passion, would be not to point the
finger in judgment but to part a curtain, that invisible shadow that falls
between people, the veil of indifference to each other's presence, each
other's wonder, each other's human plight.[2]

The struggles that humanity faces today are not new ones – how we balance the needs of the individual versus the group, the country's versus the continent's; how we balance the resources of the planet with our wants and demands. Each one of us, to a greater or lesser degree, navigates and learns how we can protect ourselves when necessary, be open in the meantime and recognize that protection and openness exist along the same continuum as violence and gullibility. In *The Cloak*, the Dead Woman advised the Unborn Spirit to weave a protection and disguise having encountered the misuse of power most familiar to all of us – 'either you must fulfil the will of others, or impose your will'. It would appear that this is the way of the world, the way of humanity. This is the nature of the cloak. The Buddha reminds us that this human realm will always possess levels of ignorance and suffering; it is its nature. If you want something else, choose to truly wake up, he tells us, see through the patterns of your own mind.[3] The Buddha offered humanity the middle path, a place where we can be in the world yet also have a degree of detachment to enable us not to become lost in the ways of the 'cloak world'. The middle path is a place where we can be connected to our thoughts, feelings, physicality and mortality, and know these are not all of who we are, where we can see that we are all players on the stage and that we are also directors, writers, stage managers and set designers too. We are also the audience. The middle path is where we can learn to accept the contradictoriness and paradox of life. Where we can ride the river of life, embracing the rapids, resting in the calm, taking in the extraordinary scenery and marvelling at the journey. Where we can let go of the idea of fixing problems, instead working collaboratively with each other and sometimes learning to enjoy the not-knowing. Life, like Cassini's engraving of the moon, is a mixture of certainty and ambiguity. The middle path offers the real possibility of shifting our perspective from what Hougham describes as 'tabloid to myth'. As Jack Kornfield says, 'in the middle we discover that the world is workable'.[4]

Once we become aware of the cloak and its qualities, however subtle, and we realize it is not all of who we are, then our perception of ourselves and others, and the world – this phenomenal planet that we share – profoundly changes. Feldman describes this way of living as 'an expression of reverence':

> It is a way of being that reveres the sacredness and dignity of all life, honours our Earth, and appreciates the implications of our fundamental interdependence and interconnectedness.[5]

Our interconnectedness with the Earth as another living being cannot be ignored. There is astonishing work being led by many individuals,[6] but we cannot leave this work to the few; we all have a shared responsibility. Awakening means a stop to regarding this work as 'alternative', which is in effect another split, another duality. We *all* need to breathe clean air. We *all* need to drink fresh water. How, then, can those speaking out on behalf of the Earth be seen as extremists?

However elaborate, intricate and richly patterned it is, the cloak is a poor reflection of who we are. Many spiritual traditions maintain that we are already awakened beings as our True nature is already present: it is always present; we just need to stop concealing it by clinging to our cloaks. One of my favourite comments on the Buddhist teachings at the Karuna Institute, particularly from Maura Sills, was, 'It's simple, but it isn't easy.' I do believe we *know* what is most skilful, most helpful and the kindest way to be, despite the many layers of obscurations and being bent and twisted out of shape by life and all its vicissitudes. So many of us live in fear, and it is fear that constricts us and stops us from being all that we can be. We can so quickly get caught up in the maelstrom of everyday irritations, worrying about the future, regretting the past. I am certainly not overlooking some of the very real suffering that so many experience and I am keen to enquire still: What is at the root of life and how do we fundamentally want to live it? As Pema Chödrön asks, 'Do the days of our lives add up to further suffering or to increased joy?'[7] I have been deeply moved and inspired by the writings of Bronnie Ware in her book *The Top Five Regrets of the Dying: A Life Transformed by the Dearly Departing* (2011, 2012) together with Sogyal Rinpoche's *The Tibetan Book of Living and Dying* (1996), and I am certain I do not want to waste this time that I have and live (and die) to regret it.

Ware reflects on her experiences with the dying and concludes that ultimately the decisions we make in our lives derive from a simple (though not easy) choice we make between love and fear. Thankfully, there are guides and guidance. The fourth of the Noble Truths, known as the Noble Eightfold Path, is such a teaching. Paradoxically, it is based not so much on learning, but on unlearning the lessons most of us have been taught in life. In English, the teachings are introduced as 'right' but the actual translation from the word *Samma* means 'proper', 'whole', 'thorough', 'integral', 'complete', 'perfect'; corresponding to the word 'summit' in English, it does not mean 'right' as opposed to 'wrong'.[8] The eight teachings include perception, resolve, speech, conduct, livelihood, effort, mindfulness and attention. Right perception concerns our understanding that our actions and beliefs have consequences beyond our personal death; our vision of the nature of reality and the path of transformation; the cultivation of loving-kindness, compassion, sympathetic joy and equanimity, and moving away from hatred and cruelty. Resolve is about cultivating an informed heart and feeling mind that are free to practise letting go. Speech relates to the way in which we communicate, practising authentic, non-harmful speech, speech that is beneficial and encouraging to others. Conduct focuses on the non-exploitation of self and others, and the protection of life. Livelihood is concerned with the ways we make a living and a commitment to avoid harming and exploiting all others. Right effort relates to consciously and courageously directing the life force to the transformative path of creative and healing action that fosters wholeness. Right mindfulness is connected to being present, being awake, developing the contemplation 'If you hold yourself dear, watch yourself well'. The final teaching relates to developing *Samadhi*, which is right attention and concentration.

For me, the instruction to 'watch oneself well' is an acknowledgement of the power of witness consciousness. This watching well arises from a basis of loving-kindness and compassion for oneself.

In the Prologue, Manjushri dropped his bundle of sticks, enlightening the elderly monk yet leaving him disorientated and confused, even though the monk was very familiar with the process of awakening. Today, we live in a world more attached to immediate rewards and gains than ever before – we want something and we want it now – and there are practices available that offer this dramatic, dynamic approach to awakening. One might ask, though, how that experience becomes integrated for the people involved. The journey requires a peeling away of the layers, like Inanna descending into the Underworld, and this needs to happen in a gradual and timely way; otherwise, we are likely to go into shock, disintegration and perhaps even psychosis. Awakening is a path, and there is no other option than to walk each step with our own feet.

Without resources, primarily the Brahma Viharas, that enable us to stay present and awake, it is likely we will fall asleep. The key question: How do we not draw a veil of oblivion over all that is painful and unpleasant and instead cultivate the resources to meet our suffering without becoming overwhelmed or dissociated? When we real-eyes the cloak is not all of who we are, then we can see that although we need the cloak for this earthly existence, we can use play in all its many guises to shape, reshape, weave and reweave it as we see fit.

We are not 'puppets in the hands of gods'; we have choices in how we live our lives. We have access to the infinite if only we can real-eyes this. If we see ourselves as puppets, in effect we give away our power, rendering ourselves helpless victims, becoming passive and estranged from ourselves. Theologian and poet Rowan Williams describes us as players in the sense of musicians bringing alive a piece of music, and maybe this is what our purpose is – to bring life, love and hope to the world just as Bax's Unborn Spirit believed.[9]

Perhaps too we can find a meaning for the suffering we experience? The field of Post-Traumatic Growth (PTG) has received much interest in the clinical and academic worlds in recent times. PTG is concerned with the positive changes we may cultivate following a traumatic event, such as positive changes in our goals, priorities, relationships with others and spirituality as a result of re-evaluating or modifying our assumptions about the world and our lives.[10] Being able to share our experiences and finding ways to express what has happened to us and the impact of those happenings through creative channels such as art, poetry, music, dance and drama allows others to see us, to connect and resonate with our suffering. Through connection with others and the telling of our stories, we are reducing the suffering and the lasting effects of trauma. David Pelzer wrote:

> One's past, no matter how severe, should never dominate nor control your future. To know that you survived an ordeal, simply put, is nothing short of courageous. Then, to realize that you in fact survived for a reason is a gift as well as an awesome responsibility. Resilience is an art that can be applied in ALL facets of life. And, it already lies deep within you! So go out and live the adventurous life you deserve.[11]

Jane McGonigal, whom we met in Act 1, created an electronic game that has been used by hundreds of thousands of people, as a direct result of her concussion and ensuing depression. Many artist players, some named in this book and some I have not had space to name, are inspired to create from their places of suffering truly beautiful works of art. Maya Angelou became mute after being raped and believing herself responsible for the rapist's death after she had named him. She did not speak for five years but in that time she read every book, poem and play she could find. When she did speak again, she had a great deal to say, and the world listened. Others transform their suffering to the service of counselling and therapy, and the term the 'wounded healer' is a notion familiar to many. We *can* grow through our suffering, but, as Alice Miller said, we have to hear and see that suffering first, we have to waken up to it. Only when we can acknowledge our own can we begin to be with the suffering of others, and we have to be resourced; otherwise, this awareness will simply overwhelm us. Play, in its many forms, is one of our fundamental resources. It can offer us a new perspective and a new way of expression, beyond the personal:

> Talent for speaking differently, rather than for arguing well, is the chief instrument of cultural change.[12]

Our play and the outcomes of play are enormously powerful mechanisms for change:

> It gives voice to democracy, and shape to a civilization. It is a platform for ideas and an agent for change.[13]

One of the most authentic and affirming ways in which we can live life is to cultivate a healthy relationship with our death. In the Prologue, I spoke about death being the backing on the glass that mirrors life back to us, giving life meaning. I imagine most of us, most of the time, do not look too often or too long into this mirror, unless we are consciously dying. When I began writing this book, my dear friend Anna Trevone did not know she would receive a diagnosis for terminal cancer. Witnessing Anna's journey has been a profound privilege (these words are all I have but truly do not reflect the experience) and a tender, heartbreaking one for me. As well as being a therapist of astonishing compassion and intuition, Anna is a shaman, and so what lies beyond her earthly existence is not based on conjecture or faith. She has not 'squandered her life in fooleries or the stirring up of strife' (as the Dead Woman observes in *The Cloak*).[14] Knowing her earthly death is imminent, Anna wrote a play, *Seven Gates*, based on the myth of Inanna. In *Seven Gates*, the female protagonist is directed by Inanna herself through each of the archways into the Underworld, discarding her earthly attributes as she enters – the first to go is her health... When the protagonist is struggling to concentrate with her discomfort, Inanna urges her to pay attention:

There's only this moment.
That's all we have.
What will you do with it?
Create?
Or focus on your wet socks?

She manages to write and accepts Inanna's offer to look after these, her last and most precious words. After the woman's death, Inanna reads her words of thanks and celebration, a dedication to the protagonist's Mother. The play closes with these lines describing the onward journey of the Woman's Spirit:

She knows where she's heading. She's been to paradise remember. She travels to the top of the waterfall at the bottom of the world. She quite simply passes through that way, moving out across the stars. All the time she is extending, growing out from inside herself, no edges, no edges at all. She becomes the night sky, Queen of Heaven, then shifts slightly.

Finding herself in the Moon she remembers. She follows the
cycle and waits for full ripeness then casts down to find pools.

Who you are will not matter, how you are will not either.
She will simply reach you with love, as the moon upon the
water.

In *The Cloak*, the Unborn Spirit succumbs to fear and takes on the
cloak of the Dead Woman. Perhaps Bax has written it so, so that we
do not need to. We each have a choice – love or fear. I know which I
want to choose.

Thank you so much, Anna, for showing me the way.
It is simple but it isn't easy. Travel well and don't forget to play.
May all beings be happy.
May all beings know the root of happiness.

Epilogue

Dear Play,

Truly the more I get to know you, the more you astonish me. You are like a mother, a lover, a child, a grandchild to me. But, hey, here I go trying to contain you within human form and I imagine you chuckling to yourself. I thank you for your benign forgiveness of me and my humanness, while I imagine hearing simultaneously, 'There is nothing to forgive.'

I want you to know that it is my wholehearted intention to serve you from the confines and gifts of my human form. I rejoice in your primordial nature – knowing you existed before and will continue to exist after my body is devoid of breath. This helps me to bear my own mortality.

I celebrate the knowledge that others have known you and brought their own wisdom to that knowing. In the workshop today, I mistakenly referred to Donald (Winnicott), imagining him sitting beside me, as Derrick. This is my father! Donald Winnicott is my forefather. One of many. I have many ancestors and I will pass the thread on to the next generation to do with what they will.

I am honoured to be a part of this tapestry. I am deeply privileged to know you. May I always be open to allow your winds to blow through me and may I always serve you.

Di Gammage
July 2016
Terapia, London

Notes

Prologue

1. Bax n.d., pp.4–5.
2. Bax n.d., p.4.
3. A bodhisattva in Mahayana Buddhism is a person who is able to reach the state of nirvana but delays doing so through compassion for all suffering beings.
4. Epstein 1998.
5. Welwood 2000.
6. Welwood 2000, p.9.
7. Core Process psychotherapy (CPP) is a mindfulness-based approach to therapy and emphasizes a deep, ongoing awareness of one's body and mental processes for self-exploration and healing. See www.karuna-institute.co.uk (accessed 27 March 2017).
8. Maslow 1968.
9. Washburn 1995.
10. Indra's Net is a metaphor to symbolize *Sunyata* – emptiness.
11. Franklyn Sills, Karuna Institute, Devon.
12. Kübler-Ross 2014.
13. Chödrön 2001, p.28.
14. Oliver 1990.
15. Chögyam Trungpa Rinpoche cited in Chödrön 2001, p.2.
16. Deadly play is a term borrowed from theatre director Peter Brook from his book *The Empty Space* (1968).
17. Richard Hougham, Dramatherapist and Course Director of the Sesame Programme in Drama and Movement Therapy, Royal Central School of Speech and Drama, London.

Act I – Scene I

1. Jacques, Act 2, Scene 7, *As You Like It*, William Shakespeare 1993.
2. Stuart Brown is a medical doctor and psychiatrist and founder of the National Institute for Play based in California.
3. Brown 2008.
4. Schierlitz 2008.
5. White 2009.
6. White 2009.
7. Sutton-Smith 1997.
8. Harris 2000.
9. McGonigal 2010.
10. Brown 2008.
11. Darwin 2006.
12. Schoemaker 2011.

13. Toumazou 2014.
14. Behncke Izquierdo 2011, 2014.
15. Macdonald 2014.
16. B. Brown 2010.
17. DeLoache and Gottlieb 1998.
18. Burghardt 1975.
19. Jenkinson 2001.
20. Young 2012.
21. *Front Row*, BBC Radio 4, 12 October 2011.
22. S. Brown 2010.
23. Winnicott 1971, p.63.
24. S. Brown 2010, p.127.
25. Winnicott 1971, p.44.
26. Göncü and Perone 2005, p.4.
27. Clarkson 1995.
28. Guerrière 1980.
29. Paracelsus 1958, p.5.
30. Hougham 2013, p.4.
31. Hougham 2013.
32. Hougham 2013, p.5.
33. Hougham 2013, p.7.
34. Preece 2006, p.3.
35. Welwood 2000, p.306.
36. Jung 1991, p.212.
37. Preece 2006, p.89.
38. Dimock 1989, p.159.
39. A bodhisattva, like Manjushri whom we met with the monk in the Prologue, is a being who has chosen to work for the benefit of all beings to bring an end to suffering. One who is aspiring to Buddhahood.
40. Hawley 1995, p.6.
41. Goodwin 1995, p.6.
42. Nachmanovitch 1990, p.1.
43. Hillman 1983, p.55.
44. Suzuki 1970.
45. Burbea 2014.
46. Watkins 1999.
47. Rob Burbea, private communication.
48. Preece, private communication 2015.
49. Sangharakshita 1999, p.209.

Act 1 – Scene 2

1. Spariosu 1989, p.ix.
2. S. Brown 2010, p.5.
3. White 2009.
4. Winnicott 1971.
5. Winnicott 1971, p.50.
6. Marks-Tarlow 2010, p.40.
7. Nachmanovitch 1990, p.43.
8. Franklyn Sills, Karuna Institute, personal notes.
9. Rosen 2010.
10. Epstein 2005, p.159.
11. Matthew 4:4.
12. Bateson 1972.
13. Eberle 2014.
14. Nachmanovitch 1990, p.43.

15. Nachmanovitch 1990, p.43.
16. Brown 2008.
17. Sutton-Smith 1997.
18. Brown 2008.
19. Hougham 2013, p.4.
20. Kipling 2011.
21. Elkind 2007.
22. Nietzsche cited in Zweig and Abrams 1991, p.xx.
23. White 2009.
24. VanderVen 2004.
25. Eberle 2014, p.215.
26. Göncü and Perone 2005, p.137.
27. Nachmanovitch 1990, p.45.
28. Negative capability is a term coined by John Keats (1817) meaning 'When man is capable of being in uncertainties, mysteries, doubts, without any irritable reaching after fact and reason' (Keats 2012, pp.193–194).
29. 'The willing suspension of disbelief' is a phrase coined by Samuel Taylor Coleridge in 1817 from *Biographia Literaria*, chapter 14.
30. Spariosu 1989, p.ix.
31. Eberle 2014, p.219.
32. Sutton-Smith 1999, p.253.
33. Eberle 2014, p.222.
34. Brook 1968, p.30.
35. There are very few instances of 'objective' reality, especially when we begin adding our own interpretations and meanings to events. Two people can hear exactly the same speech, see exactly the same film, and each will have their own narrative. In the Challenge of Change Resilience programme, the example is given of two siblings being brought up in the same household. Each will have their own unique, subjective experience that can be so wildly different that one could be forgiven for thinking they were raised in different families.
36. Harris 2014, p.53.
37. Harris 2014, p.53.
38. Eberle 2014, p.223.
39. Szpunar, Addis and Schacter 2012, pp.25, 28.
40. Eberle 2014, p.224.
41. Eberle 2014, p.222.
42. Epstein 2005, pp.158–159.
43. This might be another reason why some people fear play.
44. In my experience, when we *really* hear the Fool's words, we know we are hearing the Truth.
45. Note that Jonathan Kay uses a metaphor here to communicate his understanding.
46. I real-eyes I have met Fools before – David Cowell with his ex-spert, for instance.

Act i – Scene 3

1. Bax n.d., pp.4–5.
2. Wallace 1999, p.14.
3. Winnicott 1960.
4. Kerényi 1976, p.xxxv.
5. Kennedy 2013.
6. Harding 2014.
7. Perry 2014.
8. Baggini 2011, p.168.
9. Susan Blackmore in Baggini 2011, p.149.
10. Clifford Bax's Angel.
11. Freud 1920, p.27.
12. Baggini 2011, p.126.
13. Baggini 2011, p.5.

14. Baggini 2011, p.45.
15. Derek Parfit in Baggini 2011, p.47.
16. Bax n.d., p.45.
17. Brunt 2014.
18. Pelzer 1995.
19. Pelzer 1999.
20. Originally intended to run for two weeks, the experiment had to be aborted after only six days as there were grave concerns for the mental health of both the 'prisoners' and the 'guards' (both groups had been recruited from young male volunteers). The guards quickly fell into perpetrating acts of depravity, cruelty and humiliation against the prisoners while Zimbardo and his fellow researchers and even a Catholic priest quashed their consciences in preference to recording their data. These prisoners, like the inmates of Nazi concentration camps, were supplied with ID numbers which, after several hours, replaced their own names.
21. Jung 1938.
22. The Hakomi Method was founded by psychotherapist and author Ron Kurtz in the late 1970s. The Hopi word 'Hakomi' translates to 'How do you stand in relation to these many realms?' See www.hakomi.com.au; www.hakomiinstitute.com (accessed 27 March 2017).
23. Kurtz 1990.
24. Kalsched 1996, p.4.
25. Kalsched 1996, p.4.
26. Bax n.d., p.5.
27. Baggini 2011, p.72.
28. Baggini 2011, p.123.
29. Baggini 2011, p.123.
30. Baggini 2011, p.126.
31. Keats 1994, p.190.
32. Baylor and Parnall 1997.
33. Sills 2009, p.4.
34. Sills 2009, p.27.
35. Sills 2009, p.3.
36. Dhammapada verse 80. Translated from the Pali by F. Max Muller, Project Gutenberg EBook. Available at www.gutenberg.org/files/2017/2017-h/2017-h.htm (accessed 18 April 2017).
37. Jung 1981.
38. Sills 2009, p.7.
39. Sills 2009, p.27.
40. Sills 2009, p.28.
41. Known in Zen Buddhism as Brilliant Sanity.
42. Jung 1976.
43. Lui Hsu Chi cited in Sills 2009, p.vii.
44. Winnicott 1960.

Act 1 – Scene 4

1. Walt Whitman, 'There Was a Child Went Forth'.
2. Lowenfeld 1991, p.17.
3. Jennings 1987, 1999.
4. Slade 1954, 1995.
5. Sue Jennings, www.suejennings.com, 9 January 2016.
6. William Wordsworth, 'Intimations of Immortality'.
7. Adler 1966, p.120.
8. King Solomon, Ecclesiastes 12:7.
9. Baggini 2011, p.189.
10. Montagu 1989, p.135.
11. Burbea 2014.
12. Stern 1990, p.17.
13. Stern 1990, p.9.

14. In my work as a psychotherapist, often a client will report feeling, for example, anger, envy or contentment. It seems to help to enquire: How do you know it is this feeling? What sensations are you recognizing in your body? Exploring the tonal quality of an embodied sensation can open up a richer enquiry than resorting prematurely to naming a feeling as this or that. It is also common for apparently contradictory feelings to co-exist, such as fear and excitement.
15. Batchelor 2007, p.71.
16. Damasio 2000.
17. Wallin 2007, p.64.
18. Siegel 2015.
19. Murray and Andrews 2000, p.39.
20. Stern 1990, p.38.
21. Winnicott 1971.
22. Winnicott 1971, p.131.
23. Sunderland 2006.
24. Murray and Andrews 2000.
25. There is much research regarding children with sensory disabilities with reference to their ability to attach and the risk of inadequate attachment (Fraiberg 1977; Brazelton and Cramer 1990; Warren 1994; Swain *et al.* 2004).
26. Murray and Andrews 2000.
27. Schore 1994, p.33.
28. Bowlby 1988.
29. Ainsworth *et al.* 2015.
30. Winnicott 1971, p.173.
31. Winnicott 1971, pp.11–12.
32. Winnicott 1960.
33. van der Kolk 2005, p.2.
34. Ainsworth *et al.* 2015.
35. van der Kolk 2005, p.2.
36. Hughes 1998, 2016.
37. Fairbairn 1994.
38. Gomez 1997, p.58.
39. Winnicott 1971.
40. Winnicott 1971, p.47.
41. Preece, private communication 2015.
42. The potential space is also pivotal in the therapeutic relationship established between therapist and client, for as Winnicott said, 'Psychotherapy takes place in the overlap of two areas of playing, that of the patient and that of the therapist. Psychotherapy has to do with two people playing together' (1971, p.44). Psychotherapist Patrick Casement defines the potential space as 'a sense of inviting and a safe interpersonal field in which one can be spontaneously playful while at the same time connected to others' (1985, p.162).
43. Winnicott 1971.
44. Nietzsche in Zweig and Abrams 1991.
45. Murray and Andrews 2000.
46. Stafford 2014.
47. Eberle 2014, p.223.
48. A TV advertisement in the UK for a soap powder shows parents creeping into their child's room late at night while the child sleeps to secretly wash and dry the special teddy bear before its owner awakes. Apparently, the child does not notice the fresh, clean-smelling bear the next morning. This just would not happen!
49. Winnicott 1971, p.7.
50. Winnicott 1971, p.134.
51. Klein 1975.
52. Fairbairn 1994.
53. Winnicott 1971.
54. Gomez 1997, p.54.
55. Winnicott 1971, p.3.

56. Stern 1990, p.61.
57. Sunderland 2006.
58. Stern 1990, p.53.
59. Stern 1990, p.67.
60. Stern 1990, p.77.
61. Stern 1990, p.102.
62. Stern 1990, p.107.
63. Stern 1990, p.112.
64. Stern 1990, p.112.
65. Stern 1990, p.119.
66. Stern 1990, p.123.
67. Stern 1990, p.124.
68. Stern 1990, p.131.
69. Stern 1990, p.131.
70. Stern 1990, p.133.
71. Stern 1990, p.88.
72. Stern 1990, p.114.
73. Kalsched 1996, p.13.
74. Kalsched 1996, p.13.

Act 2 – Scene 1

1. Winnicott 1964, p.145.
2. William Wordsworth, 'Intimations of Immortality'.
3. William Blake, 'A Memorable Fancy'; Blake 1977.
4. Kalsched 1996, p.20.
5. Marvell 2005.
6. Washburn 1995, p.39.
7. Washburn 1995, p.74.
8. Washburn 1995, p.49.
9. Perry 2010.
10. Sills 2009, p.30.
11. The Angel, Bax n.d., p.41.
12. Fromm 1983, p.60.
13. Hanson 2009, p.45.
14. Winnicott 1971.
15. Long-Crowell 2015.
16. Cathy Haynes is a London-based artist, curator and writer.
17. The Human Zoo programme on Radio 4 on the subject of the psychology of ambiguity (Haynes 2013).
18. See Suzanne O'Sullivan's book It's All in Your Head (2016) for accounts of dissociative seizures where the body 'chooses' to manifest the physical symptoms rather than experience the traumatic emotional upset.
19. Herman 1992, p.33.
20. Herman 1992; Levine 1997, 2000; Rothschild 2000.
21. Herman 1992, p.8.
22. Eitinger in Herman 1992, p.8.
23. There is much research relating to the effect of maternal stress on the developing foetus: see Monk et al. 2000; Van den Bergh and Marcoen 2004; O'Connor et al. 2005; Weinstock 2005; Talge, Neal and Glover 2007; Kinsella and Monk 2009.
24. It is estimated that since 2004 there has been a 400 per cent increase in the USA of babies born addicted to drugs (Tolia et al. 2015).
25. Levendosky and Graham-Bermann 2001.
26. See Grantly Dick-Read's book Childbirth without Fear: The Principles and Practice of Natural Childbirth (1942, 2004).
27. Miller 1979, p.xv.

28. Epstein 2013, pp.1, 3.
29. The book was Ishmael Beah's *A Long Way Gone: The True Story of a Child Soldier.*
30. The international charity War Child states there are an estimated 250,000 child soldiers in the world today. Almost half of these children are girls used as sex slaves for male combatants. See www.hrw.org/topic/childrens-rights/child-soldiers (accessed 18 April 2017).
31. Dr Phil is Dr Philip Calvin McGraw, psychologist and host of the US television show *Dr Phil.*
32. Chödrön 2003, p.27.
33. Friere 1968/1970.
34. Nachmanovitch 1990, p.116.
35. May 1975, p.30.
36. Los Angeles-based street artist WRDSMTH.
37. Nachmanovitch 1990, p.116.
38. Nachmanovitch 1990, p.116.
39. Welwood n.d.
40. Welwood n.d.
41. Marshall Rosenberg often quotes Sufi poet Rumi's poem 'Out beyond ideas of wrongdoing and rightdoing there is a field. I'll meet you there' from *The Book of Love: Poems of Ecstasy and Longing* (HarperOne, 2005); see Rosenberg 2003, chapter 1.
42. Matthew 26:52; Martin Luther King 1967.
43. Interview of Marshall Rosenberg by Michael Bertrand, The Natural Child Project, www.naturalchild.org.
44. See Figley 1995.
45. See the NSPCC document 'Vicarious trauma: the consequences of working with abuse' which draws on the work of Conrad and Kellar-Guenthar 2006; Braithwaite 2007; Tehrani 2011. Available at www.nspcc.org.uk/globalassets/documents/information-service/research-briefing-vicarious-trauma-consequences-working-with-abuse.pdf (accessed 18 April 2017).
46. The Constructive Journalism Project working in conjunction with the University of Southampton in the UK is an attempt to empower audiences by presenting a more balanced picture of news reports, offering the public a means by which it may stay awake and present to world events rather than becoming secondarily traumatized, resulting in disconnection and disempowerment. See www.constructivejournalism.org.
47. Epstein 2013, pp.21–22.

Act 2 – Scene 2

1. Piaget 1951.
2. Vygotsky 1978.
3. A preoperational child, usually age 2–7 years, is not considered to have 'logical thought' or be able to imagine a situation from another person's perspective; that is, they are what Piaget terms 'ego centric'. A concrete operational child, age 7–12 years, is becoming more rational in their thoughts and beginning to use their imagination to explore the 'what if' capacity.
4. Sutton-Smith and Herron 1971, p.332.
5. Sutton-Smith and Herron 1971, p.333.
6. Sutton-Smith and Herron 1971, p.339.
7. Todd and Scordelis 2009.
8. Todd 2011.
9. Sutton-Smith and Herron 1971.
10. Göncü and Perone 2005, p.137.
11. Lowenfeld 1991, p.232.
12. B. Brown 2010, p.95.
13. Winnicott 1971, pp.119–120.
14. Gompertz 2015.
15. Greenburg 1991.
16. Perry 2010.
17. Tharp 2003.
18. Ross 2011, p.199.

19. Roy 2004.
20. B. Brown 2010, p.100.
21. Q Music Awards 2011.
22. In Act 3 we will explore Will Gompertz's idea that artists do not fail.
23. van der Kolk 2014, p.13.
24. van der Kolk 2014, p.17.
25. van der Kolk and Ducey 1989.
26. van der Kolk 2014, p.17.
27. Phillips 2010.
28. www.theguardian.com, 10 May 2016.

Act 2 – Scene 3

1. Brook 1968.
2. Brook 1968, p.32.
3. Brook 1968, p.33.
4. Brook 1968, p.11.
5. Miller 1997.
6. Chödrön 2003.
7. Maté 2008, p.1.
8. Maté 2008, pp.31–32.
9. Meltzer 2011.
10. Cesarone 1998.
11. Meltzer 2011.
12. Stuart Brown quotes *The Washington Post* in its reporting that at least ten South Korean gamers died in 2005 from blood clotting that can result in people sitting for many hours at a time.
13. Tumbokon n.d.
14. McGonigal 2012.
15. McGonigal 2015.
16. Bush 1989.
17. Nachmanovitch 1990, p.127.
18. Nachmanovitch 1990, p.126.
19. Terr 1990, p.238.
20. Freud 1991, p.315.
21. Winnicott 1965, p.145.
22. Epstein 2005, p.158.
23. The Challenge of Change Resilience programme was devised by Dr Derek Roger based on the question: What is it that makes some people more vulnerable to stress and others more resilient? See www.challengeofchange.co.nz.
24. Roger 2016, p.262.
25. Freud 1991, p.317.
26. Axline 1947.
27. Axline 1947, pp.69–70.
28. In the NSPCC (National Society for the Prevention of Cruelty to Children) Child Sexual Abuse Consultancy in Manchester and the NSPCC, Stockport, UK.
29. Kathleen Nader writes about this in her article 'Guilt Following Traumatic Events' (2001).
30. Sangharakshita 1999; Chödrön 2003.
31. Gil 2006.

Act 2 – Scene 4

1. Jung 1946.
2. Jung 1959, p.21.
3. Von Franz 1974, p.5.
4. Icon, www.icon-art.com.

5. Whitmont 1991, p.12.
6. Maté 2008, p.2.
7. Conger 1988, p.91.
8. Zweig and Abrams 1991, p.xvii.
9. Preece 2006, p.191.
10. Cipriani 2009, pp.221–222.
11. Scott Peck 1991.
12. Now Jessica Williams Ciemnyjewski.
13. Williams Saunders 2001, p.xx.
14. Personal communication 2016. Professor Jo Clarke, short biography.
15. Leviticus 16:8, 10, 26.
16. Scott Peck 1991, pp.179–180.
17. Buber 1984, p.111.
18. Preece 2006, p.183.
19. McGuire and Hull 1972, p.158.
20. May 1969, pp.136–137.
21. According to Jung, the process of individuation is one of psychic integration where the personal and the collective unconscious are brought into consciousness and assimilated into the whole personality. This process comes about through the use of dreams and active imagination. In other words, through play. See Jung 1956.
22. May 1969, p.121.
23. Diamond 1991, p.183.
24. May 1969, p.137.
25. *The Guardian*, 11 December 2012, p.11.
26. Peacock 2009, p.27.
27. Lecoq 2002, p.157.
28. Peacock 2009, p.28.
29. Sinclair 1985.
30. Lecoq 2002, p.124.
31. Peacock 2009, p.32.
32. Mason 2002, p.52.
33. Mason 2002, p.53.
34. Billington 1984.
35. Billington 1984, p.321.
36. Peacock 2009, p.118.
37. UK Council for Psychotherapy conference 'Young People and Social Networking', London 2011.
38. Ross 2011, p.199.
39. Boal 2000.
40. Frey-Rohn 2001, p.xvii.
41. Winnicott 1971, p.63.
42. Landy 1994.
43. Jung 1991, p.212.
44. Jung 1995.
45. Maté 2008, p.37.

Act 3 – Scene 1

1. Blofield 1958, p.41.
2. William Wordsworth, 'Intimations of Immortality'.
3. Wallace 1999, p.22.
4. Chödrön 2003.
5. Batchelor 1998, p.11.
6. Nirmala 2010.
7. Nelson 1994, p.xx.
8. Epstein 1998, p.xix.

9. Feldman 2005, p.39.
10. Chögyam Trungpa Rinpoche refers to the Three Lords of Materialism as the Lord of Form who rules the world of physical materialism; the Lord of Speech who rules the realm of psychological materialism; and the Lord of the Mind who rules the realm of spiritual materialism. See Chödrön 2007.
11. Sogyal Rinpoche 1996.
12. Batchelor 1998, p.22.
13. Feldman 2005, p.9.
14. Chödrön 2001, p.28.
15. Epstein 1998, p.xix.
16. Epstein 1998, p.124.
17. Wallace 1999, p.21.
18. Wallace 1999, p.12.
19. Feldman 2005, p.123.
20. The quotation is taken from Petrūska Clarkson's book *The Therapeutic Relationship* (1995). See Act 1, Scene 1.
21. Wallace 1999, p.13.
22. Wallace 1999, p.15.
23. Famously, at the Mind and Life Conference in 1990, Buddhist meditation teacher Sharon Salzberg asked the Dalai Lama how he might address the problem of low self-esteem among students. His Holiness was baffled by the question as such widespread misery was alien to him. He repeated, though, what the Buddha had said: that all human beings are seeking an end to suffering and a yearning for happiness.
24. Wallace 1999, p.89.
25. Welwood 2000.
26. *Udāna* 47.
27. Wallace 1999, p.107.
28. Wallace 1999, p.151.
29. Gil Fronsdal, 'Equanimity', Insight Meditation Center, 29 May 2004, www.insight meditationcenter.org (accessed 21 July 2009).
30. Epstein 1998, p.120.
31. Jung 1991.
32. Campbell 1988, p.5.
33. Campbell 1988, p.3.
34. Hougham 2006, p.3.
35. Anderson 1997; Perrault 2010; Zipes 2012; Grimm and Grimm 2014.
36. Perera 1981; Carter 1991, 2005; Schertmann 1993; Warner 1995; Feldman 2005; Estés 2008, 2013; Maitland 2012.
37. Bly and Woodman 1998, p.179.
38. Starhawk 1988. Starhawk is a prolific and well-respected writer and activist of contemporary 'earth-based spirituality' (https://starhawk.org, accessed 23 January 2017). She is one of the most prominent leaders in the revival of Goddess religion.
39. Perera 1981, p.21.
40. Perera 1981, p.24.
41. A powerful exercise when working with the myth is to explore the chakras and what is blocking these energy centres. For instance, the crown chakra orients to self-knowledge, so the enquiry might be: What is obstructing my relationship to my spiritual connection? Or the brow/third eye chakra which orients to self-reflection, where the enquiry may be: What is obstructing me from seeing the bigger picture? Perera was not aware that the Sumerian-Akkadian culture would have been aware of the chakras.
42. We see the Witness archetype in many other myths – for example, Ariadne in Greek mythology, who provides Theseus with the way out of the Minotaur's labyrinth using her golden thread.
43. Perera 1981, p.68.
44. Perera 1981, p.70.
45. Perera 1981, p.73.

Act 3 – Scene 2

1. Federico Garcia Lorca (1898–1936).
2. Winterson 1996.
3. Regrettably, it is impossible to do justice to their work within these pages.
4. Winterson 1996, p.12.
5. Tharp 2003, p.31.
6. Rosy Tydeman, www.devonartistnetwork.co.uk.
7. David calls himself a tradigital painter as he moved from traditional painting into the digital world. He uses the computer as an expansive tool – he has over 16 million colours available to him.
8. Gompertz 2015.
9. Tharp 2003, p.42.
10. Winterson 1996, p.6.
11. Winterson 1996, p.10.
12. Brook 1968, p.55.
13. Yentob 2010.
14. Winnicott 1971, p.114.
15. Although as can be seen in Figure 2, Act 1, Scene 4, the space in between infant and mother-figure is not an equal space. The maternal object's effect upon the infant is, arguably, far more influential than vice versa, the mother's cloak having more solidity than her baby's fledgling one.
16. Khan 2014.
17. Tharp 2003, p.40.
18. Perry 2010.
19. Ernest Hemingway quoted in Tharp 2003, p.168.
20. Grainger 2006, p.6.
21. Motion 2010.
22. Jackie Juno, https://jackiejuno.com/poetry.
23. Hillman 1983, p.81.
24. Kavran 2008; 'Karadzic: Psychiatrist turned "Butcher of Bosnia"', CNN, 22 July 2008.
25. O'Brien 2015.
26. O'Brien 2015.
27. Harris 2000; see also Gernsbacher, Goldsmith and Robertson 1992.
28. O'Farrell 2016a.
29. O'Farrell 2016b.
30. Perry 2010.
31. Perry 2016a, 2016b.
32. Haig 2016.
33. Jones 2016.
34. De Mille 1991.
35. Grotowski 1975.
36. Brook 1968, p.52.
37. Grainger 2006, p.5.
38. Bennett 1923, p.290.
39. Grainger 2006, p.6.
40. Written by Daphne Thomas.
41. Jenkyns 1996, p.136.
42. Dijana Milosevic, ECArTe Conference, Paris, France, 12 September 2013.
43. Brook 1968, p.44.
44. Brook 1968, p.44.
45. Brook 1968, p.43.
46. Herman 1992, p.33.
47. Hornstein 2012, p.xi.
48. Prinzhorn's book *Artistry of the Mentally Ill: A Contribution to the Psychology and Psychopathology of Configuration* led to psychiatric art, which later became known as 'outsider art'.

49. Introduction by Marina Warner in Baker 2008.
50. Dialectical Behaviour Therapy.
51. Baker 2008, p.81.
52. Baker 2008, p.214.
53. Baker 2008, p.214.
54. Baker 2008, p.214.
55. Baker 2008, p.214.

Act 3 – Scene 3

1. Di Gammage 2013.
2. Epstein 2005, p.159.
3. Jessica Duchen, *Jewish Chronicle*, 12 March 2010.
4. Both films made by Christopher Nupen.
5. Muller and Piechocki 2007.
6. I am aware that David Pelzer's account has been disputed by Pat Jordan ('Dysfunction for Dollars', *New York Times*, 28 July 2002), supported by contra-accounts from his maternal grandmother and younger brother. I cannot say whether David Pelzer's account is accurate or not, as I was not there; however, having worked in the field of childhood abuse for many years, I am very familiar with the denial, minimalizing and scapegoating that goes on in many families.
7. Carr and James 2008, p.70.
8. Carr and James 2008, p.204 (emphasis added).
9. The Forgiveness Project (http://theforgivenessproject.com) is a charity founded by journalist Marina Cantacuzino in 2004 as a forum for telling real stories of people whose response to experiencing injury and harm was not to seek revenge but rather a path of reconciliation and restoration. Also see Marina Cantacuzino's book *The Forgiveness Project: Stories for a Vengeful Age* (Jessica Kingsley Publishers, 2016).
10. Oddie 2008. On leaving Marjons in 2010, David Oddie established The Indra Congress (www.theindracongress.com). See also Oddie 2015.
11. www.dailylifeltd.co.uk.
12. 'Experts by experience' is a term now frequently used to identify psychiatric survivors – current and former patients. The Experts by Experience project is now a well-established organization in mental health in south-west England. See Hornstein 2012, pp.132–133.
13. Kelly 2014.
14. Esiri and Kelly 2012.
15. Sissay 2008.
16. Khaleeli 2015.
17. M. Lahad in Jennings 1992.
18. Lahad, Shacham and Ayalon 2013.
19. Lahad 2000.
20. Lahad 2000, p.38 (emphasis added).
21. Epstein 2005, p.157.
22. British Association of Play Therapy Annual Conference, SOAS, London, 2005.
23. Mary Booker (private communication, 28 September 2016) is a psychodramatist, dramatherapist, supervisor and author.
24. For further reading, see Rob Preece, *The Alchemical Buddha* (Mudra Publications, 2000) and *The Wisdom of Imperfection* (Snow Lion Publications, 2013); Radmila Moacanin, *The Essence of Jung's Psychology and Tibetan Buddhism* (Wisdom Publications, 2003); Jeremy D. Safran (ed.) *Psychoanalysis and Buddhism: An Unfolding Dialogue* (Wisdom Publications, 2003).
25. Hillman 1983, p.55.
26. Burbea 2014.
27. Winnicott 1971, p.38.
28. Epstein 2005, p.158.
29. Francis Deas, private communication, Karuna Institute.

30. Sadly, just because a child has been removed from his or her original home and placed in care does not mean the child is actually in a safe environment. Caring for a traumatized child can, and frequently does, trigger a carer's own unresolved trauma history. Any therapist working with children will know the importance of a support system that can hold both the child and the carers.
31. Lowenfeld 1991, p.17.
32. The word 'detachment' in the English language does not really do justice to this vital component so intrinsic to the healing process. To this end, I consulted colleagues Sarah Scoble and Mary Booker. We discovered a word none of us knew previously – manumit – which means to set free, release from bondage, unfetter and – one I especially like – disemprison. The word 'manumit' originates from late middle English and comes from the Latin *manumittere*, and *manu emitter* in French, which literally means 'to send forth from one's hand'.
33. Sills 2009, p.11.
34. Tolle 2009, p.6.
35. Gil 2006, p.160.
36. Psychoanalyst Ronald Fairbairn (1994) coined this term to describe how the child discovers that it is slightly less intolerable to take the blame for the abuse or neglect than to hold the parent responsible.
37. Levine 2015, p.xxi.
38. Fiona Lothian, private communication.
39. Jung 1960, p.82.

Act 3 – Scene 4

1. The Angel, Bax n.d., p.12.
2. Welty 1971, p.9.
3. With thanks to Heather Mason.
4. Kornfield 2008, p.369.
5. Feldman 2005, p.39.
6. Macy and Young Brown 1998.
7. Chödrön 2001, p.28.
8. John Allan, http://buddhanet.net, accessed 9 November 2016.
9. With thanks to Sarah Scoble for this sharing.
10. Positive Outlooks: Posttraumatic Growth, www.writingforrecovery.wordpress.com (accessed 10 November 2016).
11. Amy Jones, personal assistant to David Pelzer, personal correspondence from David Pelzer.
12. Richard Rorty in Batchelor 1998.
13. Gompertz 2015, p.174. See Popovic and Miller 2015.
14. Bax n.d., p.9.

References

Adler, G. (1966) *Studies in Analytical Psychology*. London: Hodder & Stoughton.

Ainsworth, M., Blehar, M.C., Waters, E. and Wall, S. (2015) *Patterns of Attachment*. London: Routledge.

Anderson, H.C. (1997) *The Complete Fairy Tales*. Ware, UK: Wordsworth Editions.

Axline, V. (1947, reprinted 1989) *Play Therapy*. London: Churchill Livingstone.

Baggini, J. (2011) *The Ego Trick: What Does it Mean to Be You?* London: Granta Publications.

Baker, B. (2008) *Diary Drawings: Mental Illness and Me*. London: Profile Books.

Batchelor, S. (1998) *Buddhism without Beliefs: A Contemporary Guide to Awakening*. London: Bloomsbury Publishing.

Batchelor, M. (2007) *Let Go: A Buddhist Guide to Breaking Free of Habits*. Somerville, MA: Wisdom Publications.

Bateson, G. (1972) *Steps to an Ecology of Mind*. Northvale, NJ: Aronson Publishing.

Bax, C. (n.d.) *The Cloak*. London: Samuel French.

Baylor, B. and Parnall, P. (1997) *The Other Way to Listen*. New York, NY: Aladdin Paperbacks.

Behncke Izquierdo, I. (2011) TED Talk: 'Evolution's gift of play from bonobo apes to humans', March 2011.

Behncke Izquierdo, I. (2014) *Museum of Curiosity*. BBC Radio 4, 10 November.

Bennett, A. (1923) *The Wisdom of the Aryas*. London and New York, NY: Paul, Trench, Trubner & Co.

Billington, S. (1984) *A Social History of the Fool*. Sussex: Harvester Press.

Blake, W. (1977) *The Complete Poems*. London: Penguin Classics.

Blofield, J. (1958, reprinted 2006) *The Zen Teaching of Huang Po: On the Transmission of Mind*. New York, NY: Grove Press.

Bly, R. and Woodman, M. (1998) *The Maiden King*. New York, NY: Henry Holt & Co.

Boal, A. (2000) *Theatre of the Oppressed*, 3rd edn. London: Pluto.

Bowlby, J. (1988) *A Secure Base*. London: Routledge.

Braithwaite, R. (2007) 'Feeling the pressure? workplace stress and how to avoid it.' *Community Care 1654*, 28–29.

Brazelton, T.B. and Cramer, B.G. (1990) *The Earliest Relationship: Parents, Infants and the Drama of Early Attachment*. New York, NY: Perseus Books.

Brook, P. (1968, reprinted 1996) *The Empty Space*. New York, NY, and London: Touchstone.

Brown, B. (2010) *The Gifts of Imperfection: Let Go of Who You Think You're Supposed to Be and Embrace Who You Are*. Center City, MN: Hazelden.

Brown, S. (2008) TED Talk: 'Play is more than just fun', May 2008.

Brown, S. (2010) *Play: How it Shapes the Brain, Opens the Imagination, and Invigorates the Soul*. New York, NY: Penguin Group.

Brunt, C.R. (2014) 'A Name is an Anchor and a Coffin.' Unpublished.

Buber, M. (1984) *Good and Evil*. Magnolia, MA: Peter Smith.

Burbea, R. (2014) Path of the Imaginal Parts 1, 2 and 3 (7 December). Recorded teachings on www.dharmaseed.org.

Burghardt, G.M. (1975) 'Behavioral Research on Common Animals in Small Zoos.' In *Research in Zoos and Aquariums*. Washington DC: National Academy of Sciences.

Bush, K. (1989) 'Deeper Understanding', *The Sensual World*. Columbia Records.

Campbell, J. (1988) *The Power of Myth*. New York, NY: Doubleday.

Carr, C. and James, J. (2008) *The Sky is Always There*. London: Canterbury Press.

Carter, A. (1991) *The Virago Book of Fairy Tales*. London: Virago.

Carter, A. (2005) *Angela Carter's Book of Fairy Tales*. London: Virago.

Casement, P. (1985) *On Learning from the Patient*. London: Routledge.

Cesarone, B. (1998) 'Video games: research, ratings, recommendations. ERIC Digest.' Available at https://eric.ed.gov/?q=Cesarone+Video+Games&id=ED365477 (accessed 18 April 2017).

Chödrön, P. (2001) *The Places That Scare You*. Boston, MA: Shambhala Publications.

Chödrön, P. (2003) *From Fear to Fearlessness: Teaching on the Four Great Catalysts of Awakening*. Boulder, CO: Sounds True.

Chödrön, P. (2007) 'A Guide to Fearlessness in Difficult Times and Crazy Wisdom: The Life and Times of Chögyam Trungpa Rinpoche.' Available at www.crazywisdom.myfilmblog.com (accessed 29 March 2017).

Cipriani, D. (2009) *Children's Rights and the Minimum Age of Criminal Responsibility: A Global Perspective*. Surrey: Ashgate.

Clarke, J. (2016) Private communication.

Clarkson, P. (1995) *The Therapeutic Relationship: In Psychoanalysis, Counselling Psychology and Psychotherapy*. London: Whurr Publishers.

Conger, J.P. (1988) *Jung and Reich: The Body as Shadow*. Berkeley, CA: North Atlantic Books.

Conrad, D. and Kellar-Guenther, Y. (2006) 'Compassion fatigue, burnout, and compassion satisfaction among Colorado child protection workers.' *Child Abuse and Neglect 30*, 10, 1071–1080.

Damasio, A. (2000) *The Feeling of What Happens: Body, Emotion and the Making of Consciousness*. London: Vintage.

Darwin, C. (2006) *On the Origin of Species*. London: Penguin Classics.

DeLoache, J. and Gottlieb, A. (1998) 'Pretending to be Ogre and Tricksters in Huli, Papa New Guinea.' In L. Goldman (ed.) *Child's Play: Myth, Mimesis and Make-Believe*. New York, NY: Berg.

De Mille, A. (1991) *Martha: The Life and Work of Martha Graham*. New York, NY: Random House.

Diamond, S. (1991) 'Redeeming Our Devils and Demons.' In C. Zweig and J. Abrams (eds) *Meeting the Shadow: The Hidden Power of the Dark Side of Human Nature*. Los Angeles, CA: Jeremy Tarcher.

Dick-Read, G. (1942, reprinted 2004) *Childbirth without Fear: The Principles and Practice of Natural Childbirth*. London: Pinter & Martin.

Dimock, E.C. (1989) Paper presented at 'The Concept of Līlā in South Asia' Conference, the Center for Study of World Religions, Harvard University, April 1989.

Eberle, S.G. (2014) 'The elements of play – toward a philosophy and a definition of play.' *Journal of Play 6*, 2, 214–233.

Elkind, D. (2007) *The Power of Play: How Spontaneous, Imaginative Activities Lead to Happier, Healthier Children*. Cambridge, MA: Da Capo Press.

Epstein, M. (1998) 'The Buddha goes to therapy.' *Psychology Today*, 1 May. Available at www.psychologytoday.com (accessed 6 June 2017).

Epstein, M. (2005) *Open to Desire: The Truth about What the Buddha Taught*. New York, NY: Gotham Books/Random House.

Epstein, M. (2013) *The Trauma of Everyday Life*. New York, NY, and London: Penguin.

Esiri, A. and Kelly, R. (eds) (2012) *iF: A Treasury of Poems for Almost Every Possibility*. Edinburgh: Canongate Books.

Estés, P.C. (2008) *Women Who Run with the Wolves: Contacting the Power of the Wild Woman*. London: Rider.

Estés, P.C. (2013) *Untie the Strong Woman: Blessed Mother's Immaculate Love for the Wild Soul*. Louisville, CO: Sounds True.

Fairbairn, W.R.D. (1994) *Psychoanalytic Studies of the Personality*. London: Routledge.

Feldman, C. (2005) *Woman Awake: Women Practicing Buddhism*, 2nd edn. Berkeley, CA: Rodmell Press.

Figley, C. (1995) *Compassion Fatigue: Coping with Secondary Traumatic Stress in Those Who Treat the Traumatized*. New York, NY: Routledge.

Fraiberg, S. (1977) *Insights from the Blind (Human Horizons)*. London: Souvenir Press.

Freud, S. (1920) *Beyond the Pleasure Principle*. London: Penguin.

Freud, S. (1991) 'Fixation to Traumas: The Unconscious.' In *Introductory Lectures on Psychoanalysis*. London: Penguin.

Friere, P. (1968/1970, reprinted 2001) *Pedagogy of the Oppressed*. London and New York, NY: Continuum International Publishing Group.

Frey-Rohn, L. (2001) *From Freud to Jung: A Comparative Study of the Psychology of the Unconscious*. Dorset: Shambhala.

Fromm, E. (1983, reprinted 1995) *The Art of Loving*. London: Thorsons.

Gernsbacher, M.A., Goldsmith, H.H. and Robertson, R.R.W. (1992) 'Do readers mentally represent characters' emotional states?' *Cognition and Emotion 6*, 2, 89–111.

Gil, E. (2006) *Helping Abused and Traumatized Children: Integrating Directive and Nondirective Approaches*. New York, NY, and London: Guilford Press.

Gomez, L. (1997) *An Introduction to Object Relations*. London: Free Association Books.

Gompertz, W. (2015) *Think Like an Artist...and Lead a More Creative, Productive Life*. London: Penguin.

Göncü, A. and Perone, A. (2005) 'Pretend play as a life-span activity.' *Topoi 24*, 2, 137–147.

Goodwin, R.E. (1995) 'The Play World of Sanskrit Poetry.' In W.S. Sax (ed.) *The Gods at Play: Līlā in South Asia*. Oxford: Oxford University Press.

Grainger, R. (2006) 'Why actors act?' *Dramatherapy 28*, 1, 3–8.

Greenburg, D. (1991) *How to Make Yourself Miserable*. New York, NY: Vintage.

Grimm, J. and Grimm, W. (2014) *The Original Folk and Fairy Tales of the Brothers Grimm: The Complete First Edition*. Princeton, NJ: Princeton University Press.

Grotowski, J. (1975) *Towards a Poor Theatre*. London: Methuen.

Guerrière, D. (1980) 'Physis, Sophia, Psyche.' In J. Sallis and K. Maly (eds) *Heraclitean Fragments: A Companion Volume to the Heidegger/Fink Seminar on Heraclitus*. Huntsville, AL: University of Alabama Press.

Haig, M. (2016) '*The Descent of Man* review – a man's man is yesterday's hero.' *The Guardian*, 23 October.

Hanson, R. (2009) *The Buddha's Brain: The Practical Neuroscience of Happiness, Love and Wisdom*. Oakland, CA: New Harbinger Publications.

Harding, S. (2014) *A Natural History of Me!* BBC Radio 4, 18 April.

Harris, P.L. (2000) *The Work of the Imagination*. Oxford: Blackwell Publishers.

Harris, S. (2014) *Waking Up: A Guide to Spirituality without Religion*. New York, NY: Simon & Schuster.

Hawley, J.S. (1995) 'Every Play a Play within a Play.' In W.S. Sax (ed.) *The Gods at Play: Līlā in South Asia*. Oxford: Oxford University Press.

Haynes, C. (2013) *The Human Zoo*. BBC Radio 4, 9 April 2013.

Herman, J.L. (1992) *Trauma and Recovery*. New York, NY: Basic Books.

Hillman, J. (1983) *Healing Fiction*. Barrytown, NY: Station Hill Press.

Hornstein, G.A. (2012) *Agnes's Jacket: A Psychologist's Search for the Meaning of Madness*. Ross-on-Wye: PCCS Books.

Hougham, R. (2006) 'Numinosity, symbol and ritual in the Sesame approach.' *British Association of Dramatherapy Journal 28*, 2, 3–7.

Hougham, R. (2013) Reflections on Duende ECArTE (European Consortium for Arts Therapies Education) Conference, Paris.

Hughes, D. (1998, reprinted 2006) *Building the Bonds of Attachment: Awakening Love in Deeply Troubled Children*. Lanham, MD: Jason Aronson Books.

Hughes, D. (2016) *Parenting a Child Who Has Experienced Trauma*. London: CoramBAAF.

Jenkinson, S. (2001) *The Genius of Play: Celebrating the Spirit of Childhood*. Stroud: Hawthorn Press.

Jenkyns, M. (1996) *The Play's the Thing: Exploring Text in Drama*. London: Routledge.

Jennings, S. (1987) *Dramatherapy: Theory and Practice 1*. London: Routledge.

Jennings, S. (ed.) (1992) *Dramatherapy: Theory and Practice 2*. London: Routledge.

Jennings, S. (1999) *Developmental Play Therapy: Playing and Health*. London: Jessica Kingsley Publishers.

Jones, J. (2016) 'Quote me on this, Grayson: you're not a true artist at all.' *The Guardian*, 10 October.

Jung, C.G. (1938) 'Psychology and Religion.' In *Complete Works 11. Psychology and Religion: West and East*. Princeton, NJ: Princeton University Press/Bollingen Foundation.

Jung, C.G. (1946) 'The fight with the Shadow.' *The Listener 36*, 641.

Jung, C.G. (1959) *The Archetypes and the Collective Unconscious*. New York, NY: Bollingen Foundation.

Jung, C.G. (1960) *The Structure and Dynamics of the Psyche.* East Sussex and New York, NY: Routledge and Kegan Paul.

Jung, C.G. (1976) (ed.) *The Portable Jung.* London: Joseph Campbell, Penguin.

Jung, C.G. (1981) 'Archetypes and the Collective Unconscious.' In G. Adler and R.F.C. Hull (eds and trans.) *The Collected Works of C.G. Jung: Vol. 9, Part 1.* Princeton, NJ: Princeton University Press/ Bollingen Foundation.

Jung, C.G. (1991) *The Archetypes and the Collective Unconscious: Collected Works of C.G. Jung Vol. 9.* London: Routledge.

Jung, C.G. (1995) *Memories, Dreams, Reflections.* London: Fontana Press.

Jung, F.F. (1956) *An Introduction to Jung's Psychology.* London: Penguin.

Kalsched, D. (1996) *The Inner World of Trauma.* London and New York, NY: Routledge.

Kavran, O. (2008) 'Bosnian Serb leader Radovan Karadzic arrested: what lies ahead?' *The Washington Post,* 23 July.

Keats, J. (1994) *The Works of John Keats.* Ware: Wordsworth Editions.

Keats, J. (2012) *The Letters of John Keats,* ed. H.E. Rollins. Cambridge: Cambridge University Press.

Kelly, R. (2014) *Black Rainbow.* London: Hodder & Stoughton.

Kennedy, A.L. (2013) *A Natural History of Me!* BBC Radio 4, 18 April.

Kerényi, C. (1976) *Dionysos: Archetypal Image of Indestructible Life.* Princeton, NJ: Princeton University Press.

Khaleeli, H. (2015) 'Lemn Sissay, foster child, poet and university chancellor: everything I know about myself comes from Manchester.' *The Guardian,* 26 June.

Khan, A. (2014) *What Do Artists Do All Day?* BBC Four, 15 October.

King, M.L. Jr (1967) *Where Do We Go from Here: Chaos or Community?* Boston, MA: Beacon Press.

Kinsella, M.T. and Monk, C. (2009) 'Impact of maternal stress, depression and anxiety on fetal neurobehavioral development.' *Clinical Obstetrics and Gynecology 52,* 3, 425–440.

Kipling, A. (2011) 'The Play's the Thing…' In J. Coventon (ed.) *Drama to Inspire.* Stoke-on-Trent: Trentham Books.

Klein, M. (1975) *Love, Guilt and Reparation.* New York, NY: Simon & Schuster.

Kornfield, J. (2008) *The Wise Heart: Buddhist Psychology for the West.* London and New York, NY: Random House.

Kübler-Ross, E. (2014) *On Death and Dying.* New York, NY: Scribner/Simon & Schuster.

Kurtz, R. (1990) *Body-Centred Psychotherapy – The Hakomi Method: The Integrated Use of Mindfulness, Nonviolence, and the Body.* Mendocino, CA: LifeRhythm.

Landy, R. (1994) *Drama Therapy Concepts: Theories and Practices.* Springfield, IL: Charles C. Thomas.

Lahad, M. (2000) *Creative Supervision: The Use of Expressive Arts Methods in Supervision and Self-Supervision.* London: Jessica Kingsley Publishers.

Lahad, M., Shacham, M. and Ayalon, O. (2013) *The 'BASIC PH' Model of Coping and Resiliency: Theory, Research and Cross-Cultural Application.* London: Jessica Kingsley Publishers.

Lecoq, J. (2002) *The Moving Body.* London: Methuen.

Levendosky, A. and Graham-Bermann, S.A. (2001) 'Parenting in battered women: the effects of domestic violence on women and their children.' *Journal of Family Violence 16,* 2, 171–192.

Levine, P. (1997) *Waking the Tiger: Healing Trauma – The Innate Capacity to Transform Overwhelming Experiences.* Berkeley, CA: North Atlantic Books.

Levine, P. (2000) *Healing Trauma: A Pioneering Program for Restoring the Wisdom of Your Body.* Boulder, CO: Sounds True.

Levine, P. (2015) *Trauma and Memory – Brain and Body in a Search for the Living Past: A Practical Guide for Understanding and Working with Traumatic Memory.* Berkeley, CA: North Atlantic Books.

Long-Crowell, E. (2015) 'The Halo Effect: Definition, Advantages and Disadvantages.' Available at http://study.com/academy/lesson/the-halo-effect-definition-advantages-disadvantages.html (accessed 29 March 2017).

Lowenfeld, M. (1991) *Play in Childhood.* Eastbourne: Sussex Academic Press.

Macdonald, H. (2014) *H is for Hawk.* London: Jonathan Cape.

Macy, J. and Young Brown, M. (1998) *Coming Back to Life: Practices to Reconnect Our Lives, Our World.* Gabriola Island, BC: New Society Publishers.

Maitland, S. (2012) *Gossip from the Forest: The Tangled Roots of Our Forests and Fairytales.* London: Granta.

Marks-Tarlow, T. (2010) 'The fractal self at play.' *American Journal of Play 3,* 31–62.

Marvell, A. (2005) *The Complete Poems*. London: Penguin Classics.

Maslow, A. (1968, reprinted 2011) *Toward a Psychology of Being*. Radford, VA: Wilder Publications.

Mason, B. (2002) 'The Well of Possibilities: Theoretical and Practical Uses of Lecoq's Teaching.' In F. Chamberlain and R. Yarrow (eds) *Jacques Lecoq and the British Theatre*. London: Routledge Harwood.

Maté, G. (2008) *In the Realm of the Hungry Ghosts: Close Encounters with Addictions*. Toronto: Alfred A. Knopf Canada.

May, R. (1969) *Love and Will*. London and New York, NY: W.W. Norton.

May, R. (1975) *The Courage to Create*. London and New York, NY: W.W. Norton.

McGonigal, J. (2010) TED Talk: 'Gaming can make a better world', February 2010.

McGonigal, J. (2012) *Reality is Broken: Why Games Make Us Better and How They Can Change the World*. London: Jonathan Cape.

McGonigal, J. (2015) *SuperBetter: How a Gameful Life Can Make You Stronger, Happier, Braver and More Resilient*. London: HarperCollins.

McGuire, W. and Hull, R.F.C. (eds) (1972) *C.G. Jung Speaking: Interviews and Encounters, Bollingen Series XVII*. Princeton, NJ: Princeton University Press.

Meltzer, T. (2011) 'I was a games addict.' *The Guardian*, 11 March. Available at www.theguardian.com/technology/2011/mar/11/i-was-games-addict (accessed 17 April 2017).

Miller, A. (1979, reprinted 2008) *The Drama of Being a Child*. London: Virago.

Miller, A. (1997) *Breaking Down the Wall of Silence*. London: Virago.

Monk, C., Fifer, W.P., Myers, M.M., Sloan, R.P., Trien, L. and Hurtado, A. (2000) 'Maternal stress responses and anxiety during pregnancy: effects on foetal heart rate.' *Developmental Psychobiology 36*, 1, 67–77.

Montagu, A. (1989) *Growing Young*. Westport, CT: Bergin & Garvey.

Motion, A. (2010) 'Poetry Schmoetry.' *Off the Page*. BBC Radio 4, 17 June.

Muller, M. and Piechocki, R. (2007) *A Garden of Eden in Hell: The Life of Alice Herz-Sommer*. London: Macmillan.

Murray, L. and Andrews, L. (2000) *The Social Baby: Understanding Babies' Communication from Birth*. Richmond: The Children's Project.

Nachmanovitch, S. (1990) *Free Play: Improvisation in Life and Art*. New York, NY: Jeremy P. Tarcher/Putnam.

Nader, K. (2001) 'Guilt Following Traumatic Events.' Available at www.giftfromwithin.org/html/Guilt-Following-Traumatic-Events.html (accessed 29 March 2017).

Nelson, J. (1994) *Healing the Split: Integrating Spirit into Our Understanding of the Mentally Ill*. Albany, NY: State University of New York Press.

Nirmala (2010) Endless Satsang website. Available at www.endless-satsang.com (accessed 9 April 2017).

O'Brien, E. (2015) Interview on *Open Book with Mariella Frostrup*. BBC Radio 4, 17 October.

O'Connor, T.G., Ben-Shlomo, Y., Heron, J., Golding, J., Adams, D. and Glover, V. (2005) 'Prenatal anxiety predicts individual differences in cortisol in pre-adolescent children.' *Biological Psychiatry 58*, 3, 211–217.

Oddie, D. (2008) 'How do we struggle to get a few thousand pounds when billions are spent on the arms trade?' *The Guardian*, 10 June.

Oddie, D. (2015) *A Journey of Art and Conflict: Weaving Indra's Net*. Bristol: Intellect Books.

O'Farrell, M. (2016a) *This Must Be the Place*. London: Tinder Press.

O'Farrell, M. (2016b) 'I have three seconds before she draws blood: life with extreme eczema.' *The Guardian*, 21 May.

Oliver, M. (1990) 'This Summer's Day.' *New and Selected Poems, Volume One*. Boston: Beacon Press.

O'Sullivan, S. (2016) *It's All in Your Head*. London: Vintage.

Paracelsus (1958) *Paracelsus: Selected Writings*, 2nd edn (ed. J. Jacobi, trans. N. Guterman). New York, NY: Pantheon Press.

Peacock, L. (2009) *Serious Play: Modern Clown Performance*. Bristol: Intellect Books.

Pelzer, D. (1995) *A Child called 'It': One Child's Courage to Survive*. Deerfield Beach, FL: Health Communications.

Pelzer, D. (1999) *A Man Named Dave: A Story of Triumph and Forgiveness*. New York, NY: Plume.

Perera, B.S. (1981) *Descent to the Goddess: A Way of Initiation for Women*. Toronto: Inner City Books.

Perrault, C. (2010) *The Complete Fairy Tales (Oxford World Classics)*. Oxford: Oxford University Press.

Perry, G. (2010) *Imagine – Art is Child's Play*. BBC1, 22 June.

Perry, G. (2014) *Who Are You?* Channel 4, October and November 2014.

Perry, G. (2016a) *All Man*. Channel 4, 5, 12 and 19 May.

Perry, G. (2016b) *The Descent of Man*. London: Allen Lane.

Phillips, A. (2010) *Imagine – Art is Child's Play*. BBC1, 22 June.

Piaget, J. (1951) *Play, Dreams and Imitation in Childhood*. London: Routledge.

Popovic, S. and Miller, M. (2015) *Blueprint for Revolution: How to Use Rice Pudding, Lego Men, and Other Non-Violent Techniques to Galvanise Communities, Overthrow Dictators, or Simply Change the World*. London: Scribe.

Preece, R. (2006) *The Psychology of Buddhist Tantra*. Ithaca, NY, and Boulder, CO: Snow Lion Publications.

Roger, D. (2016) 'Rumination, Stress, and Emotion.' In G. Fink (ed.) *Stress: Concepts, Cognition, Emotion, and Behavior. Handbook of Stress, Vol. 1*. Burlington, CA: Academic Press.

Rosen, M. (2010) *Imagine – Art is Child's Play*. BBC1, 22 June.

Rosenberg, M. (2003) (revised edition) *Nonviolent Communication: A Language of Life*. Encinitas, CA: PuddleDancer Press.

Ross, M. (2011) *Cultivating the Arts in Education and Therapy*. London and New York, NY: Routledge.

Rothschild, B. (2000) *The Body Remembers: The Psychophysiology of Trauma and Trauma Treatment*. New York, NY: W.W. Norton & Company.

Roy, A. (2004) *The God of Small Things*. London: HarperCollins.

Sangharakshita (1999) *The Bodhisattva Ideal: Wisdom and Compassion in Buddhism*. Birmingham: Windhorse Press.

Sax, W.S. (ed.) (1995) *The Gods at Play: Līlā in South Asia*. New York, NY, and Oxford: Oxford University Press.

Schertmann, J. (1993) *The Stepmother in Fairy Tales*. Boston, MA: Sigo Press.

Schierlitz, T. (2008) 'Why do we play?' *New York Times Magazine*, 17 February.

Schoemaker, P.J.H. (2011) *Brilliant Mistakes: Finding Success on the Far Side of Failure*. Philadelphia, PA: Wharton Digital Press.

Schore, A. (1994, reprinted 2015) *Affect Regulation and the Origin of the Self*. Mahwah, NJ: Lawrence Erlbaum Associates/London: Routledge.

Scott Peck, M. (1991) 'Healing Human Evil.' In C. Zweig and J. Abrams (eds) *Meeting the Shadow: The Hidden Power of the Dark Side of Human Nature*. Los Angeles, CA: Jeremy P. Tarcher.

Shakespeare, W. (1993) *As You Like It*. Ware, UK: Wordsworth Editions.

Siegel, D. (2015) *The Developing Mind: How Relationships and the Brain Interact to Shape Who We Are*. New York, NY, and London: Guilford Press.

Sills, F. (2009) *Being and Becoming: Psychodynamics, Buddhism, and the Origins of Self*. Berkeley, CA: North Atlantic Books.

Sinclair, M. (1985) 'La Fura dels Baus – London Docklands.' *NME*, September.

Sissay, L. (2008) *Listener*. Edinburgh: Canongate Books.

Slade, P. (1954) *Child Drama*. London: University of London Press.

Slade, P. (1995) *Child Play: Its Importance for Human Development*. London: Jessica Kingsley Publishers.

Sogyal Rinpoche (1996, reprinted 2002) *The Tibetan Book of Living and Dying*. London: Rider Books.

Spariosu, M.I. (1989) *Dionysus Reborn: Play and the Aesthetic Dimension in Modern Philosophical and Scientific Discourse*. Ithaca, NY: Cornell University Press.

Stafford, T. (2014) 'Why all babies love peekaboo.' BBC Future, 18 April. Available at www.bbc.com/future/story/20140417-why-all-babies-love-peekaboo (accessed 18 April 2017).

Starhawk (1988) *Truth or Dare: Encounters with Power, Authority and Mystery*. London: HarperCollins.

Stern, D. (1990) *Diary of a Baby: What Your Child Sees, Feels, and Experiences*. New York, NY: Basic Books.

Sunderland, M. (2006) *The Science of Parenting*. London: Dorling Kindersley.

Sutton-Smith, B. (1997) *The Ambiguity of Play*. Cambridge, MA: Harvard University Press.

Sutton-Smith, B. (1999) 'Evolving a Consilience of Play Definitions: Playfully.' In S. Reifel (ed.) *Play and Culture Studies, Volume 2: Play Contexts Revisited*. Stamford, CT: Ablex Publishing.

Sutton-Smith, B. and Herron, R.E. (1971) *Child's Play*. New York, NY, and London: John Wiley & Sons.

Suzuki, S. (1970) *Zen Mind, Beginner's Mind* (ed. Trudy Dixon). New York, NY, and Tokyo: Weatherhill.

Swain, J., French, S., Barnes, C. and Thomas, C. (2004) *Disabling Barriers – Enabling Environments*. London: Sage.

Szpunar, K.K., Rose Addis, D. and Schacter, D.L. (2012) 'Memory for emotional stimulations: remembering a rosy future.' *Psychological Science 23*, 1, 24–29.

Talge, N.M., Neal, C. and Glover, V. (2007) 'Antenatal maternal stress hormones and long-term effects on child neurodevelopment: how and why?' *Journal of Child Psychology and Psychiatry 48*, 3–4, 245–261.

Tehrani, N. (ed) (2011) *Managing Trauma in the Workplace: Supporting Workers and Organisations*. London: Routledge.

Terr, L. (1990) *Too Scared to Cry*. New York, NY: Basic Books.

Tharp, T. (2003) *The Creative Habit: Learn it and Use it for Life*. New York, NY: Simon & Schuster.

Todd, C. (2011) TED Talk: 'The shared experience of absurdity', May 2011.

Todd, C. and Scordelis, A. (2009) *Causing a Scene: Extraordinary Pranks in Ordinary Places with Improv Everywhere*. New York, NY: William Morrow & Company/HarperCollins.

Tolia, V.N., Patrick, S.W., Bennett, M.M., Murthy, K. *et al.* (2015) 'Increasing incidence of neonatal abstinence syndrome in U.S. neonatal ICUs.' *New England Journal of Medicine 372*, 2118–2126.

Tolle, E. (2009) *A New Earth: Create a Better Life*. London and New York, NY: Penguin.

Toumazou, C. (2014) *The Life Scientific*. BBC Radio 4, 14 October.

Tumbokon, C. (n.d.) 'The Positive and Negative Effects of Video Games.' Raise Smart Kids website. Available at www.raisesmartkids.com/3-to-6-years-old/4-articles/34-the-good-and-and-bad-effects-of-video-games (accessed 24 March 2017).

Van den Bergh, B.R. and Marcoen, A. (2004) 'High antenatal maternal anxiety is related to ADHD symptoms, externalizing problems, and anxiety in 8- and 9-year-olds.' *Child Development 75*, 4, 1085–1097.

Van der Kolk, B. (2005) 'Developmental trauma disorder: towards a rational diagnosis for children with complex trauma.' *The Trauma Centre*.

van der Kolk, B. (2014) *The Body Keeps the Score*. London: Allen Lane/Penguin.

van der Kolk, B. and Ducey, C. (1989) 'The psychological processing of traumatic experience: Rorschach patterns in PTSD.' *Journal of Traumatic Stress 2*, 259–274.

VanderVen, K. (2004) 'Beyond Fun and Games Towards a Meaningful Theory of Play: Can a Hermeneutic Perspective Contribute?' In S. Reifel and M.H. Brown (eds) *Social Contexts of Early Education, and Reconceptualizing Play (II)*. Bingley: Emerald Publishing.

Von Franz, M.-L. (1974) *Shadow and Evil in Fairytales*. Zurich: Spring Publications.

Vygotsky, L.S. (1978) *Mind in Society: Development of Higher Psychological Processes*. Harvard, MA: Harvard College.

Wallace, B.A. (1999) *The Four Immeasurables: Practices to Open the Heart*. Boston, MA, and London: Snow Lion.

Wallin, D. (2007) *Attachment in Psychotherapy*. New York, NY: Guilford Press.

Ware, B. (2011, 2012) *The Top Five Regrets of the Dying: A Life Transformed by the Dearly Departing*. London: Hay House.

Warner, M. (1995) *From the Beast to the Blonde: On Fairy Tales and Their Tellers*. London: Vintage.

Warren, D. (1994) *Blindness and Children: An Individual Differences Approach*. New York, NY: Cambridge University Press.

Washburn, M. (1995) *The Ego and the Dynamic Ground: A Transpersonal Theory of Human Development*. Albany, NY: State University of New York Press.

Watkins, M. (1999) *Invisible Guests: The Development of Imaginal Dialogues*. Woodstock, CT: Spring Publications.

Weinstock, M. (2005) 'The potential influence of maternal stress hormones on development and mental health of the offspring.' *Brain, Behavior, and Immunity 19*, 4, 296–308.

Welty, E. (1971) *One Time, One Place*. London: Rider Books.

Welwood, J. (2000) *Towards a Psychology of Awakening*. Boston, MA, and London: Shambhala Publications.

Welwood, J. (n.d.) 'Human Nature, Buddha Nature: On Spiritual Bypassing, Relationship and the Dharma – An Interview with John Welwood by Tina Fossella.' Available at www.johnwelwood.com/articles/TRIC_interview_uncut.pdf (accessed 29 March 2017).

White, B. (2009) 'Play, healing, and wellness as seen by a physician who clowns: an interview with Bowen White.' *American Journal of Play 2*, 1.

Whitmont, E.C. (1991) *Dreams, a Portal to the Source: A Guide to Dream Interpretation*. London: Routledge.

Williams Saunders, J. (2001) *Life within Hidden Worlds*. London: Karnac Books.

Winnicott, D.W. (1960) 'The theory of the parent–infant relationship.' *International Journal of Psychoanalysis 41*, 585–595.

Winnicott, D.W. (1964) *The Child, the Family, and the Outside World*. London: Penguin.

Winnicott, D.W. (1965) *The Maturational Processes and the Facilitating Environment*. Madison, CT: International Universities Press.

Winnicott, D.W. (1971) *Playing and Reality*. London: Tavistock.

Winterson, J. (1996) *Art Objects: Essays on Ecstasy and Effrontery*. London: Vintage.

Yentob, A. (2010) *Imagine – Art is Child's Play*. BBC1, 22 June.

Young, E. (2012) *The Week*, 11 February, Issue 855, p.30.

Zipes, J. (2012) *The Irresistible Fairy Tale: The Cultural and Social History of the Genre*. Princeton, NJ: Princeton University Press.

Zweig, C. and Abrams, J. (eds) (1991) *Meeting the Shadow: The Hidden Power of the Dark Side of Human Nature*. New York, NY: Jeremy P. Tarcher.

Index